RED ROCKS
S E L E C T

Second Edition

Compiled by
Todd Swain

Chockstone Press
Evergreen, Colorado

RED ROCKS SELECT, 2ND EDITION

Printed in the United States of America.

Front cover photo of Mount Wilson by Chuck Ward, Bureau of Land Management.
Inset cover photo of Todd Swain on April Fools, Stone Wall, 2nd Pullout.
Back cover computer art by the students of Harris Vogel, Adjunct Professor of Art,
the University of Redlands, Redlands, California.

ISBN: 0-934641-86-2

PUBLISHED AND DISTRIBUTED BY:
CHOCKSTONE PRESS, INC.
Post Office Box 3505
Evergreen, Colorado 80439

WARNING: CLIMBING IS A SPORT WHERE YOU MAY BE SERIOUSLY INJURED OR DIE. READ THIS BEFORE YOU USE THIS BOOK.

This guidebook is a compilation of unverified information gathered from many different climbers. The author cannot assure the accuracy of any of the information in this book, including the topos and route descriptions, the difficulty ratings, and the protection ratings. These may be incorrect or misleading and it is impossible for any one author to climb all the routes to confirm the information about each route. Also, ratings of climbing difficulty and danger are always subjective and depend on the physical characteristics (for example, height), experience, technical ability, confidence and physical fitness of the climber who supplied the rating. Additionally, climbers who achieve first ascents sometimes underrate the difficulty or danger of the climbing route out of fear of being ridiculed if a climb is later down-rated by subsequent ascents. Therefore, be warned that you must exercise your own judgment on where a climbing route goes, its difficulty and your ability to safely protect yourself from the risks of rock climbing. Examples of some of these risks are: falling due to technical difficulty or due to natural hazards such as holds breaking, falling rock, climbing equipment dropped by other climbers, hazards of weather and lightning, your own equipment failure, and failure of fixed protection.

You should not depend on any information gleaned from this book for your personal safety; your safety depends on your own good judgment, based on experience and a realistic assessment of your climbing ability. If you have any doubt as to your ability to safely climb a route described in this book, do not attempt it.

The following are some ways to make your use of this book safer:

1. **CONSULTATION:** You should consult with other climbers about the difficulty and danger of a particular climb prior to attempting it. Most local climbers are glad to give advice on routes in their area and we suggest that you contact locals to confirm ratings and safety of particular routes and to obtain first-hand information about a route chosen from this book.

2. **INSTRUCTION:** Most climbing areas have local climbing instructors and guides available. We recommend that you engage an instructor or guide to learn safety techniques and to become familiar with the routes and hazards of the areas described in this book. Even after you are proficient in climbing safely, occasional use of a guide is a safe way to raise your climbing standard and learn advanced techniques.

3. **FIXED PROTECTION:** Many of the routes in this book use bolts and pitons which are permanently placed in the rock. Because of variances in the manner of placement, weathering, metal fatigue, the quality of the metal used, and many other factors, these fixed protection pieces should always be considered suspect and should always be backed up by equipment that you place yourself. Never depend for your safety on a single piece of fixed protection because you never can tell whether it will hold weight.

Be aware of the following specific potential hazards which could arise in using this book:

1. **MISDESCRIPTIONS OF ROUTES:** If you climb a route and you have a doubt as to where the route may go, you should not go on unless you are sure that you can go that way safely. Route descriptions and topos in this book may be inaccurate or misleading.

2. **INCORRECT DIFFICULTY RATING:** A route may, in fact be more difficult than the rating indicates. Do not be lulled into a false sense of security by the difficulty rating.

3. **INCORRECT PROTECTION RATING:** If you climb a route and you are unable to arrange adequate protection from the risk of falling through the use of fixed pitons or bolts and by placing your own protection devices, do not assume that there is adequate protection available higher just because the route protection rating indicates the route is not an "X" or an "R" rating. Every route is potentially an "X" (a fall may be deadly), due to the inherent hazards of climbing, including, for example, failure of fixed protection, your own equipment's failure, or improper use of climbing equipment.

THERE ARE NO WARRANTIES, WHETHER EXPRESS OR IMPLIED, THAT THIS GUIDEBOOK IS ACCURATE OR THAT THE INFORMATION CONTAINED IN IT IS RELIABLE. THERE ARE NO WARRANTIES OF FITNESS FOR A PARTICULAR PURPOSE OR THAT THIS GUIDE IS MERCHANTABLE. YOUR USE OF THIS BOOK INDICATES YOUR ASSUMPTION OF THE RISK THAT IT MAY CONTAIN ERRORS AND IS AN ACKNOWLEDGEMENT OF YOUR OWN SOLE RESPONSIBILITY FOR YOUR CLIMBING SAFETY.

For Donette

AUTHOR'S NOTE

Not being a Red Rocks local (I live in Joshua Tree), I've felt a bit funny about this project from the start. When I agreed to write the first edition of this guide in 1992, I'd only done about 75 climbs in the area, and hadn't even visited major canyons such as Oak Creek.

By press time, I'd done over 200 of the climbs listed in that book, but still needed a vast amount of information, which was given to me by local climbers, land managers and friends. They were essential to producing what you saw in the first edition and what you'll see here.

By the time this edition goes to print, I'll have done 400 of the routes included in this book. There are still a multitude of crags that I even haven't visited, let alone climbed. Again, I've had to rely on information and help from others to produce what you're now holding in your hands.

Of incredible importance was the team at Chockstone Press. They are the ones that take my text, photos and topos and turn them into a useable book.

Mike and Tim Ward at Desert Rock Sports in Las Vegas were again invaluable. Not only did they have a wealth of information, they allowed me to use their shop as a meeting ground for sessions with other knowledgeable locals.

Former Gunks ranger Chuck Liff allowed frequent use of his Starbase, keeping Donette and I well rested and clean.

The extremely helpful and knowledgeable locals that contributed this time around included: Nick Nordblom, Paul Van Betten, Greg Mayer, Wendell Broussard, Mike Tupper, Randy Marsh, Leo Henson, Dan McQuade....

I also received a wealth of information from the Bureau of Land Management, particularly from Chris Miller and Chuck Ward.

To all that helped out, thanks VERY much (and be forewarned I'll be bugging you again before the third edition comes out)!

ABOUT THIS BOOK

If you want a complete climbing guide to Red Rocks, you're out of luck. Joanne and Jorge Urioste wrote the first (and only) comprehensive climbing guide to the area in 1984, and it contained 221 routes. The first edition of *Red Rocks Select* contained 500 routes (out of an estimated 1,100). This edition contains nearly 800 climbs, but is still not meant to be comprehensive, or even a true "best of" guide.

Rather, the climbs described here are meant to be representative of the Red Rocks climbing experience. With each edition I plan to add at least several hundred routes, eventually having a (mostly) complete guidebook. If I've left your favorite route or area out, I'm sorry. Let me know about new and/or overlooked routes and perhaps they'll make it into the third edition of this guide.

Calico Basin
Cow Lick Co.
Crag 5.7
Catriona and
George Reid

TABLE OF CONTENTS

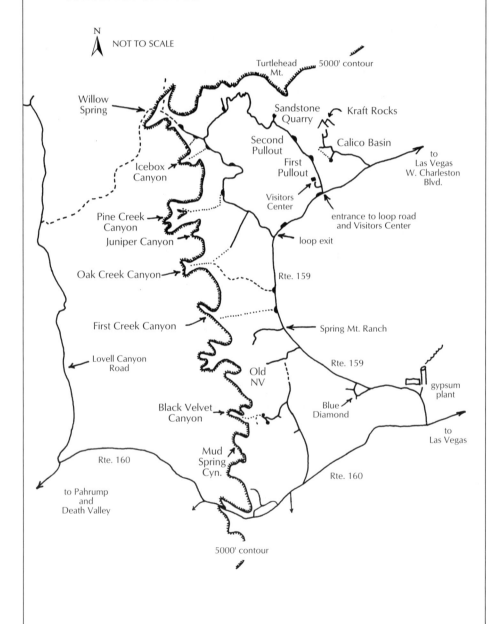

Red Rock Canyon National Conservation Area

N
NOT TO SCALE

Turtlehead Mt. 5000' contour

Willow Spring

Sandstone Quarry   Kraft Rocks

Second Pullout

Calico Basin

First Pullout

to Las Vegas W. Charleston Blvd.

Icebox Canyon

Visitors Center

entrance to loop road and Visitors Center

Pine Creek Canyon

Juniper Canyon

loop exit

Oak Creek Canyon

Rte. 159

First Creek Canyon

Spring Mt. Ranch

Lovell Canyon Road

Rte. 159

Old NV

gypsum plant

Black Velvet Canyon

Blue Diamond

to Las Vegas

Rte. 160

Mud Spring Cyn.

Rte. 160

to Pahrump and Death Valley

5000' contour

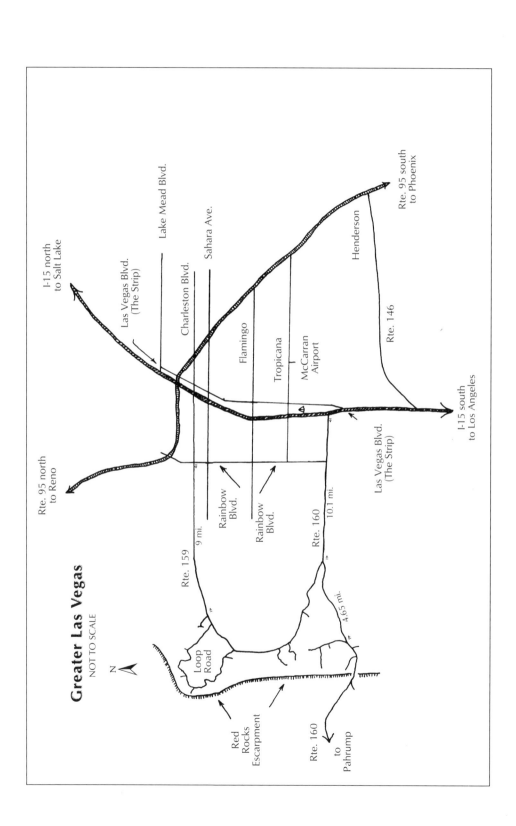

Greater Las Vegas

NOT TO SCALE

N

I-15 north
to Salt Lake

Rte. 95 north
to Reno

Las Vegas Blvd.
(The Strip)

Lake Mead Blvd.

Charleston Blvd.

Sahara Ave.

Flamingo

Tropicana

McCarran
Airport

Henderson

Rte. 146

Rte. 95 south
to Phoenix

I-15 south
to Los Angeles

Las Vegas Blvd.
(The Strip)

Rainbow
Blvd.

Rainbow
Blvd.

Rte. 159

9 mi.

Rte. 160

10.1 mi.

4.65 mi.

Loop
Road

Red Rocks
Escarpment

Rte. 160
to
Pahrump

*George Reid on **Head Case** 5.8, Case Face, Willow Spring*

INTRODUCTION

Most climbers have now at least heard of Red Rocks and know that it lies just outside of Las Vegas, Nevada. While this guidebook contains nearly 800 selected climbs, Red Rocks currently has over 1,300 different routes of all grades and lengths.

From the popular sport climbs of the Calico Hills to the multi-day routes in Juniper and Icebox canyons, the area hosts numerous climbs of world class stature. The area is officially named Red Rock Canyon National Conservation Area (RRCNCA) and is administered by the Bureau of Land Management (BLM), a federal agency within the United States Department of the Interior.

GETTING THERE

Once you arrive in Las Vegas, you'll find that it's pretty simple to get around. McCarran Airport is right off the Strip, while Interstate 15 and Routes 93/95 divide the city roughly into quarters. The Red Rock escarpment is located about 15 miles west of Las Vegas and is typically approached from West Charleston Boulevard (Route 159).

With the exception of Black Velvet Canyon and The Illusion Crags, all of the climbing at Red Rocks is accessed by Route 159 and a one-way scenic loop road. This loop road, within the National Conservation Area, is gated and closed at night. Typically, the road is open from early morning until just after dark. Check with the BLM Visitor Center or local climbing shops for current opening and closing times. Black Velvet Canyon and the Illusion Crags are accessed via Route 160.

The introduction to each chapter of this guide describes how to get to the trailhead for that certain area. The individual route descriptions will then tell you how to get from your car to the base of the climb. Hiking approach times at Red Rocks range from a few minutes to four hours and are also mentioned in the chapter and route introductions.

THE LAND

Like all climbing areas, Red Rock Canyon National Conservation Area should be treated with the utmost respect. The area was first designated as Red Rock Canyon Recreation Lands in 1967, with the scenic loop road completed in 1978.

The current designation as a National Conservation Area (NCA) came in 1990; it is defined as: "An area of the public lands managed by the Bureau of Land Management (BLM) which has been established by Congress for the purpose of protecting and conserving identified resource values of national interest. A Conservation Area is managed for multiple use and sustained yield in conformance with the Resource Management Plan, and in accordance with a general management plan which reflects the dominant and compatible uses for specific tracts."

Red Rock Canyon NCA currently encompasses 195,610 acres and hosts nearly one million visitors each year. There is a very nice visitor center, located just off the scenic loop road, that has interpretive displays, books, postcards and a helpful staff. The visitor center is typically open from 8 A.M. to 5 P.M.; (702)363-1921.

As climbing visitation increases, land managers at Red Rocks and other desert parks are becoming more concerned about a number of climber impacts. Please abide by posted regulations and closure times and be courteous to other user groups.

The following climbing-related regulations are currently in effect at Red Rock Canyon National Conservation Area:

- It is prohibited to chip, chisel, glue or scar the rock.
- Climbing is not allowed within 50 feet of any Native American rock art site (petroglyphs and/or pictographs).
- Digging, or in any way disturbing archaeological sites is prohibited.

Note: These first three regulations are extremely important. Violations will most likely lead to the closure of climbing areas.

- Camping is allowed only in designated roadside areas, or when backpacking, above 5,000 feet elevation (accessed only off the Red Rock Summit Road/Rocky Gap Road or Lovell Canyon Road). When backpacking, you must camp more than 200 feet from archaeological sites and water sources.

Note: As of press time, roadside camping was allowed at Oak Creek Campground with a fee of $5.00 per vehicle per night.

- Vehicles must be outside the gated sections of the loop road before closing time. (If there's one thing that annoys the rangers at Red Rocks, it's waiting for tardy visitors to get back to their car and exit the loop road.)
- Permits are required for backpacking and bivouacs. Contact the NCA Visitor Center for more details.
- Fires are only allowed within furnished fire grates.
- Gathering of native vegetation is prohibited; bring your own firewood.

In addition, a number of very important low impact policies should be followed:

- Do not climb on wet sandstone! The rock becomes very brittle and typically needs at least 24 hours to dry.
- Pack out all trash, whether it's yours or not.
- **Pack out all toilet paper and human waste using a Ziploc type bag; at the least, bury the waste six inches deep and carry out the toilet paper.**
- Stay on maintained trails as much as possible and try to minimize impacts to plants and soil through erosion and trampling.
- New routes should be established away from the view of the general public.
- All bolts and anchors should be painted to match the color of the rock. If webbing is used, it should also match the color of the rock.
- To help keep the visual impacts of climbing to a minimum, remove all retreat or "bail" slings you encounter.
- Do not use chalk on areas visible to the general public. This definitely applies to the boulders at Willow Spring Picnic Area and Sandstone Quarry.

The Bureau of Land Management has a number of useful handouts for planning your visit to Red Rocks. These include a park brochure and the following titles:

Climbing and Camping, *Hiking, Mammals, Birds, Geology, Plants* and *Archeology of Southern Nevada*. For more information, brochures or a list of other publications available, contact the BLM at: Las Vegas District Office, 4765 West Vegas Drive, Las Vegas, NV 89108. Telephone: (702)647-5000.

THE RULES OF THE GAME

How a route is established (whether ground up or on rappel) will never be as important as having the opportunity to climb. Do your part to minimize all impacts associated with climbing (noise, visuals, social trails, human waste, disturbing wildlife, etc.). Climb to have fun, not to aggravate others or upset land managers.

Here are the ethics currently accepted by the majority of climbers at Red Rocks:

• Not all routes are worth bolting. Toprope those routes that share anchors or are close to other established routes.

• Lead routes may be established from the ground up, or on rappel. From a boldness and historical perspective, ground up is more desirable. Hooks are typically used on ground up ascents. If you do decide to rappel bolt, toprope the route first, so that the bolts are in the proper place!

• Bolts should be at least ⅜" diameter, but preferably ½" by 4", using grade 5 material.

• All bolts and anchors should be painted to match the color of the rock.

• New routes should not be established within view of the general public.

• Climbs that are still in progress will have a red ribbon tied to the first bolt. Please do not attempt these routes until they have been completed or abandoned by the party that installed the bolts.

• A new route is completed when the leader starts at the bottom of the cliff and climbs to the top, without falling, grabbing slings or hanging on the rope.

RATINGS

The Yosemite Decimal System (YDS) is used throughout this book to rate climbs. Currently, technical rock climbs at Red Rocks range from 5.0 to 5.13. The higher the number, the more difficult the climb. To differentiate between true sport climbs (quickdraws only) and routes where gear is needed, I have used two different types of sub-grading methods.

True sport climbs have ratings subdivided by letter grades (a-d), as was introduced by Jim Bridwell of Yosemite fame. Routes that require some amount of traditional gear have the subdivisions of - and +. These "gear subdivisions" are used on climbs 5.10 or harder, with a rating of 5.10- being equal in difficulty to 5.10a.

As with any rating system, the ratings are not meant to be definitive, but are intended to give you a rough idea of the difficulty that may be encountered. Height, reach, finger size and flexibility vary for each climber, thus making the rating system somewhat inaccurate. Just because a route is rated 5.9 doesn't mean it's really 5.9. **Remember, I haven't done all of the routes in this guide; therefore, the information may be suspect.**

I also have used the protection rating system first introduced by Jim Erickson in his climbing guide to Boulder, Colorado. This system is based on the movie rating system

(G, PG, PG13, R, X), with X-rated routes being VERY dangerous. I have dropped the G ("safe") rating and use only the other four grades. These ratings assume the leader is competent at the grade, has the proper equipment for the route, and an attentive belayer. Roughly, the ratings mean the following:

PG Protection is usually considered adequate, although the leader may fall up to 15 feet. The leader will probably not get injured in the fall. These routes might seem a little bit sporty.

PG13 This is somewhere between PG and R (as you might have guessed).

R Protection is usually considered inadequate and the leader will probably get injured if he/she falls. These routes are potentially dangerous and runout.

X Protection is nonexistent. A falling leader will probably suffer severe injuries, and/or death. These are death routes or solos.

Again, there may be very dangerous climbs listed in this book that don't have an R or X rating. Use caution and good judgement when leading!

TERMS

Rad means cool. Manky means choss. Gnarly can mean rad or choss. OOPS! Wrong book.

The following climbing terms are used throughout this guide:

FA: First Ascent

FFA: First Free Ascent

FRA: First Recorded Ascent

FRFA: First Recorded Free Ascent

Generally, the person whose name appears first led the crux of the route.

Directions (left, right) assume the reader is facing the cliff.

Variations to the normal route are shown as **V1**, **V2**, etc. and are listed at the end of the route description.

Pitches are listed as **P1**, **P2**, etc.

◀ "Thumbs up" means the route is of high quality.

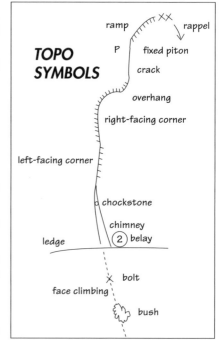

GEAR

The joy of sport climbing, is that you need only a rope, quickdraws, and strong fingers. For the traditional routes, you'll want a good selection of wires, TCUs, Friends, and slings. "Specialty" gear will be noted in the description of the climb. For the longer canyon routes, you'll usually need two ropes to descend. Again, this will be noted in the description.

WEATHER

Climbing is possible at Red Rocks all year, but most people visit the area in the spring and fall. For the latest forecast, the preferred number is (702)736-3854; you can also call (702)734-2010. "Typical" weather for each season is detailed below:

Spring   While the weather can be good, it's likely that there will be windy and wet conditions in March. Shade combined with downcanyon winds can make places like Black Velvet seem much colder than the sunny cliffs of the Calico Hills. By May, the temperatures could reach 100° Farenheit (F).

Summer   It is common for temperatures to reach 106°F or higher. Thunderstorms are the norm for late July and all of August, and these rains frequently cause flash floods. Climb in the early morning and evening hours, and avoid the sun. Drink LOTS of water!

Fall   Although the days are getting shorter, it is probably the best time to visit the area. As November rolls around, expect it to get cold in the shady canyons. Places like The Gallery are warm enough for climbing in shorts and T-shirts.

Winter   Sunny cliffs such as The Gallery and Trophy are extremely popular. Snow is common at the higher elevations and forces the closure of the loop road on occasion. Shady canyon climbs are usually out of the question. Shaded descents (such as on **Solar Slab**) may remain icy for some time.

EMERGENCIES

The BLM and Las Vegas Metropolitan Police Department (Metro) provide emergency services at Red Rocks. There are three emergency phones located on the scenic loop road at Sandstone Quarry, White Rock Spring and Icebox Canyon. Between 8 AM and 5 PM, report the accident to the NCA Visitor Center if possible. After hours, call from pay phones outside the NCA Visitor Center or in the towns of Blue Diamond, Old Nevada (Bonnie Springs Ranch) or Las Vegas.

Emergency Telephone Numbers

Red Rock Canyon NCA Visitor Center: Las Vegas Metropolitan Police: **911**
(702)363-1921 BLM Las Vegas Dispatch: **(702)647-5090**

Area Medical Facilities
University Medical Center (UMC) **UMC Quick Care - Lakes**
1800 West Charleston 2760 Lake Sahara Drive
Las Vegas, NV Las Vegas, NV
(702)383-2000 **(702)254-4900**

WHERE TO STAY

Las Vegas has over 100,000 rooms available for its visitors, ranging from astonishingly cheap to astronomically expensive. Many of the huge casinos on the Strip offer great deals and are only minutes away from the crags. As a general rule, prices are quite a bit higher on weekends and in the summer. At least one hotel offers discounts to climbers – check with the climbing shops for details.

For those that want to camp, the choices are a bit more limited. Historically, the BLM has allowed climbers and other user groups to camp at Oak Creek and at the mouth of Black Velvet Canyon. As of June 1995, Oak Creek Campground was still open, and was charging a fee of $5.00 per car, per night. Due to the huge increase in use, I foresee camping being more limited and restricted than it has in the past. Check with the BLM or local climbing shops for the latest information. There are also commercial camp-grounds in Las Vegas, some of which will provide showers to those staying elsewhere.

SUPPLIES AND OTHER IMPORTANT INFORMATION

At the intersection of West Charleston (Route 159) and Rainbow Boulevard you'll find grocery stores and numerous restaurants. Water is available at the NCA Visitor Center and at various places in town.

Numerous movie theaters can also be found in the local area. The Red Rock Cinema is about one mile east of Rainbow at 5201 West Charleston; (702)870-1423. The Torrey Pines Theater at 6344 West Sahara (at the intersection of Torrey Pines) offers cheaper, second-run movies; (702)876-4334. A new public library has been built on West Charleston, just west of Jones. There is also a branch library in Blue Diamond.

Showers are available at some commercial campgrounds and fitness centers. Check with the local climbing shops for the latest information. Do NOT use the NCA Visitor Center bathrooms for bathing.

LAS VEGAS

If you haven't been to Vegas yet, you're missing out! Before your trip, rent the follow-ing films at your local video store to get a feel for the area: *Bugsy* starring Warren Beatty, *Viva Las Vegas* starring Elvis and *Honeymoon in Vegas* starring Nicholas Cage. Here's a list of my favorite things to show first-time visitors to Las Vegas:

Caesar's Palace   The most opulent of the casinos, you'll find a higher class clientele here than at Circus, Circus. Take in a movie at the large-screen Omnimax Theater and don't miss the Forum, an amazing shopping area featuring talking statues and a "sky" that changes as the day progresses.

Circus, Circus   A bit tacky, but a brilliant idea for sucking families into a casino. Check out the free circus acts (running from about noon to mid-night), the midway and "the World's Largest Buffet." Grand Slam Canyon is attached to the rear and features an indoor roller coaster and other neat stuff.

Excaliber   The biggest (and gaudiest) hotel in the world when it was built. It sports a medieval motif and was built by Circus, Circus. Don't miss the Magic Motion Machine on the lowest level of the casino. For those with money, the dinner theater features jousting and other knightly daring do.

"Glitter Gulch"   This is the downtown part of Vegas. The buildings aren't as tall as those on the Strip, but their closeness makes the neon that much more impressive.

Luxor   It's shaped like a pyramid and has an Egyptian theme. Check out just the first Episode and the buffet.

The Mirage   Quite spiffy, with a bunch of things to experience. Don't miss the exploding "volcano" in front of the casino. It erupts on a regular basis all evening. Inside, you'll find rare white tigers (usually sleeping), a tropical jungle, a huge tropical aquarium (behind the check-in desk), and dolphin shows (behind the casino).

MGM Grand This huge, green casino/outdoor amusement park is across the street from the Excaliber. It has all sorts of shows and rides to while away those long winter nights.

Treasure Island With its pirate motif and raging battle outside (multiple times each evening), it's worth a visit.

In the works: A bunch of new theme-park-type casinos on the south end of the Strip. At least one of them will have water skiing around the hotel!

LOCAL CLIMBING SHOPS

Desert Rock Sports
W. Charleston
Boulevard
(west of Rainbow)
Las Vegas, NV
89117
(702) 254-1143

Adventure
Outfitters
(Rainbow and
Sahara)
Las Vegas, NV
(702) 252-7114

Gary's Backpacking
& Mountaineering
4251 West Sahara,
Ste. B
Las Vegas, NV
89102
(702) 368-2225

Peak Sports
3065 E. Patrick
Lane, #4
Las Vegas, NV
89120
(702)458-8870

LOCAL AUTHORIZED GUIDE SERVICES

Nevada Outdoor Connection
Scott Olsen
9025 West Desert Inn #205
Las Vegas, NV 89117
(702) 228-1426

Mountain Skills
Jim Munson
(702) 256-7078 or
(914) 687-9643

High and Wild
Mountain Guides
Jay Smith
Box 11905
Tahoe Paradise, CA 96155
(702) 254-9804 or
(916) 577-2370

Sky's The Limit
Randy Grandstaff
HCR 33 Box 1
Calico Basin
Red Rock, NV 89124
(702) 363-4533

FURTHER READING ABOUT CLIMBING AT RED ROCKS

At least three other guidebooks have been written about climbing at Red Rocks, as well as numerous articles. This is not meant to be a complete list of published material, but will get you started in your quest for more routes to do (once you've done all of the routes listed in this book!):

The Red Rocks of Southern Nevada by Joanne Urioste; American Alpine Club, 1984

Climber's Guide to North American Rock Climbs: West Coast Rock Climbs by John Harlin III; Chockstone Press, 1987

A Climber's Guide to the Red Rocks of Nevada by Randy Faulk; RT Publ., 1992.

Periodicals: *Climbing*, issues 128, 131; *Mountain Magazine*, issue 140; *Onsight Magazine*, issues 1, 2; *Rock & Ice*, issues 18, 36, 50; *Sport Climbing*, vol .1 #3, vol. 2 #4.

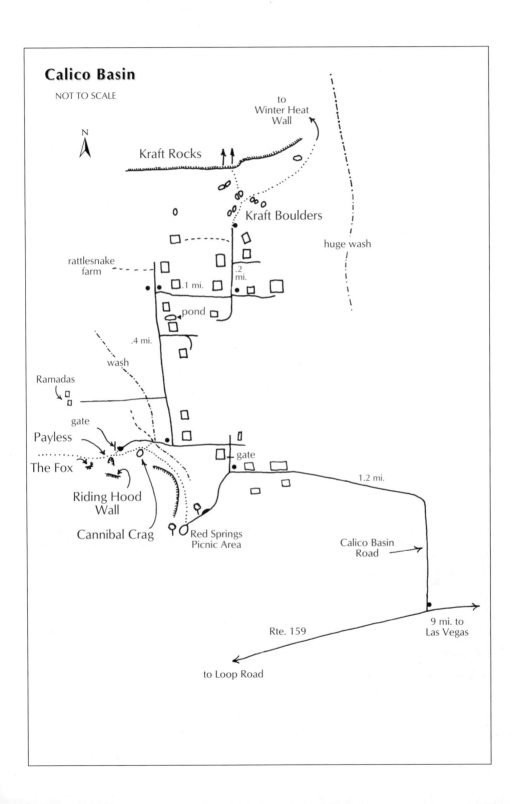

CALICO BASIN

ROCK SPRINGS AREA

Most of the routes included in this guidebook are on a series of primarily north-facing formations to the northwest of Red Springs Picnic Area. Many more routes have been done here than will be described in this guide.

To access the first climbs that are described, turn off West Charleston (Route 159) onto Calico Basin Road and follow it 1.2 miles to a "T" intersection. Turn right (the Red Springs Picnic Area will be to the left) and go through a gate marked "Private Property." Turn left about 40 yards inside the gate, and follow the street for about 200 yards. At the next curve, go left and park in front of some boulders blocking the road. Walk along this road past a wash and up a short hill to a locked gate.

The next routes described are all on the north-facing hillside to the left and left center (west) of the gate. They will be described from left to right as viewed from the parking area. **Please do not block the road and be respectful of the private landowners in this area!**

Cannibal Crag

This is actually a huge boulder that is best approached by a trail that leads up left (south) just after you cross the wash, but before you go up the steep hill to the gate at the end of the road. Follow a faint trail uphill from the closed road for 250 yards, crossing a well-defined trail that contours along the hillside just below the cliff. The

boulder is easily seen from the road, and harbors some excellent climbs. Most routes are in the sun for a good part of the day. Climbs will be described from right to left, starting on the extreme south end of the varnished west face. As you approach the cliff, you will arrive on the east face, near **Caustic**.

1. **Shishka Bob** 5.6 X   FA: Todd Swain (solo)–June 1992.
   Climb the very short, varnished face on the upper right side of the wall.

2. **Ma & Pa In Kettle** 5.7-   FA: Todd Swain, Randy and Andy Schenkel–June 1992.
   Start at a varnished left-facing corner that is at the very right edge of the face, and 20 feet right of a white boulder leaning against the cliff. Three bolts provide protection on the face above the corner, and TCUs make up the belay. Walk off right.

3. **Mac & Ronnie In Cheese** 5.10- PG13   FA: Todd Swain, Debbie Brenchley–June 1992.
   Begin on the right edge of a white boulder leaning against the west face of the cliff. Angle up and right to a bolt, then straight up past another bolt to the top. You may want to bring a few TCUs for the climb, and the belay. Walk off right (southwest).

4. **A Man In Every Pot** 5.8+   FA: Debbie Brenchley, Todd Swain–June 1992.
   Begin seven feet left of the last route, at the left edge of the white boulder leaning against the crag. Scamper up the face past three bolts to the top. Bring a couple of TCUs for pro and the anchor.

5. **What's Eating You?** 5.9+   FA: Todd Swain, Randy and Andy Schenkel–June 1992.
   Start ten feet left of **A Man In Every Pot** at a left-facing flake leading to a bulge. Saunter past three bolts to the top, where you'll need TCUs or Friends for the anchor.

6. **Elbows Of Mac & Ronnie** 5.11a   FA: Todd Swain–June 1992.
   Begin ten feet left of the previous route at a right-leaning flake/ramp. Climb up and right pasta four bolts to da cold shut anchor.

7. **Fear This** 5.11+   FA: Sal Mamusia, Paul Van Betten–September 1992.
   Three bolts lead to cold shuts, starting about ten feet left of the last route.

8. **Have A Beer With Fear** 5.11a   FA: Richard Harrison , Paul Van Betten–August 1992.
   Start 15 feet left of the last climb, at the left edge of the wall. Climb past four bolts, either lowering off the last bolt or going to the summit. The crux is by the first bolt and is per-haps height related.

The next routes are on the eastern corner of the formation, directly above the trail.

9. **Caustic** 5.11b PG ◄   FA: Paul Van Betten, Dan Krulevski, Shelby Shelton, Richard Harrison, Sal Mamusia 1991.
   This route climbs the arête separating the east and west faces, and is directly above the well worn trail that contours along the hillside. Start to the right of the arête and climb easy rock out left (a bit scary – TCU placement before reaching first bolt if you're not brave) onto the edge. Most people lower off at the fourth bolt.

10. **Pickled** 5.11c   FA: Paul Van Betten, Sal Mamusia, Richard Harrison–August 1991.
    Begin 40 feet left of the last route, and just left of some Native American petroglyphs (do not touch!). Shoot up a slabby face to a bolt, then angle up right past four bolts. It's com-mon to lower off the last bolt.

11. **Save The Heart To Eat Later** 5.12a   FA: Sal Mamusia, Paul Van Betten, Shelby Shelton, Richard Harrison–August 1991.
    Begin as per the last route, but angle up left past three bolts before lowering off.

12. **Baseboy** 5.10d PG   FA: Paul Van Betten, Richard Harrison, Sal Mamusia–August 1991.
    Rope up 15 feet left of the previous two routes at the base of a left-leaning crack. Jam up the crack for 20 feet, clip two bolts, then move right and up past one more. Lower off the fourth bolt or go to the top.

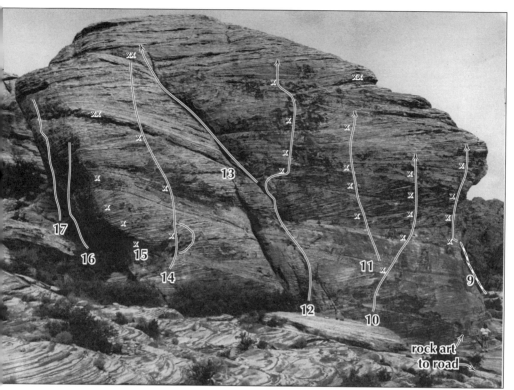

Cannibal Crag

9. Caustic
10. Pickled
11. Save The Heart To Eat Later
12. Baseboy
13. You Are What You Eat
14. Caliban
15. Project
16. Fear This Sport
17. New Wave Hookers

13. **You Are What You Eat** 5.3   FA: Unknown–early 1990s.
   Climb the obvious left-leaning crack mentioned above.

14. **Caliban** 5.8+ PG   FA: Sal Mamusia, Paul Van Betten–1993.
   A bit contrived near the bottom, but an OK route nonetheless. Begin 20 feet left of the previous route at a hole in the rock. Climb the lower-angled face past three bolts to cold shuts. The 5.8+ (and most obvious) route moves right past the first bolt, then way back left to the second (hence the PG rating).

15. **Project** 5.12?   FA: Will Gove?–after June 1995.
   Start five feet left of **Caliban**. Four bolts lead to cold shuts at the right edge of the overhanging southeast face.

The next four climbs are on the overhanging southeast face, left of the last route.

16. **Fear This Sport** 5.12b   FA: Paul Van Betten, Richard Harrison, Sal Mamusia–July 1991.
   Angle out right toward the arête, passing five bolts.

17. **New Wave Hookers** 5.12c   FA: Paul Van Betten, Richard Harrison, Sal Mamusia–July 1991.
    Begin 12 feet up and left, just above a pit, and power past six bolts heading right, then up
    past honeycombed rock.

18. **Wonderstuff** 5.12d   FA: Paul Van Betten, Richard Harrison, Sal Mamusia–July 1991.
    Rope up as per the last route, but follow the left line of six bolts. Bring a #1 or 1.5 TCU to
    get to the first bolt (or stick clip).

19. **Man-eater** 5.12a   FA: Dan McQuade–Spring 1992.
    Eight feet left you'll find another four bolts that lead to a cold shut anchor.

The next three routes are located on the hillside above Cannibal Crag.

20. **Shit Howdy** 5.10+   FA: Paul Van Betten, Nick Nordblom–1986.
    This unique climb lies above and right of Cannibal Crag, and is best approached from the
    gate at the end of the road and faces to the west. From the gate walk up and left (south)
    about 350 yards to an obvious large boulder/cliff. On the right (west) face, climb a crack
    that arches right, paralleling the slope of the hillside. Bring pro to 3".

The next two routes are near the top of the hillside, midway between **Shit Howdy**
and the Riding Hood Wall.

21. **Risk Brothers Roof** 5.11-
    FA: Paul Van Betten, Sal
    Mamusia, Richard
    Harrison–Winter 1985/86.
    From the gate, head straight
    uphill (southwest) to an east-
    facing crag with a large
    streaked roof. Climb a crack
    up and left through the roof.

22. **Zona Rosa** 5.9   FA: Robert
    Finlay (solo) –circa 1986.
    Named for the "Pink Zone"
    in Panama City where some
    American servicemen were
    killed. About 60 feet right
    and around the corner from
    Risk Brothers Roof, you'll
    find a fingers to off-width
    crack.

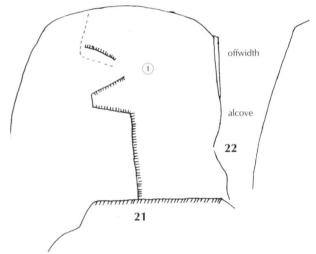

Riding Hood Wall

From the gate at the end of the closed road, walk about 50 yards southwest to a
wash. Go straight up the rocky hillside 150 yards, to the biggest section of rock visible. This cliff is in the shade in the afternoon. Descend down the gully to the right
(west) of the routes.

23. **Physical Graffiti** 5.7   FA: Jon Martinet, Randy Grandstaff, Scott Gordon–1973.
    Not too many rolling stones on this one. Start at the northeast corner of the formation at
    a varnished dihedral with a crack running up and slightly right.

    P1 Follow the crack up about 130 feet, then move right into the main crack system of
    Over The Hill... Belay above at rope's end. 150 ft, 5.7.

    P2 Continue up the easy crack and face to the top. 110 ft, 5.5

24. **Over The Hill To Grandmother's House** 5.9+ FA: Bob Logerquist, John Williamson –September 1970.
Difficult to start, no matter which way you go. Begin this journey 50 feet right of **Physical Graffiti** atop boulders and below a vertical crack running through a roof.

P1 and 2 Climb a short, smooth face to a roof, then over this at an obvious crack (crux, V1). Follow the crack to a stance 40 feet up. Rappel off jammed slings or continue up the easy but awkward crack for about 200 feet to the top of the buttress.

V1 Climb the right-leaning crack 15 feet left of the normal start until it intersects with the main crack about 40 feet up. 5.9+

Ranch Hands Crag

From the gate at the end of the closed road, walk 200 yards west to a low, overhanging buttress. The cliff has two tiers—the lower tier faces east, the upper tier to the north.

The next five routes are on the lower tier, and are in the shade in the afternoon. For all of the routes on this buttress, walk off left (southeast), and bring gear for an anchor on top.

25. **Payless Cashways** 5.11a FA: Richard Harrison, Sal Mamusia, Paul Van Betten, Shelby Shelton–June 1991.
Shelby dropped Sal's Bosch, and they had to go to Payless to buy another! Start at the left (south) edge of the lower tier at the base of a left-leaning crack that leads to a cave. Move up right past a hueco to the first bolt (½" with a blue hanger), then straight up the face past four more bolts. Bring a # 3.5 and 4 Friend for the belay.

26. **Spanky** 5.11- FA: Richard Harrison, Sal Mamusia, Paul Van Betten, Shelby Shelton–June 1991.
Begin ten feet right of the previous route and slightly downhill atop a boulder. A difficult boulder problem to a pocket leads to face climbing past four bolts. Finish up a short crack. Bring a # 3.5 and 4 Friend for the belay.

27. **Mexican Secret Agent Man** 5.11b FA: Paul Van Betten, Richard Harrison–July 1991.
Start eight feet right of the previous route off the same boulder. Climb past four bolts, trending slightly right. Many people lower off the last bolt or bring a # 3.5 and 4 Friend for the belay.

28. **Swilderness Experience** 5.11c FA: Paul Van Betten, Richard Harrison, Shelby Shelton–July 1991.
Rope up ten feet right, near the bottom of the boulder mentioned in the past two routes. Traverse out right along flakes passing one bolt, then go up past four more bolts to the top.

29. **Swilderness Permit** 5.12c FA: Sal Mamusia, Paul Van Betten, Richard Harrison–July 1991.
Begin 20 feet downhill below very overhanging, brown rock. Power past a bunch of moonscoops to lower angled rock. There are seven bolts enroute, with most folks lowering off the last one.

29a. **Roman Meal** 5.11 FA (TR): Todd Swain–December 1994.
The loose face 15 feet right **Swilderness Point** has been done.

30. **Roman Hands** 5.4 X FA: Unknown–1991.
Start 35 feet right of the previous route at the base of a lower-angled face leading to an overhanging wall. Climb the face to a ledge, then move left and up a crack system to the top.

*The next three routes are on the upper tier, which is best approached by climbing up the easy **Roman Hands** face (5.4) to the base of the overhanging wall. These three routes are in the shade all day.*

31. **Jack Officers** 5.12c   FA: Paul Van Betten, Richard Harrison, Sal Mamusia–April 1991.
Angle up left from the center of the wall past three bolts.

32. **Ranch Hands** 5.12c   FA: Richard Harrison, Paul Van Betten, Bob Conz, Sal Mamusia–January 1991.
Angle up slightly right from the center of the wall past four bolts to a two-bolt rap station.

33. **Blood Stains** 5.10 R/X   FA: Richard Harrison, Sal Mamusia, Paul Van Betten–September 1990.
Dangerously loose. If the block at mid-height comes off, there could be blood stains! Start on the ledge as per the previous two routes. Traverse out right to a loose crack, and up this to an overhang formed by a loose block. Pull the ceiling, then up the steep face past one bolt to another ceiling. Swing over this, then go left to the **Ranch Hands** rappel anchor.

To approach the next route, walk 300 yards west from the gate (about 100 yards right of the previous routes). About 250 yards up the hillside is a striking crack in a right-facing corner. This climb is in the shade all day.

34. **The Fox** 5.10+ ◀   FA: Unknown–early 1970s. FFA: Unknown–mid 1970s.
One of the finest pitches at Red Rocks. Bring a full set of camming devices, with extra of the biggest sizes. Climb the widening crack in a right-facing corner for 150 feet. Descend to the left (east) down the rocky slope.

*Apparently, there is a bolted route just left of **The Fox** (up the narrow rib), but no more is known.*

Dickies Cliff

This short formation is about 200 yards right (west) of Ranch Hands Crag and 100 yards right (west) of **The Fox**. The cliff faces north and is at the level of the desert floor. Approach time from the gate at the end of the closed road is about five minutes. Routes are described from left to right.

35. **Gigantor** 5.10   FA: Richard Harrison, Paul Van Betten, Wendell Broussard, Mike Forkash–July 1991.
Start atop a boulder in a gully at the left edge of the crag. Move out right past two bolts (crux), then up past another bolt and a couple of small TCU placements to the summit. Medium Friends are needed for the belay. Walk off either side.

36. **Guys And Ghouls** 5.6   FA: Donette Smith, Todd Swain, George and Catriona Reid (Scots)–Halloween 1994.
Begin 18 feet right of **Gigantor** at the most obvious chimney/crack system in the center of the cliff. Climb disjointed cracks up and left to an easy, right-leaning chimney.

37. **Boobytrap** 5.12c PG   FA: Sal Mamusia, Paul Van Betten–July 1991.
The first ascent party says no stick clipping the first bolt! Rope up eight feet right of the obvious crack system (**Guys And Ghouls**). After a very hard start, climb past five bolts to the summit. Some folks lower off the top bolt, others walk (or crawl) off either side.

38. **Stukas Over Disneyland** 5.12-   FA: Paul Van Betten, Richard Harrison–July 1991.
A wild ride! Begin 15 feet right of the previous route at a section of smooth rock below an 18" ceiling that is 15 feet up. Power past two bolts and the ceiling to obvious, varnished, left-leaning cracks (5.10). Bring wires and TCUs.

39. **Lancaster Levels Luxor** 5.9+   FA: George Reid (Scot), Todd Swain, Donette Smith –October 1994.
Headline news. Start 15 feet right of **Stukas...** below a prominent crack system. Scramble up to a bulge, then pull this (crux) into the main crack system, which is followed to the top.

40. **Monster Island** 5.11   FA: Paul Van Betten, Sal Mamusia–July 1991.
This route climbs a thin, vertical crack five feet right of the last route, near the right edge of the cliff. Three bolts and gear (up to #2.5 Friend) are used for protection.

Gnat Man Crag

This escarpment is located 100 feet up and right of the Dickies Cliff, and is separated by a gully forming one of the descent routes for the Dickies Cliff. The routes will also be described from left to right.

41a. **P-Coat Junction** 5.9   FA: Todd Swain, Donette Smith–December 1994.
Climb the crack system ten feet left of **P-Coat Sleeve** and just above the approach gully. Finish up a low-angled, right-facing corner as per **P-Coat Sleeve**. Bring gear up to 4".

41. **P-Coat Sleeve** 5.10-   FA: Paul Van Betten, Sal Mamusia–November 1991.
An obvious fingercrack that is eight feet left of an easy looking dihedral with a crack in its back. The start of this route is varnished and looks appealing – the upper portion is a bit lower angled and on white rock. Climb the crack, eventually joining **Ghouls Just Wanna Have Fun** to the top. Medium Friends are needed for the belay. Scramble off right (west).

42. **Ghouls Just Wanna Have Fun** 5.7   FA: Donette Smith, Catriona Reid (Scot)–Halloween 1994.
Climb the central dihedral to the summit. Carry gear up to a #3.5 Friend. Scamper off right.

43. **Gnat Man On Ranch Hands** 5.11 ◀   FA: Paul Van Betten, Sal Mamusia–November 1991.
Rope up just right of the central dihedral at a series of neat-looking vertical huecos. Power past five bolts to easy slabs and the top. Medium Friends are needed for the belay, or lower off the fifth bolt. Bring a small TCU for the flake between the first and second bolt.

44. **Knock The Bottom Out Of It** 5.10- PG13 ◀   FA: Paul Van Betten, Sal Mamusia –November 1991.
Good climbing, but a bit scary getting to the first bolt. Begin ten feet right of **Gnat Man...** below a varnished face. Climb past four bolts to lower-angled rock (TCU and Friend placements) and the summit. Bring medium Friends for the belay, then walk off right.

45. **Bottoms Up** 5.7   FA: George and Catriona Reid (Scots), Todd Swain, Donette Smith–October 1994.
A good, moderate route. Climb the left-facing corner ten feet right of the last route. Exit left at the top of the corner, then follow a lower angled, right-facing flake/corner to the top. Medium Friends for the belay; scramble off right (west).

Happy Acres

This obvious cliff sits on the left side of the canyon and gets sun in the morning. Other routes have been done here, but information was lacking at press time. The following two routes are located on the black slabby face up and right from Gnat Man Crag.

46. **The Life Chuckle** 5.8?   FA: Nick Nordblom, Paul Van Betten–1984.
This is a one-bolt route on the right side of the lower angled black face.

47. **Spontaneous Enjoyment** 5.8?   FA: Nick Nordblom, Paul Van Betten–1984.
A two-bolt route on the right-hand cliff. This route is supposed to be up and right from the last route (closer to the obvious pass-through to the loop road).

Across the canyon to the north of the Dickies Cliff is a sunny, lower-angled red formation with an obvious left-leaning overlap/ceiling.

48. **Cow Lick Co. Crag** 5.7   FA: Todd Swain, Donette Smith, Mike Dimitri–November 1993.
Follow four bolts to a cold shut anchor, passing the lower right edge of the overlap.

CALICO BASIN NORTH

Numerous routes have been done around to the north (right) of the Girl Scout picnic area and left of Kraft Rocks. I haven't explored this area at all, but have decided to include these routes nonetheless. They will be documented better in the next edition. Good luck for now!

49. **Cold Sweat** 5.11+   FA: Mike Tupper, Greg Mayer–1986.
This climb is about ten minutes up the canyon above a spring – right at the point that you have to begin scrambling. The route climbs a narrow red slab with six bolts to a two-bolt belay. You'll need wires and small Friends to supplement the bolts.

50. **Arms Left** 5.10+   FA: Greg Mayer, Mike Tupper 1986.
This route starts at a large, right-facing corner where red and black rock meet. It's about 650 yards to the right (west) of the last route. Bring a full set of Friends, some large stoppers, plus a Big Dude.

P1 Lieback a six-inch crack to a horizontal. Hand traverse left six feet, then pull over the lip to a belay in a crack. 5.10+.
P2 Climb an easy crack to the top. 50 ft, 5.6.
Descent: Walk off right.

51. **Strategic Arms** 5.12-   FA: Mike Tupper–1986.
Climb **Arms Left** to the horizontal, then go up right along a steepening crack/corner to a two-bolt belay anchor. Carry a good selection of gear.

NOTE: At least five routes in the 5.11-12 range have been done on a crag above the previous routes. The crag is named Alternative Rock and will most likely have many more routes by the time its fully developed.

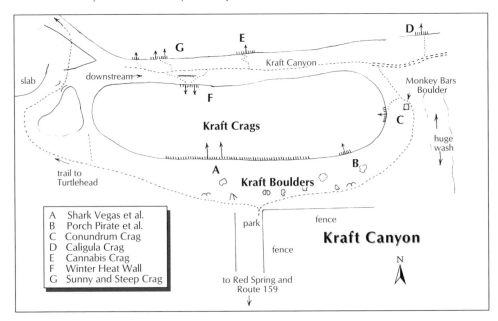

Kraft Canyon

slab

downstream→

Kraft Crags

Monkey Bars
Boulder

huge
wash

trail to
Turtlehead

Kraft Boulders

Kraft Canyon

park

fence

fence

A   Shark Vegas et al.
B   Porch Pirate et al.
C   Conundrum Crag
D   Caligula Crag
E   Cannabis Crag
F   Winter Heat Wall
G   Sunny and Steep Crag

to Red Spring and
Route 159

N

Kraft Crags and Kraft Boulders

Named for local landowner Ozzie Kraft, this is the large hill (some might call it a mountain) that forms the north wall of Calico Basin. The south face of the massif has numerous cliffs and lots of broken sections. Only a few routes will be described on the south face and they are roughly above the Kraft Rocks bouldering area, which is considered by many to be the finest in the area.

To access these climbs, turn off West Charleston (Route 159) onto Calico Basin Road and follow it 1.2 miles to a "T" intersection. Turn right (the Rock Springs Picnic Area will be to the left) and go through a gate marked "Private Property." Turn left about 40 yards inside the gate and follow the street for about 200 yards. At the next curve, go right, following the larger road for 0.4 mile. Turn right just after a house on

Kraft Crags

53.	Shark Vegas	56.	Weasel Yeast
54.	Viva Las Vegas	58.	Porch Pirate

the right with a pond and very green lawn, and about 100 yards before this road ends. Drive 0.1 mile, turn left at a series of huge adobe-like walls (the obvious way to go) and drive another 0.2 mile to the end of this road.

When viewed from the parking area, the bouldering will be spread out just right of center, and the climbs described will be almost directly in front of you, about 200 yards uphill on a pinkish cliff. **Remember, all of the climbing here is surrounded by private land – be considerate and unobtrusive!**

52. **High Roller** 5.11+ PG13   FA: Paul Van Betten, Jay Smith–1986.
    Start about 50 feet left of the **Shark Vegas** overhang/cave in the center of the cliff.

    P1 Climb a shallow left-facing dihedral over a roof (scary; thin pro). Belay at the base of an off-width crack. 80 ft, 5.11+.

    P2 Swim up the awful-width above. 80 ft, 5.10+.

53. **Shark Vegas** 5.11- PG   FA: Paul Van Betten, Nick Nordblom–1986.
    Start in the center of the cliff, below a large overhang/cave midway up the cliff and by the right of two big boulders at the cliff's base. Wander up lower-angled rock along vertical fissures to a short, varnished slab 50 feet up (bolt). Climb the striking, left-facing flake/crack up and left to the top. Photo, page 17.

54. **Viva Las Vegas** 5.11- PG13   FA: Robert Finlay, Paul Van Betten, Mike Ward, Randy Grandstaff–1986.
    Begin just right of **Shark Vegas** and climb the face to an obvious vertical crack, which is followed to the top. The small wires at the start of the route might be a bit questionable, hence the protection rating. Photo, page 17

55. **Vegas Girls** 5.11 PG13   FA: Paul Crawford, Paul Van Betten, Nick Nordblom–1986.
    Start just right of **Viva Las Vegas** and climb huecos and a shallow arête past three bolts to the top. There is an important natural thread in the ceiling.

The next three routes are located about 150 yards right and uphill from **Vegas Girls**.

56. **Weasel Yeast** 5.10   FA: Nick Nordblom, Paul Van Betten–1986.
    This route sits above the **Porch Pirate** and can be accessed by a gully system to the left (west) of the **Porch Pirate**. Climb a left-leaning handcrack to a roof. Belay above on a ledge. Photo, page 17.

57. **Weasel Cheese** 5.11- (TR)   FA: Paul Van Betten–1986.
    From partway up the **Weasel Yeast** handcrack, move out right and pull the roof into a scoop.

58. **Porch Pirate** 5.11 R   FA: Paul Van Betten, Paul Crawford, Sal Mamusia–October 1991.
    This scary but good-looking route begins about 150 yards right and uphill from **Vegas Girls**, near a large, prickly acacia bush. Scramble up and left about 40 feet on a ramp to reach a ledge, where you should find a "fixed" Hot Wheels car in a crack. Follow faint cracks up and left to a very shallow dihedral. Climb this, clipping a few bolts, then run it out up the face above to the top. Descend down the gully to the left, which is used as the approach route for the last two routes. Photo, page 17.

The Conundrum Crag

Approach by walking right (east) from the parking area through the Kraft Boulders along a well used trail. This trail will contour around the right side of Kraft Crags "mountain," going along the left (west) side of a huge wash/drainage. This sunny crag has at least two routes on it and sits about 150 yards up and slightly left from the Monkey Bars boulder (the last, huge, chalk covered boulder with a cave on its southern side). Both routes face southeast and are on a pink cliff. Approach takes about ten minutes.

59. **Satan In A Can** 5.12c   FA: Steve "Bucky" Bullock, Scott "Jimmy Dean" Carson–1992.
    Three bolts lead to chains.

60. **Drilling Miss Daisy** 5.11a   FA: "Bucky" and "Jimmy Dean" –1992.
    Four bolts lead past big holds to a chain anchor. You may wish to stick clip the first bolt.

61. **Arrowhead Arête** 5.11d   FA: Leo Henson–January 1994.
    Climb the arête that is uphill and across from the previous two routes. There are supposed to be about five bolts on the route.

KRAFT CANYON

The next four cliffs are located in the drainage on the back (north) side of Kraft Crags. While you can approach the northwestern crags by walking left (northwest) from the parking area, it is easier to approach all of these cliffs by walking right (east) past the bouldering area into the mouth of the canyon. The cliffs will be described as you encounter them while walking up canyon.

Caligula Crag

A sunny cliff located about 450 yards to the northeast of the Monkey Bars boulder, it is one of the many crags I haven't been to yet. Approach by walking right (east) from the parking area through the Kraft Boulders along a well used trail. This trail will contour around the right side of Kraft Crags "mountain," going along the left (west) side of a huge wash/drainage. This crag is on the hillside beyond the mouth of the drainage and sits above dirt roads that are visible from the Monkey Bars boulder (the last, huge, chalk-covered boulder with a cave on its southern side). Routes are described from left to right. Approach takes 15 minutes.

62. **Penthouse Pet** 5.11-   FA: Paul Van Betten, Richard Harrison–January 1990.
    Climb a thin corner on the left (west) edge of the wall, finishing up and right past a bolt to a rappel anchor on a ledge.

63. **Disguise The Limit** 5.11d   FA: Paul Van Betten–January 1990.
    Scramble up a bit, then climb an arête past three bolts, finishing on **Penthouse Pet**.

64. **Caligula** 5.12-   FA: Paul Van Betten, Richard Harrison–January 1990. Climb up to a roof, pull this (#3 Friend), then climb a thin crack to the **Penthouse Pet** anchor. Bring multiple pieces in the ¼" to 1" range.

65. **Guccione** 5.11c   FA: Richard Harrison, Paul Van Betten–January 1990. Named for the publisher of *Penthouse* magazine. Climb past about five bolts on the right (east) side of the cliff. This route is just left of a chimney.

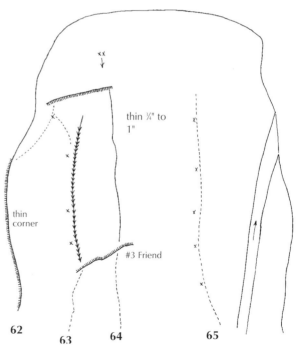

thin ¼" to 1"

thin corner

#3 Friend

62

63   64   65

Cannabis Crag

Another cliff I haven't visited. This sunny escarpment sits on the right (north) side of the drainage, about 15 minutes upstream from the Monkey Bars boulder (the last, huge, chalk-covered boulder with a cave on its southern side). It is about ten minutes downstream from the Sunny and Steep Cliff and sits about 40 yards above the drainage floor. Approach by walking right (east) from the parking area through the Kraft Boulders along a well-used trail. This trail contours around the right side of Kraft Crags "mountain," going along the left (west) side of a huge wash/drainage, then curving around the back side of the "mountain" until it joins a dirt road. Follow the road upstream for about 30 yards, then enter an obvious drainage. Continue upstream in the drainage for about ten minutes (it'll seem longer). Routes will be described from right to left as you approach up the canyon.

66. **Smokin'** 5.12b   FA: Unknown–1993.
    Four bolts lead to an anchor on the right (east) side of the formation. This route has a distinctive scar just right of the anchor, where a huge flake fell off (almost killing Paul Van Betten!).

67. **One Man's Kokopelli Is Another Man's Side Show Bob** 5.12d   FA: Paul Van Betten, Richard Harrison, Michelle Locatelli–November 1993.
    If you've seen the Simpsons and know anything about Anasazi rock art, this name will make sense! Follow a left-slanting seam off a ledge, then continue up the face to an anchor. Seven bolts.

68. **Freak Brothers** 5.13a   FA: Paul Van Betten, Shelby Shelton–October 1994.
    Start at a bolt below a ledge. Climb up and right past seven bolts to an anchor.

69. **KGB** 5.12a   FA: Dan McQuade, Jim Greg–Spring 1993.
    Start as per **Freak Brothers** but climb up and left past two bolts to a ledge. Continue past five more bolts to an anchor.

70. **Cannabis** 5.12a   FA: Dan McQuade, Jim Greg–Spring 1993.
    Begin just left of a black water streak and at the base of a left-leaning crack. Four bolts lead up and slightly left to shuts. There is one bolt in the water streak to the right, but the route hasn't been completed yet.

71. **Synapse Collapse** 5.11d   FA: Dan McQuade, Jim Greg–Spring 1993.
    Begin just left of the last route and climb up and left past four bolts to another set of cold shuts.

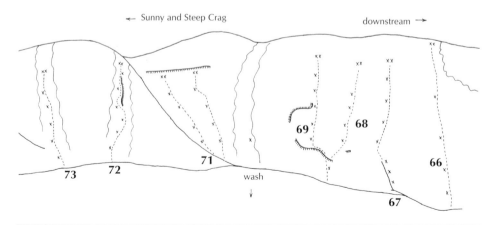

← Sunny and Steep Crag   downstream →

wash

72. **The Fiend** 5.12c   FA: Dan McQuade, Jim Greg–Spring 1993.
Rope up to the left of the last two routes at the next water streak. Six bolts lead up the water streak and past a left-facing corner to an anchor. The first bolt is apparently best clipped with a stick.

73. **Cavity Search** 5.12d   FA: Dan McQuade, Jim Greg–Spring 1993.
Five bolts lead up the next water streak to the left (west).

74. **The Felon** 5.11c   FA: Dan McQuade, Jim Greg–Spring 1993.
At the left end of the cliff is this four-bolt line that leads to cold shuts.

Winter Heat Wall

This excellent cliff is in the shade most of the day and features traditional routes. Approach by walking right (east) from the parking area through the Kraft Boulders along a well used trail. This trail contours around the right side of Kraft Crags "mountain," going along the left (west) side of a huge wash/drainage, then curving around the back side of the "mountain" until it joins a dirt road. Follow the road upstream for about 30 yards, then enter an obvious drainage. Continue upstream in the drainage for about 15 minutes (it'll seem longer). You'll pass several crags with obvious cracks and some bolts before you come to the Winter Heat Wall, which will be on your left and is characterized by a dark varnish. The crag is divided into three sections by chimney/crack systems, with the routes described herein located on the central, smoother section. Total approach time is about 30 minutes. Routes will be described from left to right.

75. **A-OK** 5.0   FA: Unknown–1980s.
Climb the short, left curving chimney at the left margin of the central wall. This route ends at a small sapling. Walk off left or rappel down **Winter Heat**.

76. **Mo Hotta, Mo Betta** 5.8 R   FA: Todd Swain, Donette Smith–October 1994.
Begin at the base of the curving chimney (**A-OK**) that is 25 feet up and left from **Couldn't Be Schmooter** and just left of a block. Follow a small ramp up and right to its top. Step left, then climb straight up the face past honeycombed rock and huecos to finish in a thin, vertical seam that is just left of a nose.

77. **Nuttin' Could Be Finer** 5.7 R   FA: Bobby Knight, Donette Smith, Todd Swain–October 1994.
Follow the previous route to the top of the ramp, then go straight up the face past numerous huecos to finish in the left-hand of two obvious vertical cracks.

78. **Couldn't Be Schmooter** 5.9 ◄   FA: Wendell Broussard, Richard Harrison, Paul Crawford–Spring 1983.
Bring gear to a # 3.5 Friend and some long slings for this excellent route. Climb the face along a very obvious crack, using huecos and the thin crack for protection. Finish in the right-hand of the two final cracks. Belay off a small oak tree and medium-sized Friends. Scramble off left (east) down ramps or rappel from the top of **Winter Heat** with one rope.

79. **Autumnal Frost** 5.11+ ◄   FA: Todd Swain–October 1994.
This route was originally attempted by Paul Crawford, who placed the first bolt on the route. If you're under 6'3", you'll be in trouble on this one! Start in the center of the crag, at a point 15 feet right of **Couldn't...** and ten feet left of **Winter Heat**. Climb up and left along a series of huecos, aiming for a shallow groove that begins 35 feet up. When the huecos end, make very height-related moves up the smooth face past two bolts, then move left into the groove. Follow this to easier face climbing and the top.

80. **Winter Heat** 5.11 ◄   FA: Paul Crawford, Jay Smith, Richard Harrison, Paul Van Betten–Spring 1983.
Bring wires and TCUs. Begin ten feet up and right of the last route at some boulders sitting at the base of crag. Climb the obvious vertical corner/groove to its end. Step right, then up another overhanging corner/groove to a two-shut anchor.

High Class Hoe *5.10-* 🔽*: Donette Smith on the route's crux fingercrack.*

81. **Vernal Thaw** 5.11 (TR)   FA: Bobby Knight, Todd Swain–October 1994.
Climb **Winter Heat** for ten feet, then move right at some huecos to a thin, vertical seam. Climb the seam and face above, finishing through an overhanging, light-colored bulge.

82. **High Class Hoe** 5.10- ◀   FA: Richard Harrison, Wendell Broussard, Paul Van Betten–Spring 1983.
Carry gear up to a #2 Friend and some long slings. Start 20 feet up and right of **Winter Heat** at a short fingercrack. This crack is just left of a huge crack/corner forming the right edge of the central section of the crag. Climb the fingercrack to a ledge (crux), then angle left over a ceiling (intimidating) to a left-leaning groove/corner. Exit left at the top of the corner to an anchor and rappel with one rope.

Sunny and Steep Crag

This relatively new sport crag became instantly popular. As the name implies, it's in the sun most of the day, although it's steep enough to be shady on summer mornings when the sun is higher in the sky. Approach by walking right (east) from the parking area through the Kraft Boulders along a well used trail. This trail contours around the right side of Kraft Crags "mountain," going along the left (west) side of a huge wash/drainage, then curving around the backside of the "mountain" until it joins a dirt road. Follow the road upstream for about 30 yards, then enter an obvious drainage. Slog upstream in the drainage for about 15 minutes (it'll seem longer). You'll pass several crags with obvious crack systems and bolts before coming to the Winter Heat Wall, which will be on your left and is characterized by dark varnish. Continue another 150 yards upstream to the Sunny and Steep Crag, which is on the right side of the drainage and partially hidden by a large flat terrace that lies below it. The approach takes about 35 minutes. Routes are described from right to left. Topo, page 24.

83. **Working For Peanuts** 5.9 PG   FA: Ward and Chris Smith, Dave Quinn–February 1994.
The Smith brothers have been putting up new routes in New England since the mid-1970s; they currently live in Massachusetts. This route follows cracks and five bolts along a lower-angled arête that is separated from the main formation by a chimney. Make sure you have an attentive belayer on the first few moves.

84. **Cirque De Soleil** 5.11b   FA: Paula King, Ward Smith, Steve Wood–February 1994.
Named for the famous circus troupe that originated in Montreal and now performs regularly in Las Vegas. Begin four feet left of the last route on the left side of a chimney. Stem up a few moves then follow a total of ten bolts to the anchor. Either rappel 100 feet to the ground with two ropes, or use one rope to lower to an intermediate anchor and then from that to the ground.

85. **Mr. Choad's Wild Ride** 5.11b   FA: Ward Smith, Steve Wood–February 1994.
Start eight feet left of the chimney mentioned in the last route at a left-facing corner. Follow ten bolts to the anchor. Either rappel 100 feet to the ground with two ropes, or use one rope to lower to an intermediate anchor and then from that to the ground.

86. **Solar Flare** 5.11d   FA: Dave Quinn, Ward and Chris Smith–February 1994.
Begin ten feet left of the last route at the base of a steep, left-leaning seam. Stick clip the first bolt, then follow five more to the anchor.

87. **Peak Performance** 5.11d   FA: Chris and Ward Smith, Dave Quinn–February 1994.
Rope up ten feet down and left of the last route, behind a boulder. Clip seven bolts enroute to a shared anchor.

88. **Turbo Dog** 5.12b   FA: Ward Smith–February 1994.
A steep route that starts eight feet left of **Peak Performance**, behind a boulder. If you can, climb past seven bolts to the same anchor as **Peak Performance**.

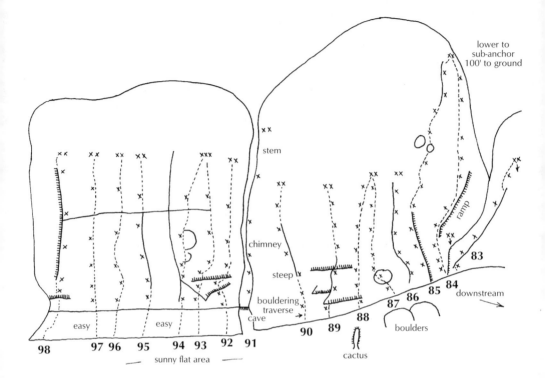

89. **Steep Thrills** 5.12a   FA: Ward Smith–February 1994.
Another overhung route that is 16 feet right of a chimney and ten feet left of the previous route. Six bolts lead to a rest at the anchor.

90. **Gimme Back My Bullets** 5.12a ◀   FA: The brothers from New England–February 1994.
The excellent, six-bolt route is eight feet right of the obvious chimney that splits the formation.

91. **The Sport Chimney** 5.8   FA: The New England dudes plus Steve Wood–February 1994.
Face climb, wiggle, and stem up the obvious varnished chimney past five bolts.

92. **Tour De Pump** 5.12a   FA: Ward Smith–February 1994.
Rope up twenty feet left of the central chimney and climb past six bolts to the anchor.

93. **Sunny And Steep** 5.12a   FA: Ward Smith, Dave Quinn–February 1994.
Begin seven feet left of **Tour De Pump** and follow six bolts to a shared three-bolt anchor.

94. **Turtle Wax** 5.11b   FA: Dave Quinn, the guys from Taxachussetts–February 1994.
A five-bolt climb five feet right of the last route. Although it's possible to climb the right-handcrack, it's easier to climb the huge huecos further right. This route shares the same anchor as **Sunny And Steep**.

95. **Scorpions** 5.11b   FA: Chris and Ward Smith, Leslie Smith, Paula King–February 1994.
Follow overhanging huecos along the left-hand of two cracks past five bolts.

96. **Blackened** 5.11d   FA: Ward Smith–February 1994.
Climb past five bolts beginning seven feet left of the last route and ten feet right of an ugly chimney.

97. **Black Happy** 5.11d   FA: The Brothers Smith–February 1994.
Follow five bolts that are five feet left of the last line and five feet right of a chimney.

98. **Claim Jumper's Special** 5.10d   FA: The Smith Brothers, Leslie Ward, Paula King–February 1994.
The leftmost route on the crag – it has five bolts and climbs just right of a chimney.

The next two routes are on a free-standing boulder that is about 150 yards to the left of the main cliff.

99. **Golden Nugget** 5.11d   FA: Chris and Ward Smith–February 1994.
This route climbs a steep face past four bolts to an anchor.

100. **Edward Silverhands** 5.10a   FA: Todd Swain, Donette Smith–April 1994.
This three-bolt route is located 20 feet left and around the corner from **Golden Nugget**.

This route sits on the next south facing formation to the left (up canyon) of the **Golden Nugget** *boulder.*

101. **Chunder Bolt** 5.12a   FA: Shelby Shelton, Paul Van Betten, Danny Reider, Richard Harrison, Michelle Locatelli–January 1994.
Climbs a vertical crack system past about eight bolts to a chain anchor.

Easy access: *First Pullout climbs feature short distances from parking.*

FIRST PULLOUT

Eleven crags are described in this chapter, probably the best of which are Dog Wall and the Fixx Cliff. The Fixx Cliff was one of the first small, modern cliffs to be developed at Red Rocks and subsequently led to establishing popular cliffs like the Gallery. All of these routes have very short approaches and generally are in the sun most of the day. To reach the first pullout, drive the scenic loop road for 1.1 miles and park in the designated area on the right. The cliffs are generally described from right (toward the loop road entrance) to left (toward the second pullout).

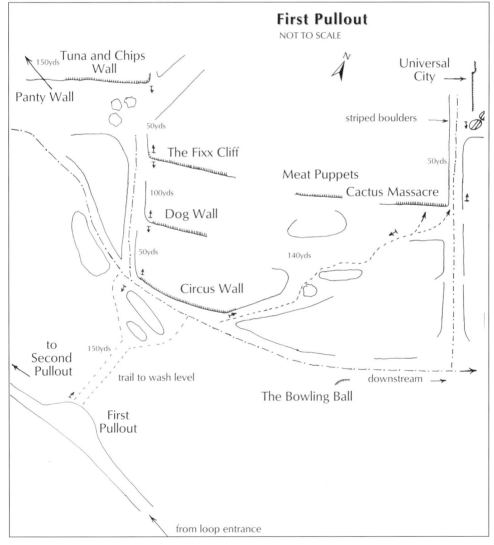

First Pullout
NOT TO SCALE

150yds — Tuna and Chips Wall

Panty Wall

Universal City →

striped boulders →

50yds

The Fixx Cliff

50yds

Meat Puppets

Cactus Massacre

100yds

Dog Wall

50yds

Circus Wall

140yds

to Second Pullout

150yds

trail to wash level

downstream →

The Bowling Ball

First Pullout

from loop entrance

VELVET ELVIS, CLIMB BOMB, UNIVERSAL CITY, CACTUS MASSACRE APPROACH

To approach the first four cliffs in this chapter, walk down the trail from the parking lot to the wash (150 yards), then go up right (southeast) on a ramp that is just right of the Circus Wall (the somewhat rotten cliff that is right at the level of the wash and is characterized by a large arch/ceiling in the middle of the cliff) for 50 yards to a small saddle (graffiti on the left side of this saddle says "T SOL").

Continue in the same direction, dropping down into a hole then scrambling back up to the same elevation (another 40 yards). The gray-colored Cactus Massacre wall is now 50 yards toward the hillside (left/north) and is characterized by a right-leaning crack crossing the cliff at ⅓ height. Walk 30 yards right from **Cactus Massacre** to a gully and go up this for about 50 yards, passing an arch formed by boulders leaning across the gully. **Universal City** will be up on the right, facing northwest (left).

Velvet Elvis and **Climb Bomb** are to the right of **Universal City** (toward the entrance to the loop road), and about 100 feet right of two boulders with right-leaning white stripes on them. Routes are described from left to right as you approach from Universal City.

Climb Bomb Cliff

This cliff is 100 feet right and just down over the crest of the ridge from **Universal City**. It is a bulbous, overhanging boulder on the right side of a short gully and a patch of scrub oak. The cliff faces toward the road and is in the sun all day. Routes are described from left to right.

First Pullout (right side overview)

A	Circus Wall	D	Universal City
B	Meat Puppet	E	Climb Bomb
C	Cactus Massacre	F	Velvet Elvis

1. **Climb Warp** 5.11- FA: Paul Van Betten, Robert Finlay–December 1988.
   Start near the left edge of the formation at some big boulders. Climb to the top of a pedestal then up an overhanging seam past one bolt. Walk off left toward the back of **Universal City**.

2. **Climb Bomb** 5.11+ R FA: Paul Van Betten, Robert Finlay–December 1988.
   Rope up 15 feet right of **Climb Warp** at a left-leaning crack that is five feet left of a gully. Climb the broken crack to a ledge, then power out a roof past two bolts and a round hueco to overhanging seams and the summit.

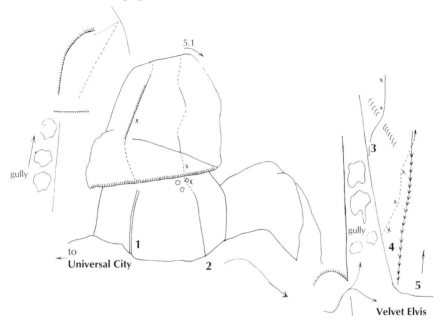

Velvet Elvis Crag

The next buttress to the right (northeast) of **Climb Bomb** has a distinct gully on its left side. Routes are described from left to right, starting about 75 feet up the gully.

3. **Black Tongue** 5.11? FA: Paul Van Betten, Sal Mamusia–1989.
   A few too many crab legs causes **Black Tongue**! Carry wires and TCUs to supplement the bolts. Begin in the midst of oak bushes below a shallow crack/dihedral that has two bolts on its left aspect. Follow the crack/dihedral past a bulge to the top. Walk off toward the top of the gully.

4. **Isis** 5.11-? FA: Sal Mamusia, Paul Van Betten–1989.
   Rope up at the mouth of the gully, on the left (west) side of a rounded arête. This is the first route you'll see as you approach the crag from **Climb Bomb**. Climb the face to the left of the arête past three bolts. Wires and TCUs needed.

5. **Velvet Elvis** 5.12- FA: Paul Van Betten, Don Welsh–November 1988.
   Start 15 feet right of the last route on the south face of the formation, below a vertical crack system. Climb the crack and seam system past three bolts. Bring wires, TCUs and Friends.

6. **Climb Bandits** 5.10 FA: Paul Van Betten, Sal Mamusia–1989.
   This route is supposed to be about 30 yards to the right of **Velvet Elvis**. It climbs a hand-crack to a roof, then finishes up a face.

7. **Claw Hammer** 5.9?   FA: "Frodo" Lybarger–1989.
   This route is somewhere down and right of the last climb and goes up a face with one bolt (which was hand drilled using a claw hammer).

Universal City

This shady crag is located near the top of the hillside, to the right (east) of the parking area. It's about 50 yards above **Cactus Massacre**, and just left of two boulders with right-leaning stripes on them. The cliff faces northwest and its routes will be described from right to left as you approach up the gully. Photo, page 28.

8. **Prime Ticket** 5.11b   FA: Randy Faulk–November 1991.
   Start atop a boulder just left of a crack/alcove. Seven bolts to cold shuts.

9. **Cameo Appearance** 5.11c   FA: Randy Faulk–November 1991.
   Begin 15 feet left of the last route, between two bushes. Climb up right to a horizontal (bolt), then cruise along a vertical seam past three bolts. Continue up the steep face past two more bolts to a shared cold shut anchor.

10. **Celebrity Roast** 5.12b FA: Leo Henson, Randy Faulk, Dan McQuade–November 1991.
    Start as per the previous route, then move left at the horizontal and power past seven bolts and one cold shut to the anchor on **Cameo Appearance**.

11. **Star Search** 5.11c   FA: Randy Faulk, Doug Henze–November 1991.
    Rope up five feet left of **Celebrity Roast** by a block on the ground. Six bolts along a vertical seam lead to the anchor.

12. **Quiet On The Set** 5.10c   FA: Louie Anderson, Bart Groendycke–December 1991.
    Begin five feet left of the last route and climb the arête that is just right of a corner. There are five bolts with black hangers on this somewhat contrived route. If you step into the corner, the route is about 5.8.

13. **Ed MacMayonnaise** 5.8   FA: Todd Swain–July 1992.
    Climb the obvious left-facing corner on the left (north) side of the face.

Cactus Massacre

This gray-colored crag has three steep and somewhat loose routes. The cliff is about 200 yards right (east) of Dog Wall, at about the same level on the hillside. It is slightly below and to the right of the parking lot, with the climbs being in the shade in the morning; it is characterized by a right-leaning crack crossing the cliff at ⅓ height. Photo, page 28.

14. **Cactus Massacre 5.11**
    FA: Paul Van Betten, Sal Mamusia, Mike Ward–December 1987.
    The left route. Begin in the center of the cliff, just right of obvious parallel, varnished, vertical seams. Scamper up 15 feet to a ledge, then climb past a bolt (either left, right or center), con-

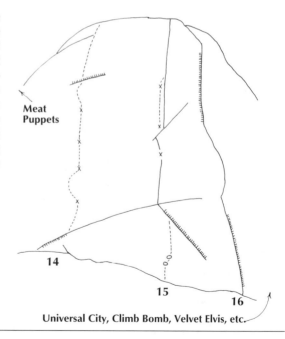

Universal City, Climb Bomb, Velvet Elvis, etc.

tinuing past three more bolts to a ledge. Either continue to the top, or downclimb and lower off the last bolt. Bring a #2.5 Friend and TCUs.

15. **Cactus Root** 5.11+   FA: Paul Van Betten, Sal Mamusia, Jim Olsen –December 1987. Bring a smattering of gear, including a #2.5 Friend. Start 30 feet right of the previous route at a left-slanting crack/corner that leads to a vertical crack. Follow the crack system past three bolts to the top.

16. **Cactus Head** 5.9   FA: Paul Van Betten, Don Welsh–1989. This route starts up a left-facing corner (right of **Cactus Root**), follows a crack, then finishes up a right-facing corner.

Meat Puppets Wall

This short, brown wall sits to the left and slightly above Cactus Massacre. Routes are described from left to right. All require gear for anchors. Photo, page 28.

17. **Blanc Czech** 5.11c   FA: Nick Nordblom, Paul Van Betten–1989. Climb past four bolts at the left edge of the wall.

18. **Hodad** 5.12-   FA: Paul Van Betten–1989. Angle out left to a bolt, then go up the face past two more bolts to finish in a crack.

19. **Crawdad** 5.11?   FA: Paul Van Betten–1989. A three-bolt route to the right of **Hodad**.

20. **Yellow Dog** 5.11-   FA: Paul Van Betten–1989. Climb past one bolt and gear placements to the summit.

21. **Ranger Danger** 5.10-   FA: Bob Conz, Bob Yoho–1989. Climb the left-hand of two crack systems in the center of the cliff.

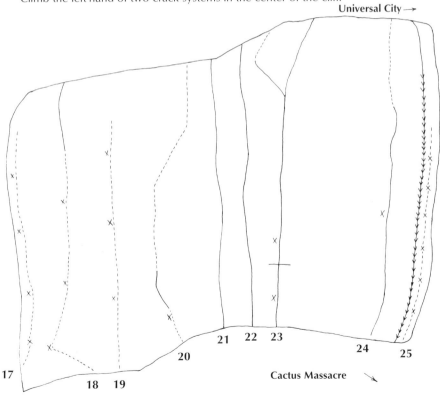

22. **Meat Puppet** 5.11- FA: Paul Van Betten, Mike Ward, Sal Mamusia–1989.
The right-hand of two central crack systems.

23. **Gay Nazis For Christ** 5.12 FA: Paul Van Betten–1989.
Climb a crack system past two bolts.

24. **Green Eagle** 5.12- FA: Paul Van Betten–1989.
Climb a crack system on the right side of the cliff past one bolt.

25. **The Max Flex** 5.11c FA: Craig Reason–1989.
Climb past a bunch of ring bolts on the extreme right side of the crag.

First Pullout (left side overview)

A	Panty Wall	**C**	The Fixx Cliff	**E**	Circus Wall (below)
B	Tuna and Chips Wall	**D**	Dog Wall		

The Bowling Ball

This small, overhanging wall is located about 50 yards right (downstream) of Circus Wall and faces toward Cactus Massacre.

26. **Take The Skinheads Bowling** 5.12 FA: Paul Van Betten–June 1988.
Three bolts and wires will get you up this route. The start uses finger pockets similar to those found on a bowling ball.

Circus Wall

This is the cliff that is right at the level of the wash, and is characterized by a large arch/ceiling in its middle and a smaller arch on its right. It is not quite visible from the parking lot, but as you walk down the trail toward the wash, it will become obvious. Climbs on this sunny cliff are listed from left to right. Photo, page 28.

27. **Human Cannonball** 5.8? FA: Kurt Mauer?
Begin in the wash at graffiti that says "Black Panthers Local 431" and five feet left of a crack. Climb past one bolt to a ledge then up to the top.

28. **High Wire** 5.10-   FA: Unknown.
Climb the fingercrack just right of the graffiti mentioned above and 50 feet left of the big arch in the center of the cliff.

29. **Carful Of Clowns** 5.10?   FA: Unknown.
Start 30 feet right of the last route and 20 feet left of the central arch at a white water streak above "Patrick Loves Michelle Feb. 23 90." Climb past two bolts to the top.

30. **Lion Tamer** 5.11? (TR?)   FA: Unknown.
Begin ten feet right of **Carful...** at a short crack that leads to the left edge of the central arch. Follow the crack to a small ceiling, then straight up the face to a vertical seam.

31. **Circus Boy** 5.11+   FA: Paul Van Betten, Sal Mamusia–December 1987.
Scamper up ledges to the left end of the central arch, then climb past two bolts, finishing up a thin seam.

32. **Main Attraction** 5.12+   FA: Paul Van Betten, Sal Mamusia–December 1987.
Climb out the center of the roof using one bolt. There are chains for rappelling.

33. **Midway** 5.12   FA: Paul Van Betten, Nick Nordblom–December 1987.
Rope up 20 feet right of the previous climb near the right edge of the main arch. Climb past three bolts, staying just right of a seam, to a chain anchor.

34. **Crowd Pleaser** 5.12-   FA: Paul Van Betten, Sal Mamusia–December 1987.
Starting 15 feet right of the right edge of the arch below a left-leaning crack. Climb up the crack, then follow a seam past four bolts.

35. **Elephant Man** 5.11-   FA: Jay Smith.
Begin as per the previous route, but move up right into a vertical crack. Climb the face above, past a drilled angle piton and a bolt.

36. **Big Top** 5.10   FA: Jay Smith.
Start five feet right, at the left end of the small arch on the right side of the wall. Climb over the arch to a flaring crack, then past a bolt to the top.

Dog Wall

A popular sport cliff with a quick approach. Walk down the trail from the parking lot to the wash, then go left 150 feet to the edge of the Circus Wall. Dog Wall is about 200 feet up a gully to the right, on the next level above the Circus Wall. This cliff is plainly visible from the trailhead, appearing as the lowest good face. Routes are described from left to right. To access the top, continue up the gully about 50 feet, then go right. From the top, walk off left. Topo, page 34; photos, pages 32 and 36.

37. **Wok The Dog** 5.7   FA: Todd Swain–January 1992.
Bring your pooper scooper. Near the left edge of the crag, and above the approach gully, climb a low-angled, right-leaning ramp to the top of the wall.

38. **Cat Walk** 5.10a ◀   FA: Don Burroughs, Alan Busby–January 1992.
Begin 40 feet right, at the left end of a right-leaning ramp/flake, about 75 feet up from the drainage. Climb past four bolts to a chain anchor.

39. **It's A Bitch** 5.10b ◀   FA: California Dudes–circa 1987.
Start five feet right of **Cat Walk**; crank past four bolts to a cold shut anchor. Rebolted by Randy Faulk and Leo Henson in 1991 after going many years with chopped bolts.

40. **Man's Best Friend** 5.10 R/X   FA: Todd Swain–January 1992.
Not exactly. Climb the right-leaning ramp/flake noted in the last two routes, finishing up the unprotected face.

41. **Here Kitty, Kitty** 5.11c   FA: Geoff Weigand–circa 1987.
Begin 30 feet right of the ramp/flake atop a block. Power past four bolts to a cold shut anchor. Rebolted in 1991 after having been chopped long ago.

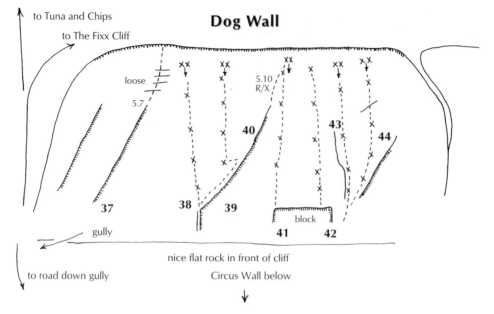

to Tuna and Chips

to The Fixx Cliff

Dog Wall

loose

5.7

5.10 R/X

37

38 39

40

41 42

block

43

44

gully

to road down gully

nice flat rock in front of cliff

Circus Wall below

42. **K-9** 5.12b   FA: Geoff Weigand–circa 1987.
Gear up eight feet right of the last route, at the right end of a block at the base of the cliff. Climb past five bolts to the bolt anchor on top. Rebolted in 1991.

43. **Cujo** 5.11d   FA: Geoff Weigand–circa 1987.
Rope up five feet right at a white streak and just left of a large flake. Climb past five bolts to a cold shut anchor. Rebolted in 1991.

44. **Poodle Chainsaw Massacre** 5.11c   FA: Randy Faulk, Karin Olson–October 1991.
Climb past four bolts to a cold shut anchor, starting at a right-leaning flake five feet right of the previous route.

The Fixx Cliff

The first semi-sport cliff to be developed in the area. Bring traditional gear for the routes here. Follow the trail from the parking lot down to the wash, then turn left (northwest) and follow the drainage about 200 feet until it turns uphill. About 250 feet up from the bottom of the wash (and 100 feet above the turnoff for Dog Wall) the drainage is split by a rock shaped like the prow of a ship. Take the right fork (straight ahead) and scramble up about 300 feet. The cliff will be on your right. Like Dog Wall, it too is plainly visible from the trailhead, being level with the road and just left of center as you view the cliff bands. Routes are again described from left to right. Descend off the right side. Photos, pages 32 and 36.

45. **The Whiff** 5.10- PG   FA: Jay Smith, Mike Ward–March 1987.
The finger-and-hand crack near the left edge of the cliff. Hard to protect.

46. **Snow Blind** 5.11 R   FA: Paul Crawford–March 1987.
Start ten feet right of **The Whiff** and climb steep huecos past one bolt to a vague arête.

47. **Stand Or Fall** 5.11-   FA: Paul Van Betten, Jim "Frodo" Lybarger–March 1987.
Begin five feet right of the last route and climb steep huecos past one bolt to a crack.

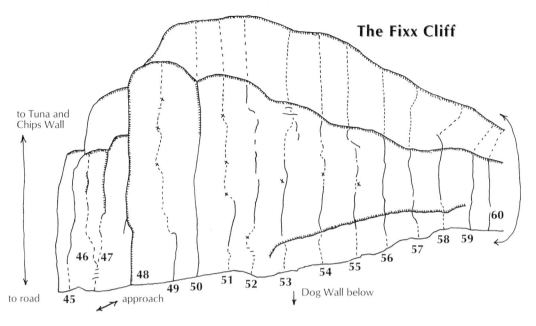

The Fixx Cliff

to Tuna and Chips Wall

to road 45 approach 46 47 48 49 50 51 52 53 54 55 56 57 58 59 60

Dog Wall below

48. **Crack** 5.11 ◄ FA: Paul Crawford, Jay Smith–March 1987.
Crank up the obvious finger crack eight feet right of the previous route.

49. **Free Base** 5.11 ◄ FA: Paul Crawford, Paul Van Betten, Jay Smith, Nick Nordblom –March 1987.
Rope up ten feet right of **Crack** and climb a vertical crack to three bolts along an over-hanging seam.

50. **Saved By Zero** 5.11 ◄ FA: Nick Nordblom, Danny Meyers–May 1986.
Climb the steep finger-and-hand crack that is ten feet right of **Free Base**.

51. **Red Skies** 5.11+ FA: Paul Van Betten, Paul Crawford–March 1987.
Follow a seam and three bolts five feet right of **Saved By Zero**.

52. **The Geezer** 5.11 FA: Jay Smith, Paul Crawford–March 1987.
Starting ten feet right, climb the pink face past a drilled angle.

53. **Cocaine Hotline** 5.11 FA: Paul Crawford, John Rosholt, Jay Smith–March 1987.
Begin eight feet right and climb a thin seam up varnished rock past one bolt.

54. **Reach The Beach** 5.11 FA: Nick Nordblom, Jenni Stone, Paul Crawford, Jay Smith–March 1987.
Rope up six feet right of **Cocaine Hotline** at the left edge of a low boulder and bushes. Climb a thin varnished seam past one bolt.

55. **Eight Ball** 5.11 FA: Paul Crawford, Jay Smith, Nick Nordblom, Jenni Stone–March 1987.
Start ten feet right of **Reach...** and face climb to a thin seam and a bolt.

56. **One Thing Leads To Another** 5.11 FA: Nick Nordblom, Jenni Stone, Paul Crawford, Jay Smith–March 1987.
Climb the thin seam eight feet right of **Eight Ball**.

57. **The Skagg** 5.11 FA: Mike Ward, Paul Van Betten, Paul Crawford, Jay Smith–March 1987.
Power up the 30-foot-high seam that is ten feet right of the last route.

58. **Running** 5.11- FA: Nick Nordblom, Jenni Stone–March 1987.
Climb the next seam ten feet to the right – also about 30 feet long.

59. **Outside The Envelope** 5.11   FA: Nick Nordblom (solo)–March 1987.
    Crank up the seam eight feet right – about 20 feet high.

60. **The Bindle** 5.11   FA: Unknown–1987 or later.
    Shoot up the very short seam ten feet right of the last route, near the crag's far right edge.

Tuna And Chips Wall

Follow the trail from the parking lot down to the wash, then turn left (northwest) and follow the drainage about 200 feet until it turns uphill. About 250 feet up from the bottom of the wash (and 100 feet above the turnoff for Dog Wall) the drainage is split by a rock shaped like the prow of a ship. Take the right fork (straight ahead) and scramble up about 300 feet. The Fixx Cliff will be on your right. Continue up the drainage past The Fixx Cliff about 150 feet to a big, plated cliff blocking the drainage. You will arrive at the center of the cliff, just right of a low-angled crack and directly below a water streak. Routes on this sunny cliff will be described from right to left. Walk off to the right (east), then follow a gully back to the base of the cliff.

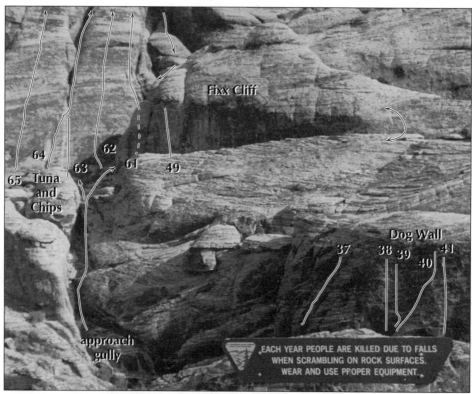

Tuna and Chips, The Fixx Cliff and Dog Wall

37. Wok The Dog	41. Here Kitty, Kitty	63. Waterstreak
38. Cat Walk	49. Free Base	64. Chips And Salsa
39. It's A Bitch	61. Chips Ahoy!	65. Tuna And Chips
40. Man's Best Friend	62. Tuna Cookies	

61. **Chips Ahoy!** 5.9 R   FA: Mike Ward, Paul Van Betten–1986.
Start 50 feet right of the crack/gully in the center of the cliff and atop boulders below left-slanting seams.

P1 Climb steep varnished rock above the left slanting seams and continue up the plated face above, passing two bolts to a two-bolt belay. 120 ft, 5.8.

P2 Power through the roof above (bolt, crux) to easier ground and the top of the formation. 100 ft, 5.9.

Descend off right.

62. **Tuna Cookies** 5.7 R   FA: National Outdoor Leadership School (NOLS) staff–1987.
If you've seen the movie *Traxx*, this route name will make sense. Begin just left of the previous route at several left-arching seams. Bring wires and gear to a #3 Friend.

P1 Climb up left to a bolt 30 feet up, then continue up the center of the long face past one more bolt to the ceiling. Climb past the left edge to a big ledge. 150 ft, 5.7

P2 Scramble to the top. 100 ft, 5.2.

Descend off right.

63. **Waterstreak** 5.8 PG ◄   FA: Jim Kessler–1987.
The difficulty is dependent on exactly where you climb – going directly up the streak could be as hard as 5.10. Gear up 30 feet left of the last route, at the base of an obvious water streak which is 20 feet right of a low-angled crack. Climb past three bolts to join the main crack/chimney system (bolt and drilled piton in the alcove). Rappel or continue up the crack to the top.

64. **Chips And Salsa** 5.3   FA: Unknown–1980s.
Rope up at the base of the central crack/chimney system and directly behind a block. Follow the crack for about 200 feet to the top. Descend off right.

65. **Tuna And Chips** 5.7 R   FA: Bob Conz, "Frodo" Lybarger–January 1987.
Start 20 feet left of the central crack at the left edge of a block. Bring up to a #2 Friend.

P1 Climb a low-angled face, keeping right of a black, left-facing flake. Three bolts will lead to a belay in a vertical crack (small gear needed). 150 ft, 5.7 R.

P2 Continue up the crack and face to the top. 60 ft, 5.3.

Descend off right.

Panty Wall

The obvious black cliff that sits 150 yards up and left from Tuna And Chips Wall is known as Panty Wall. It is easily identified by the 30 foot pine tree that sits in front of the blackest portion of the cliff. Three separate cliffs are listed here – all are considered to be part of Panty Wall.

Approach this sunny cliff from the first pullout, but do not follow the main trail to the bottom of the wash as per all the other cliffs. Instead, cut off left (toward the second pullout), aiming for the wash bottom to the left of the rock outcrop closest to the road. Hug the outside of this formation, going up over a short hill (50 yards), then down into another wash (25 yards). Scramble up the right flank of the red slab directly in front of you, then wander 100 yards up boulders to the base of the cliff. You should arrive at the center of the crag near the prominent pine tree. Climbs will be described from right to left, starting at a short buttress 200 feet up and right along a ramp.

66. **Thong** 5.7 PG   FA: Todd Swain, Marion Damiano-Nittoli–February 1994.
The next three routes are located on a small buttress about 200 feet up a ramp from the prominent pine tree mentioned in the introduction to the crag. Start 12 feet left of a left-facing flake, at a vertical crack system. Crux moves off the ground lead to easier climbing up the crack. Walk off right.

67. **Butt Floss** 5.10- (TR)   FA: Todd Swain–February 1994.
Begin ten feet left of **Thong** at a right-facing flake capped by a small ceiling. Pull past the ceiling and follow vertical seams to the top. Use medium-sized Friends for the belay.

68. **Cover My Buttress** 5.6   FA: Todd Swain (solo)–February 1994.
Climb the obvious left-facing corner that makes up the left edge of the buttress. Bring large gear to protect the route. Walk off right.

The next two routes are located midway up the ramp, about 100 feet up from the prominent pine tree. Start 50 feet down and left of the last route and five feet left of an oak bush.

69. **Scanty Panty** 5.5 X   FA: Todd Swain, Donette Smith–February 1994.
Face climb up along vertical seams, finishing right of a small ceiling. Angle left to the anchor on **Silk Panties**.

70. **Silk Panties** 5.7   FA: Donette Smith, Todd Swain–February 1994.
Begin 12 feet downhill of the last route and climb past five bolts with black, homemade hangers to a three cold shut belay.

71. **Panty Line** 5.10- R   FA: Nick Nordblom, Paul Van Betten–1987.
Rope up directly behind the rightmost of the boulders lying at the base of the cliff and just right of the pine tree. Wander straight up the right side of the black plated face aiming for a gap in the varnish at the top of the wall. Bring extra of the larger-sized wires. There is a two-bolt anchor on a ledge above the route and a rap anchor just left of that.

72. **Panty Raid** 5.10 ◄   FA: Paul Van Betten, Nick Nordblom–1987.
A quality route that's not as scary as it first appears. Begin eight feet left of the last route and climb straight up the face to a ceiling formed by the varnish. Follow a slightly right-leaning thin crack to the top. The two bolt belay anchor is directly above on a ledge.

73. **Edible Panties** 5.10 R/X   FA: Todd Swain, Donette Smith–February 1994.
Scary to lead due to the looseness, but still worth toproping. Start 40 feet left of the last route at a short, right-leaning flake/crack. Climb up and right along the fissure, then up the plated wall, finishing at a small notch. The crux is the transition from the flake to the steeper wall above. There are two cold shuts on a ledge above the route.

Panty Wall

66. Thong	71. Panty Line	75. Panty Prow
68. Cover My...	72. Panty Raid	77. Panty-Mime
70. Silk Panties	73. Edible Panties	78. Panty Shield

74. **Totally Clips** 5.11c? FA: Scott "Jimmy Dean" Carson, Steve "Bucky" Bullock (both from Salt Lake City)–1990.
The left side of the cliff is much steeper and has one known route. It begins 50 feet uphill of **Panty Raid** near a free-standing block. Follow six bolts to a chain anchor.

About 60 yards up and left from the prominent pine tree is another cliff with four very good routes.

75. **Panty Prow** 5.6 ◀ FA: Donette Smith, Todd Swain–February 1994.
Climb the right arête of the formation past five bolts to the same cold shut belay as **Panty-Mime** and **Victoria's Secret.**

76. **Victoria's Secret** 5.10 (TR) FA: Todd Swain, Donette Smith–February 1994.
No need to bolt this one, as it can easily be toproped. Climb the face between **Panty Prow** and **Panty-Mime** starting at a small block leaning against the cliff.

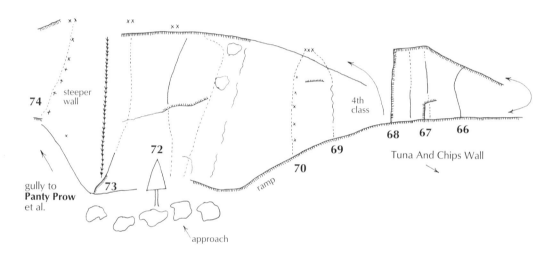

77. **Panty-Mime** 5.10c PG ◀ FA: Todd Swain, Donette Smith–February 1994.
Start atop a block 40 feet left of **Panty Prow** and 20 feet right of a right-facing corner (**Panty Shield**) at a line of bolts trending up and right. Dance past six bolts to a cold shut anchor.

78. **Panty Shield** 5.10d R ◀ FA: Nick Nordblom, Paul Van Betten–1987.
Good climbing, but a bit dangerous to reach the first bolt. Follow the obvious right-leaning corner system past four bolts. A small TCU and a #2 Friend could be carried to supplement the bolts. Bring large Friends for the belay then scramble down left.

*Above **Panty Prow** is another cliff with a huge roof split by a crack.*

79. **The Great Red Roof** A1 FA: Paul Van Betten, Sal Mamusia, Nick Nordblom–1987. This was done without pins or bolts. Have at it!

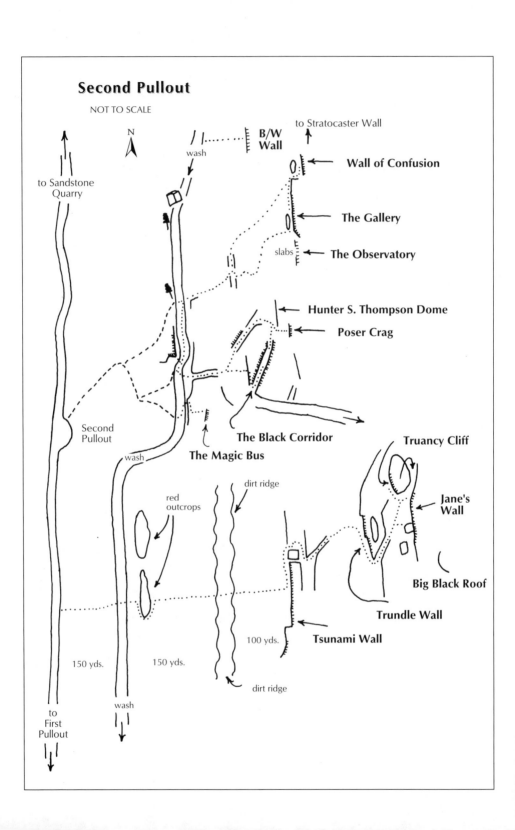

SECOND PULLOUT

This area has some of the best sport climbing cliffs at Red Rocks. The Gallery, Wall of Confusion and Black Corridor are of excellent quality, and are **extremely** popular. They are so popular, in fact, that the disposal of human waste and other environmental issues are of great concern to land managers. Please do your part to reduce impacts not only here, but at every climbing area you visit!

Park at the second pullout, 1.7 miles from the start of the scenic loop road to approach any of these crags. The cliffs at this pullout are described from right to left (from the direction of the first pullout moving left toward the Sandstone Quarry).

TSUNAMI WALL, TRUNDLE WALL, JANE'S WALL, AND TRUANCY CLIFF APPROACH

These four crags are all within 150 yards of each other and are located about 500 yards to the northeast of the second pullout. All face toward the road and sit fairly high up on the hillside. The approach described here is not the most direct way to reach the cliffs, but once you've made it to the climbs, you can figure out a better way back to the parking lot.

Tsunami Wall, et al.

To reach these routes, walk down the road from the second pullout toward the first pullout for about 300 yards, until the red rock outcrops within the drainage on your left end. Looking at the larger hillside behind these outcrops, you can now see all of the aforementioned cliffs lined up in a row.

The Tsunami Wall is the lowest crag and is easily recognized by its rectangular boxcar shape, with a huge, detached block on its left side. The other three cliffs are about 100 yards directly above. From this point along the loop road, walk down into the

Tsunami Wall
2. Barracuda
9. Abandon Ship
11. Tremor

Trundle Wall
16. Pocket Rocket

Jane's Wall
19. See Dick Fly
20. Idiots Rule

Truancy Cliff
27. Doctor's Orders
28. Iron Man

drainage, then up the other side to the top of the dirt ridge right above the outcrops (about 300 yards total). Tsunami Wall is now about 100 yards in front of you.

Tsunami Wall

Routes on this wildly overhanging wave of rock are about 40 feet long, face the road and are in the shade in the morning. The right-hand part of the wall is less steep and smaller. Climbs are described from left to right. All have anchors on top.

1. **Poseidon Adventure** 5.12b   FA: Chris Knuth, Leo Henson –January 1993.
   This climbs a very overhanging block just left of the main Tsunami Wall block past four bolts to open cold shuts.

2. **Barracuda** 5.13b ◀   FA: Chris Knuth, Leo Henson–January 1993.
   Start 30 feet right of the huge detached block at a seam that runs out a low ceiling, then up left along the wall. Four bolts lead to chains. Photo, page 41.

3. **Land Shark** 5.12b   FA: Leo Henson–January 1992.
   Rope up 40 feet right of the huge detached block at a boulder under the low roof running along the base of the cliff. Three routes start here, and share the same first two bolts. Climb up and left past a total of six bolts to the anchor.

4. **Angler** 5.12c   FA: Leo Henson–January 1992.
   Start as per **Land Shark**, but continue straight up after the third bolt to an anchor.

5. **Threadfin** 5.12c   FA: Leo Henson–January 1992.
   Begin as per **Land Shark** and follow the line of bolts straight up to chains.

6. **SOS** 5.13a   FA: Leo Henson–January 1992.
   You may need help on this one! Start ten feet right of **Land Shark** on the left edge of a block under the low roof. Move left to a horn, then up the seam past five bolts.

7. **Man Overboard!** 5.12d   FA: Leo Henson–January 1992.
   Begin five feet right of **SOS** in the center of the block under the low roof. Six bolts lead to chains.

8. **Aftershock** 5.12b   FA: Randy Faulk, Leo Henson–January 1992.
   Rope up four feet right of the last route, at the right end of the block under the low roof. Five bolts and strong fingers will get you to the cold shut anchor.

9. **Abandon Ship** 5.12a ◀   FA: Randy Faulk, Leo Henson–January 1992.
   Start ten feet right of the previous route at a dihedral that marks the right edge of the "wave." Climb up and left past five bolts. Photo, page 41.

10. **Women And Children First** 5.6+   FRA: Donette Smith, Todd Swain–Spring 1993.
    Climb the dihedral just right of **Abandon Ship**. Bring a full set of Friends. Walk off to the right (toward the first pullout), then scramble down onto a ledge below the start of the two 5.10 routes.

11. **Tremor** 5.10b   FA: Leo and Karin O. Henson–February 1992.
    Begin 25 feet right of the **Women And Children First** dihedral on a smaller, broken section of cliff. Four bolts and chains mark the route. Photo, page 41.

12. **Low Tide** 5.10b   FA: Leo and Karin O. Henson–February 1992.
    Start 30 feet right of the last route on the right side of a low ceiling, and climb up along a varnished seam past four bolts.

Trundle Wall

To reach this crag, walk down the road from the second pullout toward the first pullout for about 300 yards, until the red rock outcrops within the drainage on your left end. Looking at the larger hillside behind these outcrops in the drainage, you can now see all of the aforementioned cliffs lined up in a row.

Tsunami Wall is the lowest crag; it is easily recognized by its rectangular boxcar shape, with a huge, detached block on its left side. Trundle Wall can clearly be seen about 100 yards directly above. From this point along the loop road, walk down into the drainage, then up the other side to the top of the dirt ridge right above the outcrops (about 300 yards total). Tsunami Wall is now about 100 yards in front of you. Walk past the left (west) edge of Tsunami Wall; continue about 100 yards up the hillside to the next obvious cliff (Trundle Wall). These sunny routes are described from left to right as you approach the cliff. Photo, page 41.

13. **Before Its' Time** 5.12a   FA: Leo Henson–November 1994.
    Start to the left of a big, rotten corner and climb past about eight bolts to the anchor.

14. **Standing In The Shadows** 5.12a   FA: Greg Mayer–Winter 1990.
    Begin ten feet right of a big, rotten, right-facing corner. Climb up and left past two bolts to a left-facing flake/corner, then straight up past four more bolts to the chain anchor.

15. **Master Beta** 5.13a   FA: Scotty Gratton–October 1994.
    Rope up five feet right and zip past five bolts with homemade hangers to chains.

16. **Pocket Rocket** 5.11d   FA: Mike Tupper–Winter 1990.
    Start 15 feet right of the last route. Power past two bolts with homemade, tan colored hangers, then go up and slightly left to the chains. Photo, page 41.

17. **Life Out Of Balance** 5.11c   FA: Mike Tupper, Greg Mayer–Winter 1990.
    Begin six feet right of the previous route and just left of an obvious right-facing flake/corner leading to a huge hole. Finger traverse left, then up past four bolts to an anchor left of the hole.

18. **Bone Machine** 5.11c   FA: Danny Meyers, Scotty Gratton–October 1994.
    This line is to the right of the right-facing flake/corner. Bolts lead to a chain anchor.

Jane's Wall

Jane's Wall is a large, dark, rounded formation near the top of the ridge, with a huge, black roof just up and right of it. To reach this crag, walk down the road from the second pullout toward the first pullout for about 300 yards, until the red rock outcrops within the drainage on your left end. Looking at the larger hillside behind these outcrops in the drainage, you can now see all of the aforementioned cliffs lined up in a row.

The Tsunami Wall is the lowest crag, and is easily recognized by its rectangular box-car shape, with a huge, detached block on its left side. Jane's Wall is the second obvious cliff about 150 yards directly above. From this point along the loop road, walk down into the drainage, then up the other side to the top of the dirt ridge right above the outcrops (about 300 yards total). Tsunami Wall is now about 100 yards in front of you. Walk past the left (west) edge of the Tsunami, and continue about 100 yards up the hillside to the next obvious cliff (Trundle Wall).

Go to the right (east) end of the wall, then scramble 150 feet up a gully to the base of Jane's Wall, which is characterized by a smooth black face capped by an overhang on its left side. The cliff faces the road and is in the sun the majority of the day. All routes have anchors and are described from right to left.

19. **See Dick Fly** 5.10d   FA: Greg Mayer–Spring 1991.
    Begin atop a block near the right edge of the crag. Climb a slab to steeper rock, and the belay. The route has five bolts with homemade hangers. Photo, page 41.

20. **Idiots Rule** 5.11b   FA: Don Welsh–Fall 1990.
    Rope up 15 feet left of the last route. Scramble up a slab, step right, then up and slightly left past six bolts to a hook and chain. Photo, page 41.

21. **Pigs In Zen** 5.12b   FA: Don Welsh–Fall 1990.
Start as per **Idiots Rule** and scamper 40 feet up the slab to a cave. Exit left out of the cave, clipping a total of six bolts.

22. **Naked And Disfigured** 5.12b   FA: Don Welsh–Fall 1990.
Begin 25 feet left at the mouth of a small corridor. Go up a low-angled, right-leaning ramp to the lowest point of the overhang, pull this, then power up the steep face to the anchor.

23. **Stealin'** 5.12b   FA: Don Welsh–Winter 1991.
Done after **Every Mother's Nightmare**; it's really a variation. Start at the mouth of the small corridor and zip up to a left-leaning crack under a sculptured arête. Follow bolts up the arête, then "escape" right and clip one more bolt before reaching the anchor.

24. **Every Mother's Nightmare** 5.12b ◢   FA: Greg Mayer–Fall 1990.
Climb the overhanging, sculptured arête as per **Stealin'**, then continue up left through roofs to the anchor. A total of six bolts on the route.

Truancy Cliff

The three routes on this small cliff aren't too inspiring, but since they're within 50 feet of Jane's Wall, you can conveniently "tick" them off. To reach this crag, walk down the road from the second pullout toward the first pullout for about 300 yards, until the red rock outcrops within the drainage on your left end. Looking at the larger hillside behind these outcrops in the drainage, you can now see all of the aforementioned cliffs lined up in a row.

Tsunami Wall is the lowest crag, and is easily recognized by its rectangular boxcar shape, with a huge, detached block on its left side. Jane's Wall is the second obvious cliff about 150 yards directly above. From this point along the loop road, walk down into the drainage, then up the other side to the top of the dirt ridge right above the outcrops (about 300 yards total). Tsunami Wall will now be about 100 yards in front of you. Walk past the left (west) edge of the Tsunami, and continue about 100 yards up the hillside to the next obvious cliff (Trundle Wall).

Go to the right (east) end of the wall, then scramble 150 feet up a gully to the base of Jane's Wall, which is characterized by a smooth black face capped by an overhang on its left side. Truancy Cliff is 50 feet to the left (west), faces the road and is in the sun the majority of the day. Routes are described from right to left.

25. **Ditch Day** 5.7   FA: Todd Swain (solo)–July 1991.
Start near the right edge of the cliff below some very varnished huecos and horizontal cracks. Climb straight up the face using traditional pro (up to a #3 Friend). No anchors; walk off to the rear, then down the corridor between Truancy Cliff and Jane's Wall.

26. **Playing Hooky** 5.10a   FA: Greg Mayer–Fall 1990.
Begin eight feet left at the base of a scoop/groove with three bolts. Wander up the face past the bolts, then move left to the chain anchor.

27. **Doctor's Orders** 5.10b   FA: Greg Mayer–Fall 1990.
Climb the line of three bolts six feet left of **Playing Hooky** to the same chain anchor. Photo, page 41.

28. **Iron Man** 5.10+   FA: Jay Smith, Paul Van Betten–1983.
This route is down and right of Jane's Wall. It climbs a right-facing, right arching corner past one bolt to a bolted belay. The arch separates red and white rock and faces the road. Carry gear to a #3 Friend. Photo, page 41.

The Arena

This big, brown, overhanging wall sits on the top left side of the Rescue Wall gully. Two routes had been completed at press time. Fifteen-minute approach.

29. **Shadow Warrior** 5.13a FA: Leo Henson–June 1994.
The left route, with about six bolts to a shared anchor.

30. **Gladiator** 5.12c FA: Leo Henson–April 1994.
The right route, also with about six bolts.

Rescue Wall

This steep, east-facing cliff is hidden in a gully between Tsunami Wall and The Magic Bus. Follow the trail from the parking lot down to the wash level, then go downstream about 200 yards to a gully running north-south on the left (north) side of the drainage.

The routes are about 100 yards straight north of a bend in the main drainage, on the left (west) side of the gully. The wall is noted for its mushroom-like summit block. Approach takes ten minutes.

31. **Airlift** 5.11c FA: Randy Faulk, Bart Groendycke–before 1992.
Start at the left (south) edge and climb past two bolts. Traverse right in a horizontal, then up the face past six more bolts to the anchor.

32. **911** 5.11d FA: Randy Faulk, Bart Groendycke–before 1992.
Begin just left of a gully and about 35 feet right of **Airlift**. Climb the right arête of the wall past at least six bolts.

The Magic Bus

This small crag hosts a number of moderate routes and should become a popular cold weather spot for intermediate climbers. It is visible directly to the north of the second pullout, about halfway up the rocky hillside. The crag is an obvious black block with a small, red triangle near it's lower right corner. There are several dark, angular boulders just above this wall at the top of the ridge.

From the second pullout follow the main trail down to the wash level. Cross the wash and walk straight north toward the red outcropping. Follow a hidden gully with a smooth south wall up and right (east) for 250 feet to a fault. Scramble up left (north) along the fault/gully for 75 feet to an open, relatively flat area. The formation is located about 150 feet up and right (northeast) from this point. Routes are described from left to right as you approach. Approach takes 15 minutes.

33. **Electric Koolaid** 5.9+ (TR) FA: Donette Smith, Todd Swain–February 1994.
The loose face just right of the formation's left edge has been toproped via the anchors on **Blonde Dwarf**.

34. **Blonde Dwarf** 5.10- FA: Nick Nordblom, Paul Van Betten–1988.
The obvious thin crack that curves right and up. When the crack ends, follow two bolts up left on steep rock to a cold shut anchor. Bring a good selection of small- to medium-sized protection for the crack. Bolts were added in 1993 by some criminals. Photo, page 46.

35. **Neon Sunset** 5.8 ◀ FA: Kevin Pogue, Craig Dodson–January 1993.
Climb the center of the wall past nine bolts with red hangers to a chain anchor. This route is 15 feet right of **Blonde Dwarf** and is very well protected (some might say overbolted).

36. **Zipperhead** 5.8 PG13 FA: Paul Van Betten, Nick Nordblom–1988.
Rope up eight feet right of **Neon Sunset** at a thin, vertical crack in varnished rock. Follow the crack for 20 feet, then step right and go up another seam to a bolt. Angle either left or right to reach an anchor on one of the adjoining routes. Bring gear to a #1 Friend.

37. **Technicolor Sunrise** 5.8 PG   FA: Todd Swain, Donette Smith–December 1993.
Begin six feet right of the last line at the left edge of a smooth, triangular section of rock. Climb the left edge of the triangle, then straight up the face past four bolts to two cold shuts. Small wires are helpful near the bottom of the route.

38. **Ken Queasy** 5.8 PG13   FA: Donette Smith, Todd Swain–December 1993.
Start 12 feet right of the previous climb and eight feet left of the cliff's edge. Climb a thin, vertical seam in steep, black rock to a bolt, then straight up to another bolt. Angle up left to join **Technicolor...** from its last bolt on. A small TCU and RPs will help you reach the first bolt.

Second Pullout (right side)

| 37. Technicolor Sunrise | A. Great Red Book |
| 34. Blonde Dwarf | 62. Special Guest Posers |

THE BLACK CORRIDOR

This corridor running southeast-northwest hosts a total of 23 routes on both walls. The climbs are generally of a moderate nature, making this a popular destination. For an added challenge, try to do all of the routes in a day! This is also a good place to experience the true meaning of "generic" sport climbs. Hopefully, this sort of "development" won't be repeated in too many other places....

The approach is quite simple, although the corridor or its entrance can't be seen from the parking lot. Follow the trail down from the second pullout and take the second left (the first goes to the Gallery/Wall of Confusion). Follow this trail across a red sandy area, then turn slightly right into a drainage (the main wash curves left [west] toward the Gallery). Scramble over rocks for 100 yards (you may have to avoid water) to an open area.

Continue straight north for 50 yards until progress is blocked by a bush-filled corridor. Traverse 75 feet right (east) on a ledge system just above the bushes, then curve left toward trees at the entrance of the corridor. This sounds complicated, but once you've done it, the whole approach takes less than ten minutes. These climbs are in the shade most of the time and are described from the lower entrance moving up the corridor. All have anchors on top. Photo, page 54.

Left (south) Wall, Lower Level

39. **Bonaire** 5.9   FA: Jim Steagall, Kevin Sandefur, Chris Werner, Dave Sobocan (all from Phoenix, AZ)–Fall 1990.
    Start 75 feet in from the lower corridor entrance. Climb past six bolts with homemade hangers to a three-bolt anchor. The first bolt is stupid.

40. **Bon Ez** 5.9+   FA: Steagall, Sandefur, Werner, Sobocan–Fall 1990.
    Begin 20 feet right of the last route and climb past seven cold shuts to a three-cold-shut anchor. Again, the first bolt isn't needed.

41. **Crude Boys** 5.10d PG   FA: Steagall, Sandefur, Werner, Sobocan–Fall 1990.
    Rope up 15 feet right of the previous route, then clip six cold shuts enroute to a two-bolt anchor on top. There is an overhang in the middle of the route.

42. **Black Corridor Route 4 Left** 5.11a   FA: who knows?–1991 or later.
    This route shares the anchor with the last route. Deceptively difficult. Start eight feet right of **Crude Boys** and climb the slippery rock past two bolts to a horizontal crack. Move left and finish on **Crude Boys**.

The Black Corridor

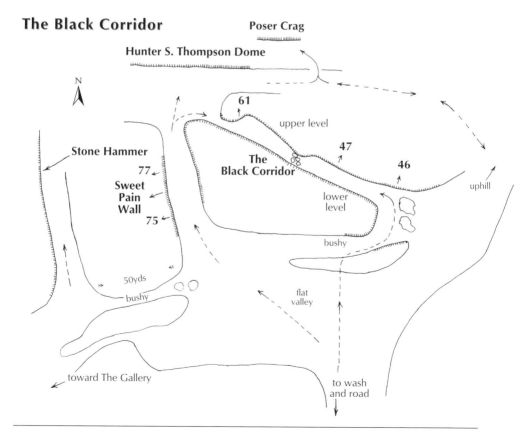

43. **BCR 5L** 5.10+   FA: Steagall, Sandefur, Werner, Sobocan–Fall 1990.
Begin ten feet right of the last route, and 20 feet left of the boulders that divide the corridor into two levels. Climb past one bolt to a thin, vertical crack and follow it to the top.

44. **Vagabonds** 5.10a   FA: Steagall, Sandefur, Werner, Sobocan–Fall 1990.
Climb the groove and face six feet right of the previous route, clipping eight cold shuts on your way to the anchor.

45. **Crude Control** 5.12a   FA: Steagall, Sandefur, Werner, Sobocan–Fall 1990.
Contrived and difficult at the start. Begin 12 feet right of **Vagabonds** and just left of the boulders that divide the corridor into two levels. Six cold shuts lead to the anchor.

Right (North) Wall, Basement

46. **Adoption** 5.11b   FA: Leo Henson, Karin Olson–November 1991.
Stiff climbing right off the ground. Start at the entrance to the corridor and climb the plated face past six bolts.

47. **Nightmare On Crude Street** 5.10d ◄   FA: Jim Steagall, Kevin Sandefur, Chris Werner, Dave Sobocan–Fall 1990.
A little loose, but that gives it some character! This route is directly across from **Bonaire** (the route with homemade hangers), and climbs overhanging, red rock past four cold shuts and one bolt to a two-shut anchor. Climbing directly between each bolt makes the climb about 5.11b and contrived.

Left Wall, Upper Level

48. **Thermal Breakdown** 5.9+ PG   FA: Steagall, Sandefur, Werner, Sobocan–Fall 1990.
Begin atop the dividing boulders and cruise past some big ledges and six cold shuts.

49. **Crude Street Blues** 5.9+ PG   FA: Steagall, Sandefur, Werner, Sobocan–Fall 1990.
Start 15 feet right of the last route at a stupidly placed cold shut. Climb past ledges and four more shuts to the anchor. Photo, page 54.

50. **Crude Behavior** 5.9+   FA: Steagall, Sandefur, Werner, Sobocan–Fall 1990.
Rope up eight feet right of **Crude Street Blues** at a ramp. Scamper past four cold shuts to a two-shut anchor.

51. **Dancin' With A God** 5.10a ◄   FA: Steagall, Sandefur, Werner, Sobocan–Fall 1990.
One of the better routes in its grade. Start 12 feet right of the last route and 35 feet right of the dividing boulders. Follow six cold shuts to a two-shut station.

52. **Live Fast, Die Young** 5.10d   FA: Steagall, Sandefur, Werner, Sobocan–Fall 1990.
This one may be harder for tall folks. Eight feet right of **Dancin' With A God,** five shuts lead to the anchor - if you can do the mantle at the start.

53. **Black Gold** 5.10b   FA: Dudes From Phoenix–Fall 1990.
Begin six feet to the right of the last route at a small flake. Five bolts with hangers lead to chains. Photo, page 54.

54. **Texas Tea** 5.10a   FA: Guys From Phoenix–Fall 1990.
From the route names, you can tell these guys watched the "Beverly Hillbillies"! Start eight feet right of the previous route at the left edge of a large flake. Climb the smooth face to a small ceiling (shut), then up past four more to a two-cold-shut anchor. The crux is at the bottom, and is contrived.

55. **Fool's Gold** 5.10b   FA: Steagall, Sandefur, Werner, Sobocan–Fall 1990.
A broken hold has made this climb harder. Begin in the same place as the last route, but walk up right on a ramp. Face climb past numerous huecos and five shuts to a two-shut anchor.

Right Wall, Second Story

56. **Oils Well That Ends Well** 5.11a   FA: Steagall, Sandefur, Werner, Sobocan–Fall 1990.
Start about 10 feet left of the dividing boulders and just left of a right-leaning crack system. Climb past five cold shuts (if you get past the second, you should be home free) to the anchor.

57. **Sandstone Enema** 5.11b   FA: Steagall, Sandefur, Werner, Sobocan–Fall 1990.
Begin ten feet left of the last route, below a short, right-leaning ramp and ten feet right of a sentry box. Tricky moves past the first two cold shuts lead to easier climbing past four more on the "slabby" face above. If you start on the left and climb by the hangerless ¼" bolt, the route is 5.10d/11a. Photo, page 54.

58. **Lude, Crude, And Misconstrued** 5.9+ PG   FA: Steagall, Sandefur, Werner, Sobocan–Fall 1990.
One of the longer routes in the corridor. Start at a sentry box/left-facing corner that is ten feet left of **Sandstone Enema** and just left of a boulder in the corridor. Power up the corner and arête past six cold shuts to the anchor.

59. **Texas Lite Sweet** 5.11b PG   FA: Rad Men From Phoenix–Fall 1990.
Rope up six feet left of the last route and climb past three bolts with hangers to a chain anchor under a ceiling.

60. **Livin' On Borrowed Time** 5.11c   FA: Steagall, Sandefur, Werner, Sobocan–Fall 1990.
Begin three feet left of the last route at smooth, varnished rock with a crescent-shaped hold by the first bolt. Four cold shuts lead to the anchor.

61. **Rebel Without A Pause** 5.11a ◀   FA: Steagall, Sandefur, Werner, Sobocan–Fall 1990.
Probably the best route here. Climb the overhanging huecos 50 feet left of the previous route and just right of the upper entrance to the Black Corridor. Four bolts to a chain anchor.

Poser Crag

Two routes have been done on this wall, which is technically part of Hunter S. Thompson Dome (named for the author of *Fear and Loathing in Las Vegas*). Poser Crag is right and slightly behind the main face on Hunter S. Thompson Dome, and directly above and behind The Black Corridor. Photo, page 54.

To approach this southeast-facing cliff, follow the trail down from the second pullout and take the second left (the first goes to The Gallery/Wall of Confusion). Follow this trail across a red sandy area, then turn slightly right into a drainage (the main wash curves left [west] toward The Gallery). Scramble over rocks for 100 yards (you may have to avoid water) to an open area. Slightly left of center is an obvious gully with a steep left wall facing northeast. This is Sweet Pain Wall and it is about 80 yards up the gully from the open area.

Routes are described from left to right as you approach the cliff. [If you continue up the gully for another 150 feet, you'll come to a large, plated face. This is Hunter S. Thompson Dome; it has numerous routes on it that aren't described in this guide. Walk right (east) along the base of this wall until you can scramble back up left to Poser Crag. It is characterized by a large, dark patch of varnish near its right edge.]

62. **Special Guest Posers** 5.11a   FA: Randy Marsh, Pier Locatelli –Fall 1990.
This is the left-hand route and climbs past four bolts to chains. Photo, p. 46.

63. **Tin Horn Posers** 5.11c   FA: Randy Marsh, Pier Locatelli–Fall 1990.
This five-bolt route climbs near the right arête of the formation.

Kitty Crag

Not much is known about this crag. It is located up a gully to the right (east) of The Black Corridor, which also forms an alternate approach for Poser Crag. Routes are described from left to right as you approach up the gully.

Follow the trail down from the second pullout and take the second left (the first goes to The Gallery/Wall of Confusion). Follow this trail across a red sandy area, then turn slightly right into a drainage (the main wash curves left [west] toward The Gallery). Scramble over rocks for 100 yards (you may have to avoid water) to an open area. Walk about 100 yards up the obvious gully to the right of center (east). The climbs are on the left wall of the gully (the sunny side).

64. **Suffering Cats** 5.11c   FA: Randy Marsh, Pier Locatelli–1994.
This route climbs a thin flake system and is protected by bolts.

65. **Titty Litter** 5.10d   FA: Randy Marsh, Pier Locatelli–1994.
The bolted route ten feet right of the last route, which leads to a different anchor.

66. **Nine Lives** 5.11d   FA: Leo and Karin Henson–Fall 1993.
A route further to the right.

The Sandbox

This shady cliff is across the canyon from the Kitty Crag and a short way uphill. At least two routes had been established as of press time.

67. **Sandblaster** 5.12b   FA: Leo Henson–Fall 1993.
The right-hand (downhill) route.

68. **Rubber Biscuit** 5.13b   FA: Leo Henson–April 1994.
This route is about 50 feet left (uphill) of the previous route.

NOTE: If you continue up the gully, you'll come to Ethics Wall. This overhanging crag is on the right side of the gully and has at least four routes on it in the 5.11/12 range.

MEISTER'S EDGE AREA

Numerous routes have been done where the trail from the second pullout first meets the wash. Six are described in this edition. Follow the trail down from the second pullout and take the second left (the first goes to The Gallery/Wall of Confusion). Follow this red, sandy trail for 50 yards along the base of a red, crumbly cliff. Photo, page 54.

69. **Sand Man** 5.11 (TR)   FA: Paul Van Betten–1987.
This neat-looking route climbs an obvious series of huecos and pockets directly above the trail and to the left of **Meister's Edge**.

70. **Meister's Edge** 5.11a ◀   FA: (TR) Joe Herbst–early 1970s.
This short but striking arête is located just above the wash as you approach The Black Corridor, or Sweet Pain Wall. Bolted in 1988 after being soloed by at least a couple brave locals. The route starts off giant angular blocks, has three bolts and no anchor.

71. **Yucca** 5.11+ (TR)   FA: Paul Van Betten–1987.
Climb a series of huecos on the wall above **Jonny Rotten**.

72. **Jonny Rotten** 5.11-   FA: Paul Van Betten, Sal Mamusia–January 1986.
A typical Navajo sandstone crack climb. Not as good as **The Fox**, but maybe you'll like it. Climb the steep, loose, right-leaning crack that is 50 feet right of **Meister's Edge** and right above the stream bed. Like its neighbor, **Jonny Jamcrack**, it's in the shade most of the day.

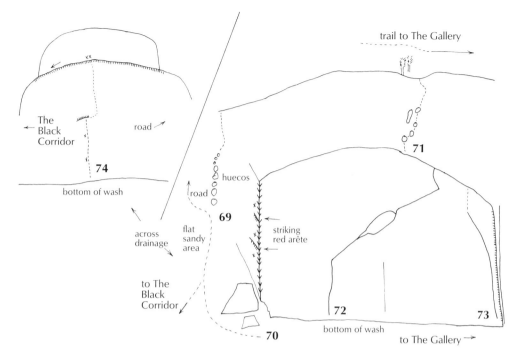

73. **Jonny Jamcrack** 5.8 R   FA: Sal Mamusia, Paul Van Betten (both solo)–January 1986.
Begin 75 feet right of **Jonny Rotten** and just left of a low-angled chimney/gully. Climb the left-curving handcrack to a ledge, then follow a left-slanting seam to an unprotected face and the top. Bring gear to 4 inches for the crack and small TCUs for the belay.

The following route is located on the sunny face directly across the wash from the Meister's Edge formation.

74. **Shut Up And Dance** 5.10   FA: Danny Meyers–1985.
Follow a seam system past two bolts to a two-bolt anchor. Walk off left (toward The Black Corridor).

Sweet Pain Wall

Although this small crag can't be seen from the parking lot, the approach is fairly straightforward. Follow the trail down from the second pullout and take the second left (the first goes to The Gallery/Wall of Confusion).

Follow this trail across a red sandy area, then turn slightly right into a drainage (the main wash curves left [west] toward the Gallery). Scramble over rocks for 100 yards (you may have to avoid water) to an open area. Slightly left of center is an obvious gully with a steep left wall facing northeast. This is Sweet Pain Wall; it is about 80 yards up the gully from the open area. Routes are described from left to right, as you approach the cliff. Photo, page 54.

If you continue up the gully for another 150 feet, you'll come to a large, plated face. This is Hunter S. Thompson Dome; it has numerous routes on it that aren't described in this guide. From here you can easily access the top entrance of The Black Corridor, simply by walking down and right about 50 feet.

75. **Sweet Pain** 5.12a ◄ FA: Leo Henson, Randy Faulk–1991.
Start in the center of the cliff at the bottom of a rotten, right-leaning crack with blocky ceilings above. Five bolts lead up and left through angular ceilings to a chain anchor.

76. **Glitter Gulch** 5.11b FA: Guys From Colorado–1991.
Begin 40 feet right, on a ledge 15 feet off the ground. Angle up and left past six bolts to chains. Holds broke on this former 5.10 route, making it more difficult.

77. **Slave To The Grind** 5.11b FA: Guys From Colorado–1991.
Start as per **Glitter Gulch**, but climb straight up, passing a right-leaning gash with a bush at mid-height. Seven bolts with a cold shut anchor.

78. **Sister Of Pain** 5.11c FA: Leo and Karin Henson–Fall 1992.
Rope up 15 feet right of the last two routes at the right edge of a low scoop that is just left of a chocolate brown streak. Climb past four bolts to an obvious right-leaning crack, then follow three more up the steep, rounded arête above to cold shuts.

79. **Lee Press-On** 5.12b FA: Leo and Karin Henson–Fall 1992.
Start six feet right of the last route at the blankest section of the wall. Clip six bolts enroute to the obvious right-leaning crack, then past one more bolt while climbing a left-leaning crack above.

80. **Pain In The Neck** 5.10a PG13 FA: Nobody will admit to this one–pre-August 1993.
A contrived start leads to better climbing. Begin at an obvious right-leaning crack near the right end of the cliff. Climb up into a bowl (bolt), follow the obvious big holds up and slightly right, then move back left just above the second bolt. A total of five bolts lead to chains. If you climb up and left from the first bolt to the second, it's 5.10c (and stupid).

81. **A-Cute Pain** 5.8 FA: Todd Swain, Donette Smith–November 1993.
Named for my sweetie. Rope up eight feet right of the previous route at a shallow, left-facing, varnished corner. Climb past a bolt to the obvious right-leaning crack and follow that up right for 15 feet (small TCUs needed). Break out left and climb the plated face past two more bolts to a cold shut anchor.

The Stone Wall

This crag was incorrectly located in the last edition and has since had a number of additional lines developed. The cliff faces east and receives sun in the morning. It is located in the first gully running north-south to the west of Sweet Pain Wall.

The Stone Wall approach is fairly straightforward, although like Sweet Pain Wall, it can't be seen from the parking lot. Follow the trail down from the second pullout and take the second left (the first goes to The Gallery/Wall of Confusion).

Follow this trail across a red sandy area, then turn slightly right into a drainage (the main wash curves left [west] toward the Gallery). Scramble over rocks for 100 yards (you may have to avoid water) to an open area. Slightly left of center is an obvious gully with a steep left wall facing northeast. This is Sweet Pain Wall; it is about 80 yards up the gully from the open area.

Continue west past the mouth of the Sweet Pain gully to a narrow, bushy gully running east-west. Follow this west for 50 yards until a narrow gully opens up on your right (uphill/north). Go up this gully about 100 yards to reach The Stone Wall, which will be on your left. Routes are described from left to right as you approach the cliff up the gully. Photo, page 54.

82. **Purple Haze** 5.10d FA: Don Burroughs, Alan Busby–1993.
The leftmost line on the wall. Start 25 feet right of a left-facing corner at a point where the solid desert varnish ends. Climb past six bolts to chains.

83. **Haunted Hooks** 5.10d   FA: (TR) Brad Stewart–August 1992. FA: (lead) Don Burroughs, Alan Busby–1993.
Begin 15 feet right of the last route at the smaller of two left-leaning arches located at the base of the crag. Nine bolts lead to rappel bolts.

84. **Roto-Hammer** 5.10c   FA: Daryl Ellis–August 1992.
Rope up 12 feet right of **Haunted Hooks** at the larger of two left-leaning arches at the base of the wall. Follow seven bolts with colored hangers to chains, passing the left side of a small ceiling between the fifth and sixth bolts.

85. **Nirvana** 5.11a   FA: Don Burroughs, Alan Busby–1993.
Start 12 feet right of the last route at a vertical, left-facing flake. The first bolt on this route has a colored hanger. A total of seven bolts lead to rappel bolts.

86. **Stonehenge** 5.11b   FA: Don Burroughs, Mike Ward, Alan Busby–1993.
Begin eight feet right of **Nirvana** at a small, left-facing flake that is just left of a bush. Eight bolts will (hopefully) get you to the chains.

87. **Stone Hammer** 5.10+   FA: Mike Ward, Mike Clifford–1986.
The original route on the wall, you'll need traditional gear to supplement the bolts. About 25 feet to the right of **Stonehenge** is a vertical crack with an oak tree in front of it. Climb this crack for 35 feet to reach the first bolt, then climb past more bolts to the rappel anchor, which is to the right of the climb.

88. **Birthstone** 5.10d   FA: Leo and Karin Henson, Karl Williamson–April 2, 1993.
Completed on Karin's birthday. Climb straight up to the anchors on **Stone Hammer**.

89. **April Fools** 5.10b   FA: Don Burroughs, Alan Busby–1993.
Start 40 feet right of the oak tree and crack at the base of **Stone Hammer**, between two scooped caves at the base of the cliff. Clip six bolts enroute to the rappel bolts.

The Observatory

This section of cliff was once included under the Gallery listing, but further development and the difference in climbing experience have warranted a separation. Bring a selection of gear to protect the climbs and two ropes for rappelling.

From the parking area, walk down the main trail, then take the first trail leading off to the left (about 120 yards from the lot; as per The Gallery). Follow this lesser-used trail about 400 yards up and over a red outcrop (the top of the **Meister's Edge** and **Jonny Rotten** formation), then down to a wash and pine tree.

Cross the wash immediately (well before another pine and a large, red cube of rock) and follow a well-trodden path up broken slabs for 100 yards to a small corridor running parallel to the hillside. Scramble up the far wall of the corridor (about 30 feet of scrambling), then angle right across slabs for 35 yards to the base of the slabby wall.

The right (east) end of the crag has the best staging area, under an overhanging section of rock. This approach takes about 15 minutes and involves some scrambling. The cliff is visible from the road, is characterized by its prominent right arête and is in the sun most of the day. Routes are described from right to left.

90. **Witches' Honor** 5.8 R   FA: Danny Meyers (rope solo)–circa 1988.
A good but scary route – you need to be very solid leading 5.8. Gear up at a human-sized hueco that is almost directly above the scrambling in the approach corridor. This hueco is located on a low-angled slab about 60 yards left of the cliff's right edge. From the hueco, scramble about 60 feet up along a right-leaning crack to a pedestal on the right side of a vertical crack. Follow the vertical crack past a horizontal to a bolt, then up to another bolt. Traverse right and up to a third bolt, then up and left on a slab to a two-bolt anchor. Rappel with two ropes down to a point just above the initial hueco, or use one rope to reach the pedestal, then downclimb the right-leaning crack to the hueco.

Second Pullout (as seen from parking area)

90. Witches' Honor
91. Which Hunters?
92. Warlock
93. Bewitched
99. Yaak Crack
110. Range of Motion

117. Desert Pickle
*The following routes are in the
Sandstone Quarry chapter:*
49. Cut Loose
53. The Choad Warrior
57. Stratocaster

91. **Which Hunters?** 5.10- R FRA: Todd Swain, Donette Smith–February 1994.
An unknown party placed the first four bolts, but apparently did not finish the climb.
Bring small TCUs, a #1.5 Friend, the two smallest Tricams, some long slings and your
rabbit's foot. You can back up the highest bolt with all of the gear mentioned, but you'll
still have to run it out above. Begin 40 feet left of the flat staging area (located below an
overhang at the right edge of the cliff) on a low-angled slab. Climb past four bolts, then
angle up and right (no protection) to the shared cold shut belay. Rappel with two ropes.

92. **Warlock** 5.9 R FA: Todd Swain, Donette Smith–February 1994.
Have your protective spells and incantations ready in case of a fall! Carry gear to 1.5",
lots of slings and a #3.5 Friend. Start about 20 feet left of the overhang and flat ledge.
Climb straight up the face past a bulge to a vertical crack that passes between two over-
hang/cave formations. At a horizontal crack, either traverse straight right, or climb up
and right to the arête. Belay at two cold shuts as per **Which Hunters?** and **Bewitched**.
Rappel with two ropes. This route can easily be toproped after doing **Bewitched**.

93. **Bewitched** 5.3 ◀ FA: Unknown–1970s.

This route was soloed long before it was developed as described here. Bring long slings for the climb and two ropes for rappelling. Rope up on a large terrace at the very right (southeast) edge of The Observatory/Gallery face, approximately 200 feet right of the man-sized hueco on **Witches' Honor**. Climb the slab just left of a big overhang, aiming for the right side of a cave-like formation above. Pass two bolts, moving up and left past the second bolt into the cave. Move straight right from the cave (bolt) to the arête, then up past three more bolts to a cold shut anchor that is just right of another, smaller cave-like formation.

The Gallery

The most popular sport climbing cliff at Red Rocks, and probably the best place to meet climbers. Human waste is a *BIG* problem here! Do your part – pack it out and chastise those that don't.

From the parking area, walk down the main trail, then take the first trail leading off to the left (about 120 yards from the lot). Follow this lesser-used trail about 400 yards up over a red outcrop (the top of the **Meister's Edge** formation), then down to a wash and pine tree. Cross the wash immediately (well before another pine and a large, red cube of rock) and follow a well-trodden path up broken slabs for 100 yards to a small corridor running parallel to the hillside. Either scramble up the far wall of the corridor (about 30 feet of scrambling) then angle up left across slabs for 75 yards to the base of the wall, or go left in the gully then walk up slabs.

You should arrive at the right (east) end of the crag, under the most overhanging section of rock if you did the scrambling; and at the left (west) end if you took the easy way. This approach takes about 15 minutes. The cliff is visible from the road (although it looks very small and insignificant) and is in the sun most of the day. Routes are described from right to left. All routes have anchors from which to grab, lower, rappel or toprope.

94. **Glitch** 5.12c FA: Mike Tupper–Winter 1990.

Start ten feet left of an alcove on the right side of The Gallery wall. Follow a right-leaning flake past four bolts, then continue up right past a hueco and two more bolts to the anchor.

95. **Nothing Shocking** 5.13a FA: Don Welsh–Winter 1989/90.

Climb **Glitch** to the third bolt, then power straight up past three more bolts to join the end of **The Sissy Traverse**.

96. **Who Made Who** 5.12c FA: Mike Tupper–Winter 1989/90.

Climb **Glitch** to the second bolt, then continue up past three more.

97. **Where The Down Boys Go** 5.12d FA: Mike Tupper–Winter 1989/90.

Start at the bottom of the flake the previous three routes climb, and go up and slightly left past five bolts.

98. **The Gift** 5.12d ◀ FA: Boone Speed–Winter 1989/90.

Start at the base of **Yaak Crack** and climb up very steep rock past six bolts.

99. **Yaak Crack** 5.11d ◀ FA: Bill Boyle–Winter 1989/90.

Begin eight feet left of the last four routes and below the obvious left-leaning crack. Climb the crack past six bolts. Photo, page 54.

100. **The Sissy Traverse** 5.13b ◄ FA: Don Welsh–Fall 1991.
Start in the corridor behind the right edge of a huge boulder that is 15 feet left of **Yaak Crack**. The bolts on this route have been painted black, so that you know you're on the right route! Climb up to the first bolt (V1), then angle right and up past eight more bolts.
V1 Start at the base of **Yaak Crack** and climb past the first three bolts on **The Gift** before going up right past five more bolts. This seems to be the more logical line.

101. **Minstrel In The Gallery** 5.12b FA: Mike Tupper–Winter 1989/90.
The first route on the cliff. Start as per **The Sissy Traverse** and climb the face just left of **Yaak Crack** past five bolts.

102. **A Day In The Life** 5.11b FA: Bill Boyle–Winter 1989/90.
Begin ten feet left, behind the huge boulder and on the left side of a cat's claw bush. Cruise out the right side of the pod past five bolts.

103. **Social Disorder** 5.11d FA: Scott (aka Jimmy Dean), "Bucky" and Jonathan Knight–1991.
Rope up as per the previous route, then climb straight up from the pod past five bolts.

104. **Gridlock** 5.11c FA: Greg Mayer–Spring 1990.
Start as per the past two routes but exit out the left side of the pod, passing four bolts with homemade hangers. It's a little easier to go left then back right between the second and third bolts.

105. **Running Amuck** 5.10c FA: Greg Mayer–Spring 1990.
Rope up ten feet left, below a short, left-facing flake and up on a ledge. Run past four bolts to the same anchor as **Gridlock**.

106. **Pump First, Pay Later** 5.10b FA: Greg Mayer–Spring 1990.
Don't run out of gas before you get to the anchor! Start six feet left of the previous route; clip four bolts.

107. **Gelatin Pooch** 5.10a FA: Greg Mayer–Spring 1990.
Begin six feet left and climb past four bolts (three have homemade hangers) to chains.

108. **Buck's Muscle World** 5.9- FA: Greg Mayer–Spring 1990.
Eight feet left of **Gelatin Pooch** you'll find this three-bolt route with homemade hangers.

109. **Sport Climbing Is Neither** 5.8 FA: Unknown–Winter 1991.
Start ten feet left of **Buck's...** at a short, curving crack. Three bolts to an anchor.

110. **Range Of Motion** 5.10d FA: Todd Swain, Dick Peterson, Peggy Buckey–May 1990.
Start about 75 feet left of **Buck's Muscle World** and 20 feet left of a right-facing corner that doesn't reach the ground. Climb up through a pod, passing four bolts. Photo, page 54.

Wall Of Confusion

This cliff is about 150 feet left of The Gallery, on the same level. Routes are described from right to left, as the normal approach is from The Gallery. All routes have anchors. Believe it or not, these routes were done before The Gallery was developed. Photo, page 54.

111. **Resin Rose** 5.11+ FA: Paul Crawford, Jay Smith–April 1987.
This traditional route climbs the right-leaning crack/roof that is up and right of the bolted routes.

112. **Body English** 5.12c FA: Mike Tupper–Winter 1988.
Start 30 feet up and right from **Fear And Loathing** at the very right end of the cliff. Climb the steep corner past four bolts to chains (or go left to the **Fear...** anchor).

113. **Fear And Loathing III** 5.12a ◂ FA: Bill Boyle, Boone Speed–Winter 1988.
One of the steepest routes you've seen – until you go to **The Trophy**. This is at least the third "**F&L**" at Red Rocks. Start atop a boulder in an alcove and power past several roofs on an overhanging wall. Nine bolts provide convenient places to hang and rest.

114. **Promises In The Dark** 5.12b FA: Mike Tupper–Winter 1988.
Begin 12 feet left of the last route at a short dihedral capped by a ceiling. Zip past seven bolts to the anchor.

115. **Big Damage** 5.12b FA: Boone Speed–Winter 1988.
Start six feet left of **Promises In The Dark** at a right-curving crack, and climb up and slightly left past seven bolts.

116. **Sudden Impact** 5.11c FA: Boone Speed, Bill Boyle–Winter 1988.
Climb the face eight feet left of the previous route passing five bolts.

117. **Desert Pickle** 5.11b FA: Bill Boyle, Boone Speed–Winter 1988.
Power up the wall six feet left of the last route, using four bolts. Photo, page 54.

118. **American Sportsman** 5.10c FA: Boone Speed, Bill Boyle–Winter 1988.
Another four-bolt route six feet left.

119. **The Runaway** 5.10b PG FA: Greg Mayer–Spring 1989.
The furthest left route on the cliff, this starts up on a ledge. Four bolts with homemade hangers provide the pro.

Wall Of Confusion

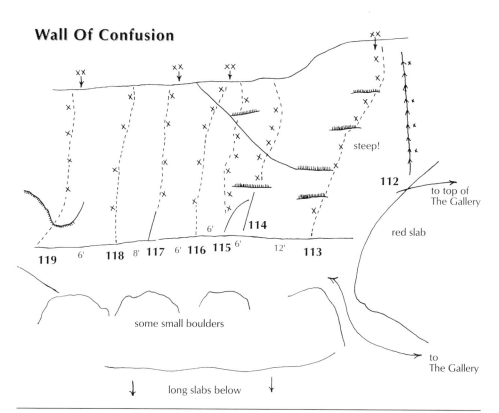

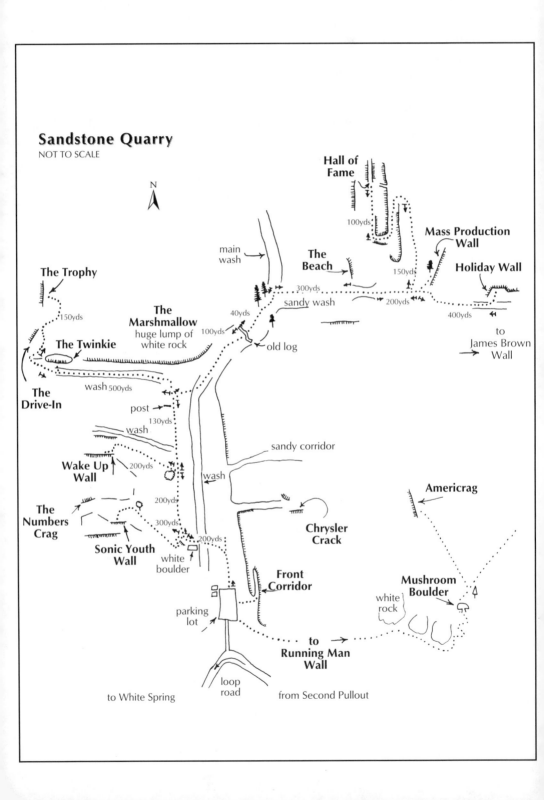

Sandstone Quarry
NOT TO SCALE

N

Hall of Fame

100yds

Mass Production Wall

The Trophy

The Beach

Holiday Wall

150yds

main wash

300yds

sandy wash

200yds

400yds

150yds

to James Brown Wall

The Marshmallow
huge lump of white rock

40yds

100yds

old log

The Twinkie

wash 500yds

The Drive-In

post

130yds

wash

sandy corridor

Wake Up Wall

200yds

wash

The Numbers Crag

200yds

Americrag

300yds

Sonic Youth Wall

200yds

white boulder

Chrysler Crack

Front Corridor

Mushroom Boulder

white rock

parking lot

to Running Man Wall

to White Spring

loop road

from Second Pullout

SANDSTONE QUARRY AREA

This area has a host of worthwhile crags, containing climbs of all difficulties. The approaches range from 1 to 25 minutes, with most of the climbs being in the shade. Among the best of the cliffs here are The Trophy, Holiday Wall and Sonic Youth Wall. Follow the scenic loop road 2.7 miles and park in the large Sandstone Quarry parking lot. The first routes described are to the right (southeast) of the parking lot (toward the second pullout); they are listed as encountered – from left to right.

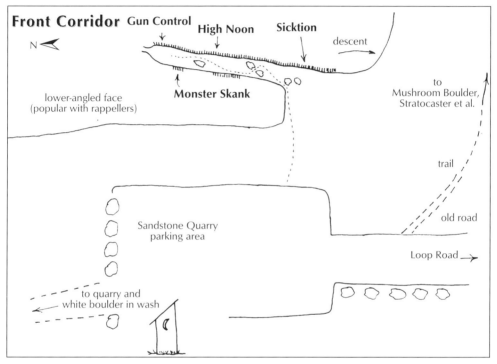

SANDSTONE QUARRY EAST
The Front Corridor

Walk 75 yards due east from the Sandstone Quarry parking lot to reach this obvious north-south running corridor. Routes in this corridor are good, but certainly not the best sport climbs at Red Rocks. Some may need some traditional gear to supplement the bolts mentioned, as well as some courage. The climbs are described from right to left as you enter the corridor, with some on the right (east) wall getting sun in the afternoon.

1. **Sicktion** 5.9   FA: Nick Nordblom, Randy Marsh–Fall 1988.
    Start at the mouth of the corridor on the right (east) wall, below a flake ten feet up and by an oak tree. Follow a vertical seam past three bolts to the top. Belay in a large recess (TCU, #2.5 and 3 Friends), then walk off right.

2. **Prescription Gription** 5.10 R   FA: Nick Nordblom, Jenni Stone–Spring 1988.
   Begin 20 feet left of the previous route. Climb past two bolts to a left-leaning seam/corner, then up a vertical crack, passing one more bolt. Bring a #2.5 Friend or bigger for the belay. Walk off right.

3. **Friction Addiction** 5.10 PG13   FA: Bob Conz, Shelby Shelton–Spring 1988.
   Start at the right edge of a tree clump that is 15 feet left of the previous climb. Power past three bolts, then follow a seam up left. Follow this past two more bolts. Bring a #2.5 Friend or bigger for the belay. Walk off right.

4. **Affliction For Friction** 5.11a R   FA: Mike Ward, Danny Meyers–Fall 1989.
   Begin at a horizontal oak tree in a clump of four trees that is ten feet left of **Friction Addiction**. Make a difficult mantle, then climb past two bolts, angling way left (dicey crux) to a seam. Continue up the seam past three more bolts. Bring a #2.5 Friend or bigger for the belay. Walk off right.

5. **Crumbling Community** 5.10 PG   FA: Paul Van Betten, Danny Meyers–1989.
   Start 15 feet left at a gray water streak. Dance up the streak past a low bolt to a seam, then follow a left-leaning crack to its top. Angle up right past two more bolts to the top. Walk off right.

6. **A Thousand New Routes** 5.11 R   FA: Paul Van Betten, Nick Nordblom–Summer 1986.
   The first route done in the corridor. Climb the left-leaning diagonal crack, then go up right from the last bolt to the belay station. Three bolts on the route.

7. **High Noon** 5.11 R   FA: Nick Nordblom, Jenni Stone–Spring 1988.
   Begin 110 feet left of the previous route, below a right-facing corner with varnish on its right side. There are six bolts on the route. Rappel with two ropes.

8. **Hair Today, Gone Tomorrow** 5.11a   FA: Nick Nordblom, Paul Van Betten–Spring 1988.
   Start 25 feet left of **A Thousand New Routes**, near a shrub. Climb along a left-trending seam past seven bolts, the first being a Metolius about 30 feet up. A 120-foot rappel will get you back to the ground or you can traverse off right

9. **To Bolt Or Toupee** 5.10c   FA: Mike Ward, Paul Van Betten–Spring 1988.
   Rope up 40 feet left of **Hair Today...**, and 30 feet right of the end of the corridor. Climb up to a right-facing corner capped by a ceiling, then follow bolts up and right to the rappel anchor. There are seven bolts.

10. **Gun Control** 5.11b   FA: Bob Conz, Shelby Shelton, Nick Nordblom–Summer 1988.
    Start ten feet left of the previous route and 20 feet right of where the corridor narrows down. Follow bolts up into a large scoop, then exit out the left side (crux) to the belay anchor. There are eight bolts. Rappel with two ropes.

The next two routes share a common start, and are in the shade all day. They are on the left (west) wall of the corridor, directly across from **High Noon**.

11. **Churning In The Dirt** 5.12b   FA: Mike Tupper, Craig Reason–November 1988.
    The left-hand route, ending at a chain anchor.

12. **Sound Of Power** 5.12a ◀   FA: Craig Reason, Mike Tupper–November 1988.
    The right-hand route, following thin flakes to a chain anchor.

12a **Sunsplash** 5.13c   FA: Dan McQuade – April, 1995
    One of the hardest routes at Red Rocks. Follow the bolts (if you can) between **Sound of Power** and **Monster Skank**.

13. **Monster Skank** 5.13b ◀   FA: Dan McQuade–January 1993.
    This route is located 30 feet right of **Sound Of Power**. Climb past eight bolts to chains.

Americrag

For a while, the patriotic first ascent party had an American flag flying on the wall! The crag faces northeast, is visible from the loop road and has a fairly straightforward approach. From the southeast corner of Sandstone Quarry's parking lot, walk down an old roadbed back toward the second pullout for 50 yards; trend left along a path, aiming for the outermost section of exposed white rock (about 275 yards).

Continue east on this trail along the right (south) slope of a small canyon, then drop down left (north) between two red outcrops to the bottom of the drainage. You'll pass a mushroom shaped boulder just before reaching the drainage bottom. At this point you will be able to see the crag for the first time. It is a large, tan overhanging wall on the left (west) side of a gully that is 500 yards to the northwest of the mushroom boulder. Turn slightly left (north) and hike up red slabs just right of the drainage to the base of the wall. Routes are listed from left to right as you go up the gully.

14. **Toxic Playboy** 5.12   FA: Paul Van Betten, Richard Harrison, Sal Mamusia, Bob Conz–April 1990.
Quite a test piece, as the pitch ratings imply. Start at the base of a long, left slanting crack/seam system that is 50 feet uphill from a pine tree in the gully.

    P1 Climb the face and vertical seam using four bolts and traditional gear to reach a three bolt anchor. 80 ft., 5.12-.

    P2 Power past six bolts to a two bolt belay. 80 ft., 5.12b.

    Descent: Rappel the route.

15. **Mr. Moto** 5.11   FA: Paul Van Betten, Richard Harrison, Shelby Shelton–April 1990.
Begin 15 feet uphill of the last route at a short, curving crack leading to a ceiling. Start up the crack, move left under the ceiling to a bolt, then pull the ceiling. Climb a left-leaning seam past three more bolts to the first belay on **Toxic Playboy**. You'll need gear to supplement the bolts on the route.

16. **Jimmy Nap** 5.11c   FA: Paul Van Betten, Richard Harrison, Sal Mamusia–April 1990.
Start as per the last route at the curving crack that leads to a ceiling. Zoom up the face right of **Mr. Moto** past five bolts, rapping from a two-bolt anchor.

17. **Americragger** 5.12-   FA: Paul Van Betten, Richard Harrison–April 1990.
Begin 20 feet uphill of the last two routes, directly across from a short, gnarled pine tree. Ascend overhanging slots using dynos and other neat tricks. There are four bolts for pro and a bolted belay from which to rap.

18. **Rebel Yell** 5.11+   FA: Paul Van Betten, Danny Meyers, Jenni Stone–September 1990.
Start 40 feet uphill of **Americragger** and 25 feet uphill of a vertical thumb of rock in the gully. Follow three bolts out left along a seam, then up to a fourth bolt in a varnished plate. Step left and climb a vertical seam, then up the face past three more bolts to a two-bolt belay.

THE RUNNING MAN WALL AREA

This collection of sunny cliffs are located to the southeast of the parking lot, back toward the second pullout. From the southeast corner of the Quarry parking lot walk down an old roadbed for 50 yards. Trend left along a faint path, aiming for the outermost section of exposed white rock (about 275 yards). Continue east on this trail along the right (south) slope of a small canyon for another 250 yards, then drop down left (north) between two red outcrops to the bottom of the drainage. You'll pass a mushroom shaped boulder just before reaching the drainage bottom. Walk 50 yards down the drainage, passing two pine trees, then veer left (north) and

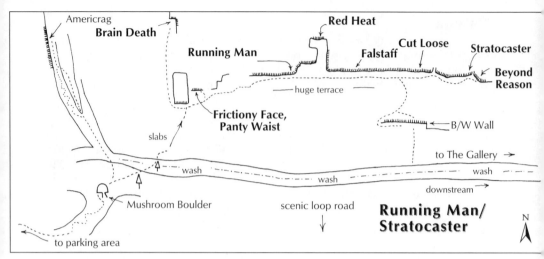

scramble 100 yards up red slabs to a huge terrace with a large, black block above (Boschton Marathon Block).

19. **Brain Damage** 5.11 R/X   FA: Robert Finlay, Mike Ward, Paul Van Betten–circa 1987.
    This route is located about 400 yards north of Boschton Marathon Block and ascends a very striking dihedral that faces southwest. Bring double ropes, wires, and Friends. Start to the right of the base of the dihedral on a ledge/ramp. Climb a right-arching flake to a small ramp, then move down and left into the corner. Finish up the dihedral using your second rope.

Boschton Marathon Block

20. **Boschton Marathon** 5.12b   FA: Geoff Wiegand–circa 1987.
    This route is located on the front of the large, black block mentioned in the approach description. It is clearly visible from the loop road, has six bolts and a slightly tricky down-climb from the summit. Photo, page 64.

21. **Frictiony Face, Panty Waist** 5.8+ ◀   FA: Danny Meyers, Brad Stewart–February 1989.
    This popular route is located just right of **Boschton Marathon** on a red slab. Start 20 feet up above the huge terrace, on a ledge right of the huge black block and behind a large cat's claw (acacia) bush. The route has six bolts and ends at a two-bolt belay station 85 feet up. Photos, pages 63 and 64.

Running Man Wall

From the Boschton Marathon Block, angle right (east) on the terrace for 125 yards to Running Man Wall, which faces the loop road (south). It is characterized by a long, low roof running along the majority of the crag.

Routes are described from left to right; the majority of routes in this guide are near the right edge of the formation. Two ropes are needed to get off most routes.

22. **Calico Terror** 5.11   FA: Mike Ward, Paul Van Betten–December 1987.
    Sounds appealing, huh? Near the left edge of Running Man Wall, climb past two bolts into a varnished, right-leaning crack, which is followed up and right past one more bolt to a two-bolt rap station. Photo, page 63.

23. **There Goes The Neighborhood** 5.11+   FA: Greg Mayer–1989.
    Start 15 feet right of a tree near the right edge of the long, low roof, atop a block and cheater stones. Climb past 11 bolts with black, homemade hangers to an anchor. Bring a #1.5 Friend.

Running Man Wall (as seen from Loop Road)

Boschton Marathon	Running Man Wall	26. The Predator
21. Frictiony Face...	22. Calico Terror	27. Running Man

24. **Second Fiddle To A Dead Man** 5.11d   FA: Greg Mayer–November 1993.
Start atop the right edge of the block where **There Goes...** starts and climb past ten bolts to a chain anchor.

25. **New Traditionalists** 5.11d   FA: Mike Tupper–1989.
Begin 20 feet right of the last route below a line of bolts with SMC hangers on very smooth rock. Climb straight up past a total of 11 bolts to the anchor. There is a superfluous bolt just left of the start of the route.

26. **The Predator** 5.10+ R   FA: Nick Nordblom, Paul Van Betten–1988.
Start as per **Running Man**, then follow a prominent left-leaning crack that leads to a two-bolt belay.

27. **Running Man** 5.11 ◄   FA: Paul Van Betten, Sal Mamusia, Mike Ward–November 1987.
Definitely better than the movie! One of the classic pitches at Red Rocks. Start 40 feet uphill and to the right of the last route below an obvious vertical seam system that trends slightly up and left. Use your Schwarzenegger-like muscles to power past lots of bolts to a bolt anchor. You may want to bring a few TCUs and small wires to supplement the bolts. Photos, pages 63, 64 and 65.

28. **Graveyard Waltz** 5.11d PG ◄   FA: Mike Tupper–1989.
Rather sporty, but great climbing. Start at the same spot as **Running Man**, but climb straight up past nine bolts with homemade hangers. Photo, page 65.

29. **Commando** 5.12b ◄   FA: Louie Anderson, Bart Groendycke–1992.
Begin ten feet right of the previous route at the left edge of a low ceiling that is just left of a right-facing corner. Nine bolts lead to a three-shut anchor. At press time, there was an unfinished route just right of this.

Running Man et al.

B. Marathon Block	**Running Man Wall**	42. Swedish Erotica
20. Boschton...	27. Running Man	
21. Frictiony Face...	38. Falstaff	

30. **Galloping Gal** 5.11a   FA: Folks from Spudland (Idaho)–1990.
    Being tall helps on this one. Rope up 45 feet right of the last route and three feet left of a left-facing chimney/corner. Climb past ten bolts to a chain anchor 85 feet up.

31. **Vile Pile** 5.10 PG   FA: Mike Ward, Danny Meyers, Jessie Baxter–Fall 1989.
    Bring #1.5 and #2 Friends to place between the fourth and fifth bolts. Start five feet right of **Galloping Gal** and zip past 6 bolts to the top of the block. Rap from three cold shuts.

32. **Project** 5.11c?   FA: Mike Ward– Spring 1995.
    Four bolts currently go up the wall 30 feet left of **Red Heat**. The route may have as many as nine bolts.

33. **Red Heat** 5.10+ 🍖   FA: Nick Nordblom, Mike Ward, Danny Meyers–Fall 1989.
    Another excellent route. Scramble 100 feet up the obvious gully that is 100 feet right of **Vile Pile** to ledges. Climb a right-facing varnished groove past five bolts, then continue up the face past more bolts to an anchor in a hueco. Nine bolts total; bring some units. Plan on a two-rope rappel.

34. **Synthetic Society** 5.11a FA: Mike Ward, Louie Anderson, Bart Groendycke–December 1990.
    A bit contrived. Scramble up the **Red Heat** gully for 40 feet. On the right (east) wall of the gully, climb past the left edge of a ceiling and seven bolts to a chain anchor shared with **Plastic People**.

35. **Plastic People** 5.10b   FA: Louie Anderson, Bart Groendycke–December 1990.
    Start as per the previous route, 40 feet up the **Red Heat** gully. Trend out right to the arête, then up to the shared chain anchor, clipping eight bolts enroute.

Running Man Area

27.	Running Man	35.	Plastic People
28.	Graveyard Waltz	36.	Fibonacci Wall
30.	Galloping Gal	37.	Northern Lights
31.	Vile Pile	38.	Falstaff
33.	Red Heat	39.	Yodritch

36. **Fibonacci Wall** 5.11+   FA: Paul Van Betten, Don Welsh–1987.
    If you're not a math major, you'll need to look this one up in the dictionary. The name *should* go with a 5.8 climb. No hooks were used on the first ascent – all the bolts were placed free on the lead. Climb the rounded arête on the right edge of the **Red Heat** gully past seven bolts.

37. **Northern Lights** 5.11d   FA: Folks from Idaho–1991.
    Begin 40 feet down and right of the **Red Heat** gully on a slab and just right of a rounded overhang at the base of the cliff. Stick clip the first bolt, then zoom past eight bolts to chains, keeping ten feet left of a vertical crack (**Falstaff**).

38. **Falstaff** 5.10- R   FA: Nick Nordblom, Paul Van Betten–1985.
    Begin 30 feet right of the last route at a line of bolts. Climb past two bolts, then angle left to the obvious sickle shaped crack, which is followed to the top. You'll probably have to finish the route with a short second pitch. Descend a gully to the west with one short rappel. Photos, pages 64 and 65.

39. **Yodritch** 5.11 R   FA: Paul Van Betten, Mike Ward–Fall 1987.
    Gear up in the same spot as **Falstaff**. Climb up and right past three bolts on a slab to a varnished crack (traditional pro here), then past one more bolt in steep rock to the belay. The second pitch has only one bolt and is runout 5.8 to the top.

*NOTE: There are at least two routes between **Yodritch** and **Super Nova**. Both start about 50 feet up on a ledge. The right route is supposed to be 5.9; the left route about 5.10-.*

40. **Super Nova** 5.10+ R   FAP1: Paul Van Betten, "Frodo" – 1988. FAP2 Nick Nordblom, Jay Smith – 1988.
This two pitch route is supposed to be scary on both pitches.

Begin about 300 feet right of **Falstaff/Yodritch** at a short, right-facing corner at the lower left margin of a large face. There is a small cat's claw bush at the base of the 15-foot-high corner.

P1 Climb the right leaning, right facing corner to its top. Angle up right on a slab to a bolt, then up the steepening face past at least two more bolts to a belay anchor near a horizontal crack. 150 ft, 5.9+ R.

P2 Pull the bulge above the belay and follow a seam/crack to a bolt then continue upward to the top. Belay at some holes and fixed slings. 150 ft, 5.10+ R.

Descent: Rappel the route with two ropes.

41. **Spikes And Twine** 5.9   FA: Nick Nordblom, Jenni Stone – 1988.
How do they get the rope up there? Rope up 40 feet right of the last route below a vertical seam/crack that is just left of a cat's claw bush.

P1 Climb the crack for 40 feet then step left to the base of another crack. Follow this up to a belay at a horizontal below a bulge. 100 ft.

P2 Pull the bulge (bolt) then move up left into an obvious crack, which is followed to the top.

42. **Swedish Erotica** 5.10-   FA: Paul Van Betten, Katja from Sweden – 1988.
Bring gear to a #3 Friend, including wires and TCUs. Start ten feet right of the previous route on the right side of the cat's claw bush.

P1 Climb a lower-angled face past two bolts to an obvious crack. Up this, traverse right (crux), then up the easier crack/ramp to a belay niche. 100 ft, 5.10-.

P2 Continue up the easy crack above, traverse left and climb the second pitch of **Spikes And Twine**, or traverse 30 feet right and rappel with two ropes from the **Flame Ranger** anchor.

43. **Flame Ranger** 5.11+/5.12-   FA: Bob Conz, Paul Van Betten, Sal Mamusia, Shelby Shelton – February, 1991.
Begin about 30 feet right of **Swedish Erotica** and 45 feet left of a chimney/chasm, at a slightly left-leaning fingercrack. Climb the fingercrack to a right leaning fissure. Move right eight feet, then climb past seven bolts to a three-bolt anchor. Rappel with two ropes.

44. **Tier Of The Titans** 5.12   FA: Paul Van Betten, Bob Conz, Shelby Shelton, Sal Mamusia – February, 1991.
Climb the **Flame Ranger** fingercrack, then angle up and right about 20 feet. Power past about seven bolts to an anchor. Rappel with two ropes.

45. **Titan Rocket** 5.12a   FA: Paul Van Betten, Bob Conz, Sal Mamusia, Shelby Shelton – October, 1991.
Begin about 20 feet right of the last two routes at the left edge of a varnished chimney/chasm. Climb the face just left of the gully past eight bolts to an anchor. Two ropes are needed for the rappel.

NOTE: The next routes are about 100 yards to the right, past a lower-angled, broken area.

The Stratocaster Wall

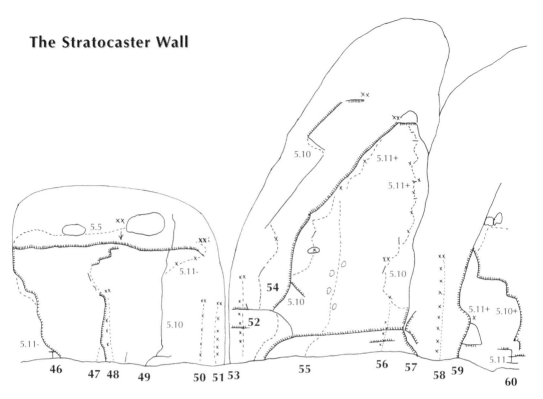

THE STRATOCASTER WALL

This excellent cliff can be approached from either the second pullout, or the Sandstone Quarry. It is located about 400 yards right (east) of Running Man Wall, on the same level. The Stratocaster Wall has two sections, the left of which is characterized by a deep chimney/corridor on its left side, and a large roof in the center. Routes will be described from left to right as approached from the Sandstone Quarry parking area.

45a. **Project** 5.12?   FA: After May, 1995.
   Start 25 feet right of a chasm at the left edge of the cliff. Two bolts head out the bulge thus far...

46. **Break Loose** 5.11-   FA: Jay and Jo Smith – Spring, 1988.
   Rope up 20 feet right of the last route and 40 feet from the left edge of the cliff. This route climbs the wide, slightly left leaning crack system that goes up through the left side of the giant roof.

47. **Diablo** 5.10 A2+   FA: Paul Van Betten, Sal Mamusia – 1988.
   This was done originally without pins or bolts. Start 40 feet right of **Break Loose** under the center of the roof. Free and aid the left facing, left-slanting corner to the center of the giant roof, then out the tongues in the roof to a huge hueco.

48. **Pablo Diablo** 5.12d   FA: Paul Van Betten, Sal Mamusia Spring, 1993.
   A wild route up the arête just right of the **Diablo** corner system. This route has five bolts and meets **Diablo** at mid-height with a two bolt belay. The giant roof is currently being worked on as a free climb!

49. **Cut Loose** 5.11- ◀
FA: Jay Smith, Nick Nordblom – Spring, 1988.
An excellent line. Bring gear up to a #2.5 Friend. Start 20 feet right of **Diablo**. Jam and lieback up the obvious dihedral to a roof that is 40 feet up. Traverse out right past two bolts (crux) to a chain anchor.

50. **One-Eyed Jacks** 5.11b
FA: Donny Burroughs, Alan Busby – 1993
The route is named after the eye-like formation above the first bolt (which can be used as a natural thread). Begin about 35 feet right of **Cut Loose** at the right edge of the cave and eight feet left of a chasm. Four bolts lead to a chain anchor. A second pitch could be done up the arête to connect with the **Footloose** belay.

51. **Footloose** 5.11b   FA: Craig Reason – 1991
Start 42 feet right of **Cut Loose**, at the right edge of the buttress and just left of a rotten, gray gully with huge huecos. Climb up a short arête, then up the steep, blank face past a total of seven bolts to an anchor.

Stratocaster

48.	Pablo Diablo	57.	Stratocaster
49.	Cut Loose	58.	Beyond Reason
51.	Footloose	**B/W Wall**	
53.	The Choad Warrior	63.	The Darkroom
55.	Marshall Amp	65.	Red Light

51a. **Unknown** 5.10?   FA: Unknown.
Scramble about 30 feet up on ledges just right of **Footloose**. Climb the left margin of the face past about seven bolts.

52. **Party Line** 5.10+ R   FA: Nick Nordblom, Jay Smith, Jo Bentley, Jenni Stone – 1988.
Scramble up about 30 feet (as for the previous route) into the bottom of the gully until you are below a lightning-bolt-shaped crack system on the right wall of the gully. Climb a thin, slabby face (dicey) past bolts, then follow the dogleg thin crack, which ends at an enormous hueco with a two bolt rap station. Another short pitch leads onto the terrace above (5.10-; single bolt for anchor).

52a. **Party Down** 5.12b (TR)   FA: Dan McQuade – May, 1995.
Begin 60 feet right of **Footloose** at the left edge of an amphitheater. Horizontal slashes and pockets will get you to a two-bolt anchor on a ledge.

52b. **Choad Hard** 5.12c   FA: Unknown – Tim Roberts – February, 1995.
Start at a boulder midway between the left edge of the wall and the first obvious crack system in the amphitheater. Nine bolts lead to an anchor.

53. **The Choad Warrior**   5.12c   FA: Dan McQuade – Spring, 1992.
Steep! Rope up 75 feet right of **Footloose** at the left side of an amphitheater, and eight feet left of two rotten, gray, right-slanting cracks. Follow five bolts to a ledge, then climb out a huge bulge past six more bolts. There is a chain anchor in the middle of the route.

54. **When The Shit Hits The Fan**   5.11+ R   FA: Jay Smith, Paul Crawford – April, 1987.
This three-pitch route climbs an obvious crack/corner system just right of **The Choad Warrior**. At least two of the belay anchors are visible from the ground.

55. **Marshall Amp**   5.11   FA: Bob Conz, Shelby Shelton, Jay Smith, Paul Van Betten – March, 1991.
If you decide to do this route, more power to you. Begin 50 feet right of **The Choad Warrior** and 30 feet left of the deepest part of the cave at a right-slanting crack.

P1 Large holds will get you to a ledge 20 feet up, then climb huecos past seven bolts to a belay station. 150 ft, 5.11.

Descent: Rappel with two ropes.

56. **Stratocaster Direct**   5.12b   FA: Dan McQuade – Spring, 1992.
Begin 15 feet left of **Stratocaster**, and just right of the deepest part of the cave. Power past five bolts to join **Stratocaster** at two cold shuts.

57. **Stratocaster**   5.11+   FA: Jay Smith, Nick Nordblom – Spring, 1988.
You'll be wired after doing this one! Bring a variety of gear, and two ropes. Start 65 feet right of **Marshall Amp** at the base of a chimney with a prominent black water streak.

P1 Climb the chimney/corner to a pod 20 feet up, then move left (two cold shuts) and go up to a belay station. 80 ft, 5.10 R.

P2 Follow cracks and huecos up the right arête of the wall, using bolts and natural gear for pro. Belay in the big hueco. 100 ft, 5.11+.

Descent: Rappel the route.

58. **Beyond Reason**   5.13b ◀   FA: Dan McQuade – Spring, 1992.
Start 15 feet right of **Stratocaster** and climb past seven bolts to a three-bolt anchor that is 40 feet up. You may want to stick clip the first two bolts.

58a. **Purple Haze II**   5.12c   FA Dan McQuade – February, 1995
Start off a block as for **The Bristler**. Traverse out right to the arête, then up and left on the face to rejoin **The Bristler**. Cross that route onto the overhanging prow, and go up to an anchor. Six bolts and a thread provide the protection.

59. **The Bristler**   5.12-   FA: Sal Mamusia, Paul Van Betten – 1987.
Richard Harrison's term for a bolt, amongst other things (i.e.: "The Black Corridor is chock full of Bristlers."). This route climbs out the overhanging corner just right of **Beyond Reason** past two bolts, then up and over the next corner. Traverse right and scramble down.

60. **Telecaster**   5.11   FA: Jay Smith, Paul Crawford – Circa 1988.
Climb the overhanging crack/corner ten feet right of **The Bristler**, then follow the left facing arch/roof around left to a notch. Join **The Bristler** through the notch, then move right and scramble down.

61. **Cowboy Cafe**   5.12a   FA: Don Welsh–1990.
This route climbs a dark, south-facing boulder directly above The Observatory (described in the Second Pullout chapter). It is about 400 yards to the right of **Stratocaster**. Six bolts lead to a chain anchor.

B/W Wall

This sunny wall has at least four climbs and all have apparently been led. As of press time, I had only done one of the routes, hence the sketchy descriptions.

Located directly below **Cut Loose**, this cliff has a prominent black water streak on it. The crag is clearly visible from the loop road, but is best approached from above at the level of Stratocaster Wall. Scramble down from the huge terrace below Stratocaster Wall to the lowest ledge. Walk right (west) and downclimb a short crack to a ramp. Follow this down until you can cut back east along the base of the cliff (you'll be about 75 feet above the drainage bottom). The routes are described from left to right (west to east) as you encounter them. Photo, page 66.

62. **The Negative** 5.9? FA: Unknown.
    Near the left edge of the wall is a left-facing corner. Climb the corner until it ends, then continue up the face above to the top.

63. **The Darkroom** 5.10- R? FA: Wendell Broussard, "Little Rick"–1982.
    This was originally led without the bolts. Bring a #2.5 Friend and some Tri-cams for solution pockets you'll encounter. Climb the obvious black water streak to an alcove just below the top of the cliff.

64. **Snapshot** 5.9? R? FA: Dave Wonderly, Jack Marshall–1988.
    A sparsely-bolted face route located atop a boulder to the right of the water streak. It begins at a right-leaning crack and will require a belay somewhere before the top (no anchors visible). Good luck!

65. **Red Light** 5.10- R ◀ FA: Jack Marshall, Eric ? –1988.
    A very good route but not for the faint of heart! Bring gear to a #2 Friend, including several small TCUs, small Tricams, long slings and wires. Begin in a corridor running north-south at a shallow dihedral with two bolts on its varnished left half. There may be a pool of water at the base of the dihedral.

    P1 Climb the dihedral past two bolts to a stance in a scoop. Move right (bolt) and up over a scary bulge to a belay stance with two bolts. 80 ft., 5.10- R.

    P2 Follow a crack to face climbing past two bolts and, eventually, the top. Belay by sitting down in a chasm (no anchors). 130 ft., 5.8 R/X.

    Descent: Walk left (west) and downclimb a short crack to a ramp. Follow this down until you can cut back east along the base of the cliff (you'll be about 75 feet above the drainage bottom).

SANDSTONE QUARRY CENTRAL
Sandy Corridor

There are dozens of climbs in this corridor, but only five routes are described in this guide. To reach this area, walk 150 yards north from the parking lot, staying close to the base of the obvious west-facing cliff on your right and walking past numerous quarried blocks. Continue across slabs for another 50 yards, then turn right (east) into the first corridor (Sandy Corridor). Walk to the back of the corridor, then scramble up the drainage about 100 yards, passing a few pine trees. Just before the red rock ends on the left (north) wall of the canyon, head up left on a ramp toward two HUGE detached boulders. The southwest face of the right (east) boulder is the Requiem Wall. Approach time is about 15 minutes; routes are in the shade in the aaearly morning. The three routes on this crag are described from left to right.

66. **Integrity Of Desire** 5.12a FA: Mike Tupper–Spring 1991.
    Start ten feet right of the gap between the huge boulders below a vertical white seam that begins in a corner. Six bolts lead to chains. This route was done for the movie *Moving Over Stone II*.

Mass Production Wall

Requiem Wall

69

Sandy Corridor

Sandstone Quarry Central

69.   Chrysler Crack

67. **Flying Cowboys** 5.12d   FA: Don Welsh–Spring 1991.
Rope up 45 feet right, and around the corner from the previous route. Start up a vertical seam, then move left and up to the cold shut anchor. Six bolts total.

68. **Plastic Pistol** 5.12b   FA: Don Welsh–Spring 1991.
Begin six feet right of the last route and 20 feet left of the east edge of the boulder. Climb past five bolts to shuts.

69. **Chrysler Crack** 5.9 ◀   FA: Randy Grandstaff, Jon Martinet–1970s.
This fine off-width (some might say those two words shouldn't appear in the same sentence) is high on the right wall of the gully, across from and above Requiem Wall. Bring Big Bros., Big Dudes, or be brave!

To approach this route, walk 150 yards north from the parking lot, past numerous quarried blocks. Continue across slabs for another 50 yards, then turn right (east) into the first corridor (Sandy Corridor). Walk to the back of the corridor then scramble about 200 yards up the canyon until you reach a large, left-leaning pine tree (this is about 30 yards before the canyon chokes off). Turn right (south) and go up a gully for 50 feet until it narrows into a corridor. Scramble out right (west) onto a ledge, then continue up and right past bulges and ledges for 150 feet to the base of the route. The climb ascends an amazing varnished corner with a pine tree at its base. Descend off left.

70. **The Deep West** 5.12b   FA: Geoff Wiegand–1987.
Climb the bolted face right of **Chrysler Crack**, stick clipping the first bolt. You might be able to get a stopper in before the first bolt.

Sonic Youth Cliff

This crag faces north and really can't be seen from the parking lot, although the rock formation is clearly visible. From the parking lot, walk 200 yards northwest past a white boulder in the main wash toward an old roadway. Turn left about 50 yards from the boulder, at the right end of a low, white rock formation. Follow a faint path up a hill, then across a plateau for about 300 yards to some pine trees. Angle slightly left toward a canyon with a large, steep, brown wall on its right. About 100 yards from the pines, you'll see Sonic Youth Cliff on your left. It is dark brown, overhanging and in the shade all day. Most of the routes do not have rappel anchors and finish on a ledge system dividing the cliff into lower and upper tiers. Routes are described from left to right.

71. **Hooligans** 5.11c   FA: Greg Mayer–July 1992.
    Begin about 25 feet left of a bush and just right of a left-leaning crack/ramp. Follow six bolts to a rap station that is about 15 feet below a bush on a ledge.

72. **GBH** (Great Bodily Harm) 5.11d   FA: Richard Harrison, Kevin Biernacki, Paul Van Betten, Don Burroughs –September 1989.
    Named for a band, not the scary nature of the climb! Start about ten feet left of a bush and near the left end of the ledge system at the base of the cliff. Climb past numerous holes and six bolts to the ledge. Walk and scramble off right.

73. **Black Flag** 5.11c   FA: Paul Van Betten, Bob Conz–June 1989.
    Rope up 15 feet right of **GBH**, at the right side of a bush. Ascend the cliff, passing five bolts enroute. Topo, page 72.

74. **Loki** 5.12a   FA: Don Welsh–April 1991.
    Named for a sci-fi movie character that was half black and half white. Begin five feet right of **Black Flag**, at the right edge of an obvious black streak. Climb past seven bolts to a chain anchor. Topo, page 72.

Sonic Youth Cliff

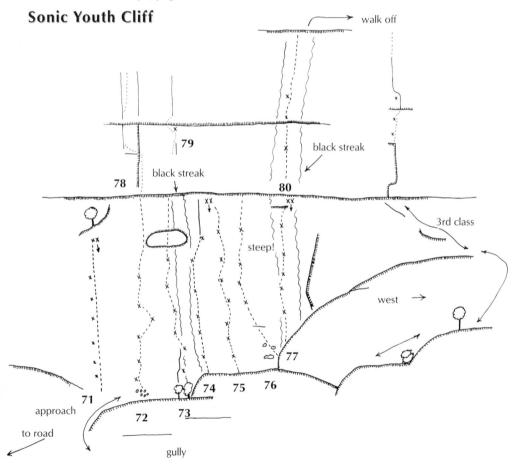

75. **Agent Orange** 5.12b   FA: Paul Van Betten, Bob Conz–June 1989.
Start ten feet right and cruise past seven bolts to the top. Topo, page 72.

76. **Sonic Youth** 5.11+ ◀   FA: Paul Van Betten, Sal Mamusia, Bob Conz–May 1989.
Begin 20 feet right of the previous route at an assortment of huecos near the left edge of a black streak. Bring a couple of small Friends to give you the courage to reach the first bolt and the top! Four bolts lead to the ledge system. Walk off right. Topo, page 72.

77. **Everybody's Slave** 5.11c ◀   FA: Don Welsh–April 1991.
A very good route – luckily, the holds get bigger the higher you get! Rope up about eight feet right of **Sonic Youth**, in the middle of a black streak, then climb past five bolts to a chain anchor. Topo, page 72.

The next four routes start on the ledge system splitting the cliff and can be approached by either doing a climb on the lower level or scrambling up to the ledge from the right (west). The scramble is a little bit dicey, but obvious – you'll angle up and left from the terrace to a big ledge.

78. **Hip-Hopin' With The Hutterites** 5.8 PG   FA: Todd Swain, Donette Smith–August 1994.
Carry gear up to a #3.5 Friend and some long slings to reduce rope drag. Begin at an obvious 40-foot-high right-facing corner that is 50 feet left of the **Crankenstein** waterstreak. Climb the corner for 20 feet, then traverse left around the corner to a crack. Climb 20 feet up to a bulge, pull this (crux), then wander up the easier face above following seams. Use a #1 Friend and TCUs for the belay, then walk off right. Topo, page 72.

79. **Seka's Soiled Panties** 5.11   FA: Richard Harrison, Paul Van Betten–September 1989.
Start 30 feet left of **Crankenstein** and 20 feet right of an obvious right-facing corner. Climb vertical seams to the ceiling. Pull through the ceiling, moving slightly left at a bolt, then up along more seams to the top. Carry gear to a #3 Friend, using a #2.5 and 3 for the belay. Walk off right. Topo, page 72.

80. **Crankenstein** 5.10c ◀   FA: Danny Meyers (rope solo)–April 1988.
This route is well worth doing. Climb the central, black water streak past three bolts. This route is located directly above **Everybody's Slave**. Use #2.5 to 3.5 Friends for the anchor, then walk off right (west). Topo, page 72.

81. **Slam Dancin' With The Amish** 5.9+ ◀   FA: Paul and Pauline Van Betten–June 1989.
A route as good as its name! Start about 60 feet right of the **Crankenstein** water streak and just above the end of the scramble up to this tier (you can start this route on the large, lower terrace and include the scramble as part of the route). Bring extra TCUs and Friends to #2.5. Climb an obvious right-facing corner/flake to its top, then follow three bolts and some seams to the summit. Save #1.5 to #2.5 Friends for the belay anchor, then walk off right. Topo, page 72.

Broast And Toast Cliff

This sunny cliff is visible from the parking lot and is located about 100 yards above Sonic Youth Wall on the right-hand side of the canyon. It is the highest and most prominent cliff in the canyon. These are traditional routes; they are described from right to left as you approach up the canyon.

82. **Fairy Toast** 5.10   FA: Richard Harrison, Paul Van Betten, Wendell Broussard– November 1989.
Begin ten feet left of a low-angled, right-facing corner that forms the right margin of the cliff. Climb a seam through the left side of a ceiling (bolt), then follow the rightmost seam/crack system past another bolt to the summit. Photo, page 75.

83. **Burnt Toast** 5.10   FA: Paul Van Betten, Bob Conz, Sal Mamusia, "Frodo" Lybarger–December 1988.
Start down and left of **Fairy Toast** at a left-slanting overhang/corner with a boulder at the base. Climb up the face past the very left edge of the **Fairy Toast** ceiling to a prominent, curving seam. Follow the seam/crack past at least two bolts. Photo, page 75.

84. **Rap Bolters Need To Be Famous** 5.11   FA: Richard Harrison, Paul Van Betten–November 1989.
Don't we all? Rope up 50 feet left of **Burnt Toast** at the left side of a smooth, varnished section of rock. Step out right from some boulders at the right edge of a cave then climb up the face past a horizontal band of varnish. Follow a left-leaning crack to the top. There are supposed to be five bolts on this route.

85. **Roasted Ramen** 5.9+ FA: Sal Mamusia, Paul Van Betten, Don Burroughs–November 1988.
Follow the previous route to the horizontal band of varnish, then trend left to an obvious, jagged crack system which is followed upwards. It looks like you'll need TCUs and wires to supplement the bolts on the route.

86. **Calico Jack** 5.11-   FA: Richard Harrison, Paul Van Betten, Don Burroughs–November 1989.
Start at the left edge of the cave mentioned in the last two routes (or up and left off a higher ledge) and climb up to an obvious notch formed by a left-leaning crack. Follow the crack up a few feet above the notch, then climb up the steep varnished streak past three bolts.

The next two routes begin on a series of left sloping ledges up and left from the cave at the base of the cliff. Scramble up about 50 feet to reach the base of the rightmost of the two routes described.

87. **Desert Sportsman** (aka Broast and Toast) 5.11   FA: Paul Van Betten, Sal Mamusia–December 1988.
From the right (lowest) edge of the sloping ledge, scramble out right on blocks, then go back left to a brown, varnished streak. Follow the streak past numerous bolts, finishing in a crack. There should be seven bolts on the route, plus a bolt anchor.

88. **C.H.U.D.** 5.11c   FA: Paul Van Betten, Bob Conz, Richard Harrison, Sal Mamusia, Shelby Shelton–April 1989.
Rope up 25 feet up and left of **Desert Sportsman**. Climb up the steep, varnished face along right-facing flakes past six bolts.

The Numbers Crag

This sunny cliff sits down and left from Broast and Toast Cliff. Routes are described from right to left as you approach up the canyon. Walk off to the right (toward Broast and Toast Cliff) after doing any of the climbs here. Photo, page 73.

89. **#6** 5.11d   FA: Paul Van Betten, Sal Mamusia, Richard Harrison–January 1992.
Start in a huge hueco at the right side of the crag. Follow three bolts up good looking varnished rock.

90. **#5** 5.12b   FA: Paul Van Betten, Sal Mamusia, Richard Harrison, Bob Conz–January 1992.
Begin in the hueco as per **#6,** but climb up and left past five bolts. A single belay bolt is located on top, about 40 feet back from the cliff edge.

91. **#4** 5.12a   FA: Paul Van Betten, Sal Mamusia, Richard Harrison–January 1992.
Rope up 15 feet left of the huge hueco. Follow four bolts up a seam and waterstreak.

92. **#3** 5.11d   FA: Shelby Shelton, Richard Harrison, Paul Van Betten–1991.
Begin eight feet left of **#4** at a short white slab that leads to four bolts.

93. **#2** 5.11d   FA: Richard Harrison, Shelby Shelton, Paul Van Betten, Sal Mamusia–Winter 1990.
Start eight feet left of **#3** and just right of a ledge that is six feet off the ground. Zoom past four bolts to a belay bolt on top with a large, homemade hanger.

94. **#1** 5.11d   FA: Sal Mamusia, Paul Van Betten, Richard Harrison–January 1992.
Rope up eight feet left of **#2** on a ledge that is six feet above the ground. There are several huecos below the first bolt. Climb along an overhanging seam past five bolts.

95. **#.5** 5.12c FA: Sal Mamusia, Paul Van Betten–January 1992. Begin 20 feet left of the last route at the base of right-leaning cracks. Clip three bolts along an overhanging seam.

96. **#0** 5.10 PG FA: Paul Van Betten, Sal Mamusia, Richard Harrison–January 1992. Start 20 feet left of the previous route at a line of scoops near an arête. Follow two bolts to a vertical seam, which will provide some thrilling moves before you reach the top (or lower off!). There's a pine tree way back from the cliff edge for an anchor.

Common Time

This crag is located about 150 yards up canyon from The Numbers Crag, up a trough on the right side of the canyon. Both routes face east (left side of the gully) and get morning sun.

Broast And Toast Cliff and The Numbers Crag

| 95. | #.5 | 83. | Burnt Toast |
| 96. | #0 | 82. | Fairy Toast |

97. **Parradiddle Riddle** 5.11b FA: Phil Bowden–July 1992.
This is the left route and climbs past four bolts to chains.

98. **Myxolidian** 5.11b FA: Greg Mayer–July 1992.
The right route, which also has four bolts to chains.

NOTE: There are two excellent boulders 50 yards up the canyon from the last two routes.

The Wake Up Wall

As the name implies, you have to get there early (at least in the winter) to have much sunshine. The routes are short and all have rappel/lowering anchors. This crag caused another uproar between the two local climbing factions due to its large number of bolts. To get there, walk 200 yards northwest from the parking lot past a white boulder in the main wash to an old roadway. Follow the roadway for about another 200 yards to an obvious oak bush on the left side of the trail. Turn left off the road and follow a faint footpath up over a dirt hump (about 200 yards). Angle slightly left (a wash will be on your right) into a corridor with a larger brown and white wall on its left side. The base of the cliff is flat, white rock and, as you approach, the climbs are described from left to right. Topo, page 76.

99. **Monkey Rhythm** 5.10+ FA: Paul Van Betten, Robert Finlay–1983.
At the crag's extreme left end is a shallow dihedral with a varnished crack in the back.

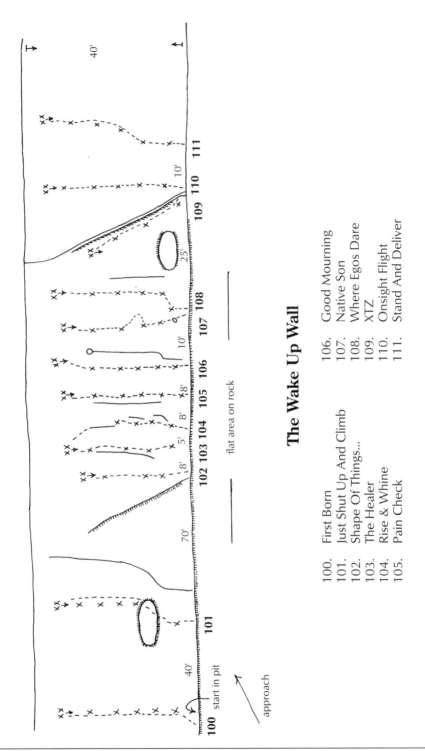

The Wake Up Wall

100. First Born
101. Just Shut Up And Climb
102. Shape Of Things...
103. The Healer
104. Rise & Whine
105. Pain Check

106. Good Mourning
107. Native Son
108. Where Egos Dare
109. XTZ
110. Onsight Flight
111. Stand And Deliver

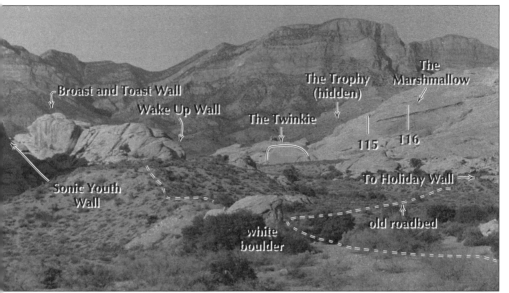

Sandstone Quarry (view from parking area)

115. Mojave Green   116. Dime Edging

---

100. **First Born** 5.10b   FA: Ed Prochaska–1990.
     Start in a pit eight feet right of boulders at a right-trending flake and climb past five bolts to the anchor.

101. **Just Shut Up And Climb** 5.11b ◄   FA: Randy Faulk, Rick Denison–June 1991.
     The best route on the cliff (and the last one done). Begin 40 feet right of the previous route and clip five bolts as you climb past the right side of a hole.

102. **Shape Of Things To Come** 5.11a   FA: Greg Mayer–Winter 1989.
     Rope up 70 feet right, and just right of an obvious left-leaning ramp. Power past three bolts to the anchor.

103. **The Healer** 5.11d   FA: Greg Mayer–Spring 1990.
     Start eight feet right and climb past four bolts to a shared belay with **Rise & Whine**.

104. **Rise & Whine** 5.12a   FA: Mike Tupper–Spring 1990.
     Climb along seams five feet right of the previous route, clipping four bolts on the way.

105. **Pain Check** 5.12a   FA: Bill Boyle–Spring 1990.
     Begin eight feet right and hobble past five bolts to the rap station.

106. **Good Mourning** (aka The Burrito) 5.11b   FA: Bill Boyle–Spring 1990.
     Another five-bolt route that begins eight feet right of **Pain Check**.

107. **Native Son** 5.11c   FA: Mike Tupper–Spring 1990.
     Starting at a pocket ten feet to the right, stroll past five bolts.

108. **Where Egos Dare** 5.12a   FA: Greg Mayer–Summer 1991.
     Begin as per **Native Son**, but climb up right, passing the left side of a large hole, and four bolts.

109. **XTZ** 5.9   FA: Greg Mayer–Spring 1990.
     The easiest route on the cliff, but not too aesthetic. Rack up 25 feet right at the base of a right-leaning ramp. Climb past three bolts to the rappel anchor.

---

110. **Onsight Flight** 5.12b   FA: Don Welsh–Spring 1990.
Start four feet right of the ramp and fly past five bolts.

111. **Stand And Deliver** 5.12b   FA: Mike Tupper–Spring 1990.
Rope up ten feet right of **Onsight Flight** and climb past five bolts that are slightly right trending.

SANDSTONE QUARRY NORTH
The Twinkie

These routes aren't all that great, but you walk right by them to get to good routes. This is a small, white formation that gets sun all day and is visible from the parking area. It is north of the lot, at the left end of the biggest, white lump of rock (The Marshmallow). The approach directions aren't the most direct way to the crag, but by following them, you shouldn't get lost.

From the parking area, walk 200 yards northwest past a white boulder in the main wash to an old roadway. Follow the roadway to its end (a bit over 300 yards), passing an oak bush, a small drainage and a cedar post (this is marked as the trail to Calico Tank). Turn left (northwest; off the trail) and walk about 500 yards up the wash, paralleling the big white lump, to reach The Twinkie. Routes are described right to left and begin in the wash.

112. **Like Mom Used To Make** 5.11c   FA: Anthony Williams, John and Ralph Day–Winter 1988.
Start just left of an easy-looking bulge at the base of the cliff, below four bolts. The route begins with difficult moves and finishes in a very short crack. There is a rappel anchor on top.

113. **Flake Eyes** 5.10+   FA: Anthony Williams, John and Ralph Day–Winter 1988.
Begin ten feet left of the previous route and behind a bush. Climb up and slightly left past three bolts. There are belay bolts on top. Walk off the rear of the formation, then around left to regain the base of the route.

114. **Short But Sweet** 5.10 R/X   FA: Anthony Williams, John and Ralph Day–Winter 1988.
Start 30 feet left at a right-leaning ramp/corner and just left of a low cave. Climb to the top of the corner, then move up and right about ten feet to the first bolt (scary). Continue past one more to the top. Belay from bolts, then walk off as per the previous route.

The Marshmallow

At least two routes have been done on the large white formation that is up from and right (north) of The Twinkie. This sunny formation has a distinctive horizontal band running across it and is visible from the parking lot. Scramble about 150 feet above the wash to get to the base of the routes.

115. **Mojave Green** 5.8+ PG13   FA: Jim Lybarger, Bob Conz–late 1980s.
The left route on the formation, which climbs a slabby white face past three bolts. It is located about 100 feet left (west) of **Dime Edging**. The route starts on the left side of some oak bushes. Bring a ¾" TCU for the climb, plus a #3.5 Friend for the anchor. Make difficult moves up to the first bolt (scary), then climb past two more to the summit. Belay from a bolt and #3.5 Friend. Walk off left (west) toward The Twinkie, then cut through a drainage to a ramp that leads back up to the base of the route.

116. **Dime Edging** 5.10 R   FA: Bob Conz, Mike Ward–1989.
Rope up in the center of the cliff on the highest ledge below numerous varnish patches. Move out right from the ledge onto the varnish patches, then go up past two bolts to the ceiling formed by the horizontal band. Get gear in the vertical seam at the lip of the ceiling, then pull this (crux) to another bolt. Friction up the face above to a single drilled angle on top; TCU placement 25 feet further back toward Satellite Wall. Bring a long rope!

The Bull Market

To reach this sunny cliff, walk 200 yards northwest from the parking lot past a white boulder in the main wash to an old roadway. Follow the roadway for a bit over 300 yards to its end, passing an oak bush, a small drainage and a cedar post (this is marked as the trail to Calico Tank). Turn left (northwest; off the trail) and walk about 500 yards up the wash, paralleling the big white lump (The Marshmallow), to reach The Twinkie. Walk just past The Twinkie, then turn right toward a smooth, brown wave of rock (The Drive-in). The Bull Market is a large, brown, bulging formation that is up and right (northeast) from the rear of The Twinkie (The Trophy and Avian Wall will be to the northwest). It sits between two obvious gullies and has routes on three aspects. These lines are described from left to right, starting in the left gully.

117. **20th Century Ultra** 5.11c   FA: Mike Tupper–1992.
Start up the chimney at the left edge of the cliff, then step right and follow eight bolts up the overhanging wall.

118. **Scudder Global** 5.11b   FA: Mike Tupper–1992.
Start ten feet right of the last route above a bush and on the left edge of a smooth recess. Follow four bolts up the left side of an arête to chains.

119. **Fidelity Select** 5.12b   FA: Mike Tupper–1992.
Begin on a ledge 25 feet up in a smooth recess. Climb up the right side of the arête on smooth rock, past three ceilings. There are at least six bolts.

120. **Liar's Poker** 5.11b   FA: Mike Tupper–1992.
This is the first route you'll come to as you approach up the gully. Start at the lower left end of the right gully. Five bolts lead out left then up to a communal chain anchor.

121. **Leveraged Buyout** 5.11b   FA: Mike Tupper–1992.
Start and end as per the last route, but climb past a different set of bolts in the middle. Five bolts total.

122. **Hostile Takeover** 5.11c   FA: Mike Tupper–1992.
Rope up ten feet uphill from the last route. Climb along a vertical seam passing four bolts to a communal chain anchor.

123. **Pinkies For The Dean** 5.11c   FA: Mike Tupper–1992.
The title refers to "Jimmy Dean" of Salt Lake, not Wendell Broussard of Las Vegas! Start as per **Hostile Takeover** then branch right after the first bolt and go up a vertical seam past four more bolts to the shared anchor.

Satellite Wall

This crag sits about 100 feet uphill from The Bull Market. Approach up the right-hand gully that runs past the base of **Liar's Poker** et al. Routes are described from left to right on this sunny escarpment.

124. **Stargazer** 5.12c   FA: Leo and Karin Henson–Winter 1993.
This seven-bolt route goes by numerous huecos on the left end of the formation.

125. **Sputnik** 5.12a FA: Leo and Karin Henson–Winter 1993.
Start five feet right of **Stargazer**; climb up brown rock past six bolts to a chain anchor.

126. **Supernova II** 5.12c ◀ FA: Randy Faulk, Jim Tobish, Tony Becchio–December 1991.
An excellent route. Begin five feet right of the previous route and ten feet left of a large flake. Eight bolts lead up the edge of brown rock to cold shuts.

127. **Cosmos** 5.12d FA: Leo and Karin Henson–Winter 1993.
Clip the first three bolts of **Supernova II**, then head up right past five more to chains.

The Avian Wall

These routes are located on a north-facing wall just below The Trophy. All are on primarily white rock and have anchors from which to lower. To get there, walk 200 yards northwest from the parking lot past a white boulder in the main wash to an old roadway. Follow the roadway for a bit over 300 yards to its end, passing an oak bush, a small drainage and a cedar post (this is marked as the trail to Calico Tank). Turn left (northwest; off the trail) and walk about 500 yards up the wash, paralleling the big white lump, to reach The Twinkie. Walk just past The Twinkie, then turn right toward a smooth, brown wave of rock (The Drive-in). Go east up the canyon about 100 yards to the cliff, which makes up the right (east) wall of the canyon. The Trophy (described next) is 200 feet up slabs to the left. Routes are described from right to left as you head up the gully.

The Bull Market et al.

118. Scudder Global
119. Fidelity Select
120. Liar's Poker

122. Hostile Takeover
Satellite Wall
126. Supernova II

128. **Spotted Owl** 5.11a   FA: Don Burroughs, Alan Busby–March 1992.
No redwoods here! Start 20 feet right of a large oak tree at a flat sandy spot. Climb up along vertical seams, clipping five bolts before you reach the chain anchor.

129. **Thunderbird** 5.11b PG   FA: Don Burroughs, Alan Busby–March 1992.
Not your typical crimper – this one requires a bit of technique. Begin in a pit 80 feet left of the last route and follow six bolts along a vertical seam to chains.

130. **Coyote Moon** 5.9   FA: Don Burroughs, Dr. Alan Busby–March 1992.
Start 15 feet left of the last route at a block in the pit and eight feet right of an oak tree. Zip past four bolts to chains.

131. **Spotted Eagle** 5.10a   FA: Don Burroughs, Alan Busby–March 1992.
Rope up 25 feet left, at the left end of the pit and ten feet right of a large, right-facing flake. Clip four bolts on your way to the chains.

The Trophy

This sunny cliff redefines the word steep! As with the approach for The Twinkie, these directions aren't the most direct way to the crag, but by following them, you shouldn't get lost. From the parking area, walk 200 yards northwest past a white boulder in the main wash to an old roadway. Follow the roadway for a bit over 300 yards to its end, passing an oak bush, a small drainage and a cedar post (this is the trail to Calico Tank). Turn left (northwest, off the trail) and walk about 500 yards up the wash, paralleling the big white lump (The Marshmallow), to reach The Twinkie. Walk just past The Twinkie, then turn right toward a smooth, brown wave of rock (The Drive-in). Go east up the canyon about 150 yards to the obvious overhanging wall on the left (north) side of the canyon. Routes are described from left to right. Total approach time is about 15 minutes.

132. **Fifi Hula** 5.11a   FA: Don Burroughs, Alan Busby–January 1992.
This sunny route isn't on the main Trophy wall, but is about 150 feet left, in the middle of a large white face. Start 40 feet left of a gray water streak and climb past six bolts to a chain anchor. There is at least one route to the left of this, a bolted arête.

133. **Shark Walk** 5.13a ◄   FA: Mike Tupper–February 1992.
Start just right of a cave and a scrub oak at the left (west) end of the main cliff. Climb past six bolts to the anchor.

134. **Indian Giver** 5.12c   FA: Mike Tupper–January 1992.
Begin six feet right of the previous route and climb past five bolts to a chain anchor.

135. **Project** 5.12b?   FA: probably Greg Mayer–sometime in 1995.
Seven bolts lead to chains.

136. **Midnight Cowboy** 5.13a   FA: Mike Tupper–March 1992.
Start 40 feet right of **Indian Giver**. Angle up and left past two bolts, continue left past five bolts, then up past two more bolts.

137. **Twilight Of A Champion** 5.13a ◄   FA: Mike Tupper–February 1992.
Start as per the previous route. Angle up and left past two bolts, then straight up past six more bolts to a chain belay.

138. **Pet Shop Boy** 5.12d ◄   FA: Mike Tupper–February 1992.
Named after Tupper's hairdo. Begin ten feet right of the last route; stick clip the first bolt, then climb straight back (!) past five more bolts.

The Trophy: **Mike Tupper (top) and Leo Henson**

134. Indian Giver	138. Pet Shop Boy	141. Caught in the...
136. Midnight...	139. Keep Your...	142. Dodging...
137. Twilight Of A...	140. The Trophy	143. Meatlocker

139. **Keep Your Powder Dry** 5.12d ◄ FA: Mike Tupper–January 1992.
Rope up 60 feet right of the last route, at the left side of the central cave. Follow nine bolts up very overhanging rock to chains.

140. **The Trophy** 5.12c FA: Mike Tupper–January 1992.
Makes **Fear and Loathing III** look like a slab climb! Starting eight feet right, climb out the right side of the central cave along a horizontal crack past ten bolts to the anchor.

141. **Caught In The Crosshairs** 5.12a FA: Greg Mayer–March 1993.
Begin 30 feet uphill of the central cave on a ledge. Power past seven bolts to the safety of the anchor.

142. **Dodging A Bullet** 5.12a FA: Greg Mayer–Spring 1991.
Start about 45 feet right of the central cave; climb along vertical seams, clipping five bolts en route.

143. **Meatlocker** 5.? FA?–after June 1995.
As of press time, this route *still* had a red ribbon on the first bolt, indicating that the route hadn't yet been redpointed. Begin at the very right edge of the cliff below a flat ceiling. Five bolts lead to chains.

SANDSTONE QUARRY NORTHEAST
Blister In The Sun Cliff

This large, white formation faces south and has a distinctive right-leaning crack/ramp system on it. It is about 500 yards to the left (north) of the approach to the Mass Production Wall and up and left of The Beach. Not much is known about these routes, which are described from left to right.

144. **Teenage Mutant Ninja Turtles** 5.11-   FA: "Frodo," Bob Conz, Sal Mamusia–December 1989.
   This is the leftmost of the routes. You'll need traditional gear to supplement the bolts and get you to the fixed anchor.

145. **Blister In The Sun** 5.11b   FA: Bob Conz, Shelby Shelton–December 1988.
   Seven bolts lead to the top. Bring #2.5 and #3 Friends for the belay.

146. **Tortugas Mutante** 5.11d   FA: Richard Harrison, Jimmy Dunn (of New Hampshire and Colorado fame)–1989.
   The rightmost route, which also has bolts.

147. **High Scalin'** 5.7   FA: Paul Van Betten, Nick Nordblom (both solo)–1987.
   This is the prominent right-leaning ramp/crack. Climb the face to the bottom of the feature, then follow that up and right to the summit. It's two pitches long (if you use a rope!). Bring gear to a #4 Friend. Scramble down the gully to the right (southeast).

The Beach

This sunny crag sits just left of the approach to Mass Production Wall, The Holiday Wall, and Calico Tank. It is just above the drainage bottom, has an overhanging red-colored right side (southeast) and a shorter, white left side (northwest). Only five routes were actually completed as of press time, but several more are in the works. Routes are described from right to left (starting closest to the drainage).

148. **Project** 5.1? FA?–after January 1995.
   Begin 40 feet to the left of the cliff's right edge at an obvious right-facing corner. Eight bolts lead to chains.

149. **Southern Cross** 5.12b   FA: Leo Henson–October 1994.
   Start 30 feet left of the previous route at a bulging arête that forms the right side of a left arching crack/corner. Seven bolts lead to chains.

150. **Looks Like Craps** 5.9?   FA: Unknown.
   Climb the obvious left-leaning crack/corner in the center of the cliff. Watch out for loose rock.

151. **Wizard Of Odds** 5.12a   FA: Greg Mayer–Winter 1992.
   Begin 100 feet left of the prominent crack/corner at the left edge of a many-layered bulge and just right of an arête. Starting at a small pine, climb along a vertical crack system past seven bolts with homemade hangers to chains.

152. **Static** 5.6   FA: Unknown–1980s.
   Rope up just left of the last route in a left-facing corner. This climb ascends the wide crack in a corner just right of a huge boulder.

153. **Squelch** 5.10+ ◀   FA: Kurt Mauer–1987.
   This route is to the left of **Static**, starts behind the huge boulder, and climbs a varnished crack and a small right-facing corner.

Blister in the Sun et al.

147. High Scalin'   149. Southern Cross   154. RF Gain

154. **RF Gain** 5.10 PG13 ◄ FA: Nick Nordblom (rope solo)–1987.
Climb the smooth, brown arête five feet left of **Squelch** and at the right edge of a low-angled gully past two bolts.

NOTE: The cliff continues to the left about 100 yards and becomes smaller and white in color.

Mass Production Wall

From the Sandstone Quarry parking area, follow the trail markers for Calico Tank. The trail goes something like this: walk 200 yards northwest past a white boulder in the main wash, to an old roadway. Follow the roadway for 250 yards past a bush and small drainage to a cedar post in the road. Angle right (northeast) into the obvious pebbly wash and follow it between two rock formations. You'll cross over an old log after about 100 yards and then reach some pine trees after another 40 yards.

The main wash will curve left (north) at this point, with a subsidiary wash continuing east. Follow this sandy wash east for about 300 yards, then continue straight east along the same wash through a canyon with red rock for another 300 yards. Just before the red layer of rock ends, you'll see Mass Production Wall uphill to the left center (northeast). The cliff is in the shade most of the day and is primarily a white-colored rock with pine trees at its base. This approach takes about 15 minutes from the parking area. Routes are described right to left, running uphill from the approach.

155. **Some Assembly Required** 5.10c FA: Greg Mayer–Spring 1991.
Start behind a gnarled pine tree and climb up along parallel, left-leaning seams, then up the face right of a cave. Six bolts to chain anchors.

156. **Kokopelli** 5.10c PG FA: Don Burroughs, Alan Busby–April 1992.
Named for the hunchbacked flute player commonly seen in Native American rock art. Begin 50 feet uphill of the previous route below the right center of a cave. Face climb past bolts, then out the ceiling at a right-facing corner to chains.

157. **Parts Is Parts** 5.8   FA: Todd Swain, Jeff Rickerl–April 1992.
The chain anchor was installed by Mayer in 1991, then bolted in 1993 after Swain and Rickerl had done the route using only traditional gear (5.8 X). Begin 100 feet uphill of **Some Assembly Required** behind two pine trees. Wander up the face past four bolts to reach the chain anchor.

158. **Battery Powered** 5.9   FA: Greg Mayer–Spring 1991.
Rope up ten feet left of the previous route and ten feet right of a right-facing corner. Climb past six bolts to the chain anchor.

159. **Foreman Ferris** 5.11b   FA: Leo Henson–October 1994.
This bolted route goes through the right side of the large varnished patch shaped roughly like Australia at a thin seam. There are supposed to be six or seven bolts.

160. **Trigger Happy** 5.10a ◀   FA: Greg Mayer–Spring 1991.
Start 90 feet uphill of **Battery Powered** below a seam leading through the left edge of a large varnished patch shaped roughly like Australia. Scamper past five bolts to a chain anchor.

161. **Hit And Run** 5.9   FA: Greg Mayer–Spring 1991.
Begin ten feet left of **Trigger Happy** behind a pine tree with a broken top. Climb past five bolts to a chain anchor, keeping just right of a seam/crack.

The Hall of Fame

From the Sandstone Quarry parking area, follow the trail markers for Calico Tank. The trail goes something like this: walk 200 yards northwest past a white boulder in the main wash, to an old roadway. Follow the roadway for 250 yards past a bush and small drainage to a cedar post in the road. Angle right (northeast) into the obvious pebbly wash and follow it between two rock formations. You'll cross over an old log after about 100 yards and then reach some pine trees after another 40 yards.

The main wash will curve left (north) at this point, with a subsidiary wash continuing east. Follow this sandy wash east for about 300 yards, then continue straight east through a canyon with red rock for another 300 yards. Just before the red layer of rock ends, you'll see Mass Production Wall uphill to the left center (east).

For The Hall of Fame, head up left (northeast) along a gully for 300 yards to the base of a large, white, south-facing cliff with a steep gully/cleft running north-south.

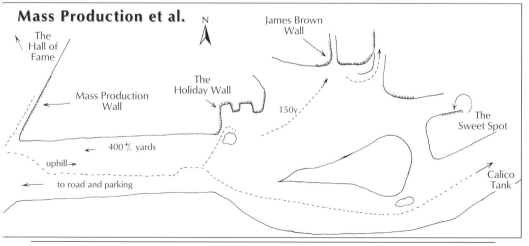

Mass Production et al.

156. Kokopelli   160. Trigger Happy

From the base of the cleft, contour around left (west and then north) on ledges above one cliff band and below another for 100 yards (there should be cairns along this section). Scamper 50 yards up the first gully you reach and you should be at the lower entrance to The Hall of Fame.

The Hall runs in a north-south direction, with the routes all being on the right (south) wall. They are in the shade all day, although it's very easy to reach sunshine to warm up on cooler days. The approach to this cliff is an additional ten minutes from Mass Production Wall, or a total of 25 minutes from the parking area. Routes are described right to left, running up The Hall from the approach.

162. **Yearnin' And Learnin'** 5.11a   FA: Don Burroughs, Alan Busby–April 1992.
Begin about 15 feet inside the corridor below two lines of bolts with a common start. Climb up and right past five bolts to chains.

163. **Repeat Offender** 5.10d   FA: Greg Mayer–Spring 1991.
Start as per the previous route, but climb slightly left past six bolts to a chain anchor, moving left then back right between the second and third bolts (V1).

     V1 If you climb straight between these bolts, the route is 5.11c.

164. **Armed And Dangerous** 5.10d   FA: Phil Bowden–Spring 1991.
Begin six feet left of **Repeat Offender**. After a difficult lieback move, climb past huecos to the left side of a bulge. Follow a total of six bolts to the chain anchor.

165. **Bad Reputation**   5.11b   FA: Phil Bowden, Guy Pinjuv–Spring 1991.
Climb the face 15 feet left of **Armed and Dangerous** past six bolts to the same chain anchor. There is a difficult ceiling down low, but the crux is up higher.

166. **Innocent Bystander**   5.10a   FA: Greg Mayer–Spring 1991.
Start 30 feet uphill of **Bad Reputation** and power past five bolts to a chain anchor.

167. **Ms. Adventure**   5.7   FA: "Chucky" Mayer–Spring 1991.
Begin 30 feet left of the previous route and about 20 feet downhill from the upper entrance to the corridor. Climb past three bolts to the anchor. The crux is off the ground.

At least four routes have been done to the left (north and west) of The Hall of Fame. The first two routes are located just left (west) of the upper entrance to The Hall of Fame.

168. **Hero Worship**   5.10b   FA: Liz Tupper–December 25, 1993.
This is the left route, which has four bolts and climbs near an arête.

169. **Computer Virus**   5.12c   FA: Mike Tupper–December 25, 1993.
This is the right route, which has nine bolts. Tupper was ill on the first ascent.

170. **Sand Illusion**   5.11c   FA: Greg Mayer–Spring 1991.
This route climbs a prominent arête about 150 yards to the west of The Hall of Fame. It faces southeast and has three bolts and a chain anchor.

171. **Unknown Arête**   5.12a   FA: Jim Greg–Fall 1993.
Somewhere to the right of **Sand Illusion** is an arête with five bolts.

The Holiday Wall

This crag has a number of very good sport routes that are in the sun most of the day. Total approach time is about 20 minutes. From the Sandstone Quarry parking area, follow the trail markers for Calico Tank. The trail goes something like this: walk 200 yards northwest past a white boulder in the main wash to an old roadway. Follow the roadway for 250 yards past a bush and small drainage to a cedar post in the road. Angle right (northeast) into the obvious pebbly wash and follow it between two rock formations. You'll cross over an old log after about 100 yards and then reach some pine trees after another 40 yards.

The main wash will curve left (north) at this point, with a subsidiary wash continuing east. Follow this sandy wash east for about 300 yards, then continue straight east through a canyon with red rock for another 300 yards. Just before the red layer of rock ends, you'll see Mass Production Wall uphill to the left center (northeast).

Continue up the main drainage beyond Mass Production Wall, heading slightly right to gain a trail that contours along the hillside. About 200 yards beyond the end of the red rock, the trail will drop down into a drainage and the red rock will appear again. Continue up the valley another 200 yards to reach The Holiday Wall, which will be on the left (northeast). The trail to Calico Tank will continue for about another 500 yards. Routes here are described from left to right as you approach on the trail.

172. **The Grinch**   5.12c   FA: Mike Tupper–Christmas 1990.
Start near the left edge of the wall and 50 feet right of a medium-sized oak at smooth, overhanging, varnished rock. Climb past three bolts (there were four, but the first is missing) to chains.

173. **Death Before Decaf** 5.12b   FA: Don Welsh–January 1991.
Bolted by Kevin Lawler and Sandy Carrick, then led by Welsh much later. Begin 20 feet uphill of the previous route on a red slab. Fire past six bolts to chains.

174. **Gift Rapped** 5.11b   FA: Karen Peil–Christmas 1990.
"Given" to Peil by Tupper as a Christmas present! Start ten feet uphill behind a pine tree, at a shallow, left-facing corner. Clip six bolts as you climb along seams to a chain anchor.

175. **Red Sky Mining** 5.11a   FA: Karen Peil–December 1990.
Climb past seven bolts to chains, starting ten feet right of **Gift Rapped** and behind a gnarled pine tree.

176. **Red Storm Rising** 5.11b   FA: Karen Peil–December 1990.
Begin as per the last route and climb up along a left-facing flake/corner past five bolts to chains.

177. **When The Cat's Away** 5.11b ◀   FA: Greg Mayer–December 1990.
Rope up 15 feet right at the base of a buttress with a small ceiling at the bottom. Pull the ceiling and clip six bolts as you climb up small, opposing flake systems.

178. **Saddam's Mom** 5.11d   FA: Karen Peil–December 1990.
Could it be Laura SCUDder? Begin eight feet right of the previous route at the right arête of the buttress. Shoot past six bolts to a chain anchor.

179. **Moments To Memories** 5.11a   FA: Greg Mayer–December 1990.
Start 40 feet right of **Saddam's Mom** and 30 feet right of a striking dihedral (a future test piece) at the left arête of a short buttress. Climb the arête past four bolts to chains.

180. **Fast Moving Train** 5.11a ◀   FA: Greg Mayer–December 1990.
Begin just right of **Moments...** and climb past five bolts up the right arête of the buttress.

JAMES BROWN AREA

From the Sandstone Quarry parking area, follow the trail markers for Calico Tank. The trail goes something like this: walk 200 yards northwest past a white boulder in the main wash to an old roadway. Follow the roadway for 250 yards past a bush and small drainage to a cedar post in the road. Angle right (northeast) into the obvious pebbly wash and follow it between two rock formations. You'll cross over an old log after about 100 yards and then reach some pine trees after another 40 yards.

The main wash will curve left (north) at this point, with a subsidiary wash continuing due east. Follow this sandy wash east for about 300 yards, then continue straight east through a canyon with red rock for another 300 yards. Just before the red layer of rock ends, you'll see Mass Production Wall uphill to the left center (northeast).

Continue up the main drainage beyond Mass Production Wall, heading slightly right to gain a trail that contours along the hillside. About 200 yards beyond the end of the red rock, the trail will drop down into a drainage, and the red rock will appear again. Continue up the valley another 200 yards to reach The Holiday Wall, which will be on the left (northeast).

The James Brown Area is 150 yards diagonally up right (east) from the right edge of The Holiday Wall and 200 yards above wash level. The cliff forms the left side of a corridor and is characterized by a prominent brown water streak on the left arête of the corridor. Total approach time is about 25 minutes to this sunny crag. Routes are described from left to right.

181. **James Brown** 5.11b PG 🍴   FA: Randy Marsh, Pier Locatelli–Winter 1991.
Dance up the brown water streak on the left arête of the corridor, clipping seven bolts en route to chains. An excellent route.

182. **Brand New Bag** 5.10d   FA: Randy Marsh, Pier Locatelli –Winter 1991.
Paper or plastic? Start 20 feet right and uphill from **James Brown** and just left of a bush. Four bolts lead to chains.

183. **Soul Power** 5.11d   FA: Randy Marsh, Pier Locatelli–Winter 1991.
You'll *feel good* after completing this one! Begin ten feet uphill, between two bushes. Climb past eight bolts to a chain anchor.

The Next Wall

This cliff has two sections and is immediately right (east) of James Brown Wall.

184. **Project** 5.12?   FA: Greg Mayer–sometime in 1995 (hopefully).
Start on a terrace 40 feet right of James Brown Wall, below an overhanging brown and white wall. Nine bolts lead up along a seam in the overhanging wall to chains.

The next two routes are down and around to the right about 60 feet from the last route, on a south-facing wall.

185. **They Just Don't Make Outlaws Like They Used To** 5.12a   FA: Greg Mayer–Spring 1993.
The left route, which has an overhanging start into a pod. Climb out the right side of the pod and up the face above. There are 11 bolts total and a chain anchor.

186. **The Heteroclite** 5.11c   FA: Greg Mayer–Spring 1993.
The right route, which has ten bolts and a separate chain anchor.

The Sweet Spot

When looking up canyon (east) from The Holiday Wall, the canyon is divided roughly in half by a dark brown rock formation. The trail to Calico Tank passes to the right (south) of this, while the two established routes are in a corridor on the north side of the formation. To approach these north-facing routes, stay in the smaller, left-hand drainage east of The Holiday Wall (but well below James Brown Wall).

187. **Absolute Zero** 5.12a   FA: Greg Mayer–Summer 1993.
The right route, which has five bolts and a chain anchor.

188. **Disposable Blues** 5.11c   FA: Greg Mayer–Summer 1993.
Start about 25 feet left and climb past five bolts to a chain anchor.

White Spring Overview

NOT TO SCALE

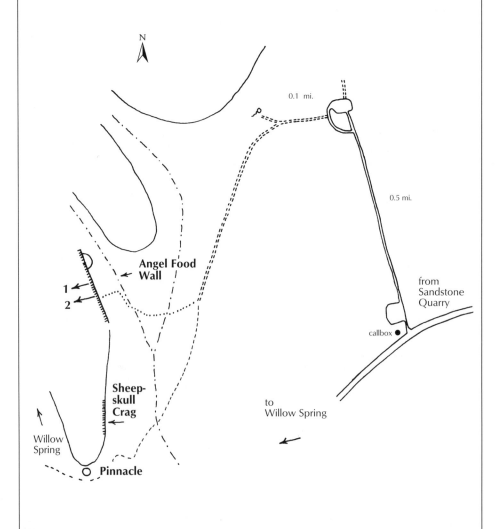

N

0.1 mi.

0.5 mi.

from
Sandstone
Quarry

callbox ●

**Angel Food
Wall**

1

2

**Sheep-
skull
Crag**

Willow
Spring

○ **Pinnacle**

to
Willow Spring

WHITE SPRING

Angel Food Wall

While numerous routes have been climbed and documented on this crag, only three will be described in this guide (of which I've only done one). To reach the parking area for White Spring, drive 5.8 miles along the scenic loop road to the sign for White Spring. Turn right off the loop road and drive 0.5 mile to a parking area at a cul-de-sac.

1. **Tunnel Vision** 5.7 ◀ FA: Joe Herbst, Randy Grandstaff–1974.
   A unique route that involves a bit of spelunking. Similar in nature to **The Tunnel** at Skytop Cliff in the Shawangunks of New York. Bring a good selection of gear, including large Friends.

   From the cul-de-sac, walk down the obvious, dirt road. Take the first left (White Spring is about 150 yards down the main road) on a lesser-used road and follow this until you are almost to a drainage. Go cross-country toward the big cliff to the west, entering another drainage that runs parallel with the cliff. Head up this drainage for about 100 yards, then go up the hillside to the base of the wall. Aim for a point at the base of the wall that is roughly 100 feet left of the right end of a pink rock band. The approach takes about 30 minutes.

   Start 30 feet above the ground on a cleared section of ledge and 15 feet right of a chimney/alcove.

   P1 Climb a short corner to a ceiling 15 feet up, then traverse right eight feet to an obvious crack system. Stem up the crack past loose blocks forming a roof, then continue up to a ledge (60 feet). Climb the chimney above to another ledge and belay in an alcove. 120 ft., 5.6.

   P2 Continue up the chimney system, belaying on the flattest section you can find (large gear needed for the anchors). 100 ft., 5.4.

   P3 Continue up the steep and exposed chimney to a spacious ledge below an overhanging wall. There's room for 15 people to sit comfortably here! 120 ft., 5.7.

   P4 Climb straight up past an overhang to a lower-angled face. Ascend the delightful varnished face and right-facing corner to another huge ledge at the mouth of the tunnel. 130 ft., 5.5.

   P5 Turn on your head lamps! Angle up left through the tunnel on water-polished, poorly-protected rock to a ledge. Walk left to reach daylight, then climb the obvious crack system to a belay ledge. 150 ft., 5.3 X.

   P6 Climb either of two cracks above, escaping left below a final ceiling or continuing straight up to the top. 150 ft., 5.5.

   Descent: Head down and left (southeast) in a series of easy chimney/gullies for 100 yards. Contour around right (west) to the top of a huge gully leading southeast. Go down this to an obvious drop-off (possible 60-foot rappel here) and move right over a small saddle into a parallel gully. This will easily take you down to the open slope at the left (southeast) end of Angel Food Wall. The descent should take about 15 minutes.

2. **Group Therapy** 5.7   FA: Joe and Betsy Herbst, Randy Grandstaff, Matt McMackin – Spring, 1974.
   This route starts to the right of **Tunnel Vision** in a recess with a pine tree.

   P1 Scamper up an easy face to a belay. 150 ft.

   P2 Jam up a crack in the center of a white face. 150 ft.

Tunnel Vision 5.7

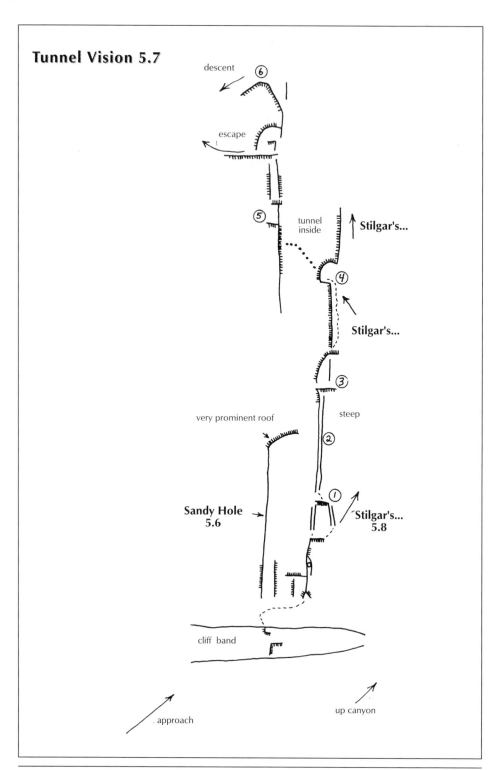

descent

⑥

escape

⑤

tunnel inside

Stilgar's...

④

Stilgar's...

③

very prominent roof

steep

②

①

Sandy Hole 5.6

Stilgar's... 5.8

cliff band

approach

up canyon

P3 Continue up cracks and the face above to a belay at a tree. This is about 80 feet below a prominent left-facing corner with a roof.

P4 Climb a left-facing corner and chimney to just beneath the roof.

P5 Climb the crack through the roof, then continue up to a belay. 150 ft.

P6 Go off to the left (V1) to reach the summit.

V1 Continue up a vertical crack (5.8).

Descent: Head down and left (southeast) in a series of easy chimney/gullies for 100 yards. Contour around right (west) to the top of a huge gully leading southeast. Go down this to an obvious drop-off (possible 60-foot rappel here) and move right over a small saddle into a parallel gully. This will easily take you down to the open slope at the left (southeast) end of Angel Food Wall. The descent should take about 15 minutes.

3. **Goobies For Gumbies** 5.10+ ◄ FA: Paul Van Betten, Randy Grandstaff, Nick Nordblom–1985.
   A classic pitch of crack climbing. Bring lots of #2- to #3-sized Friends and two ropes. Start as per **Group Therapy** in a chasm. Climb the striking handcrack on the left wall to an anchor 140 feet up.

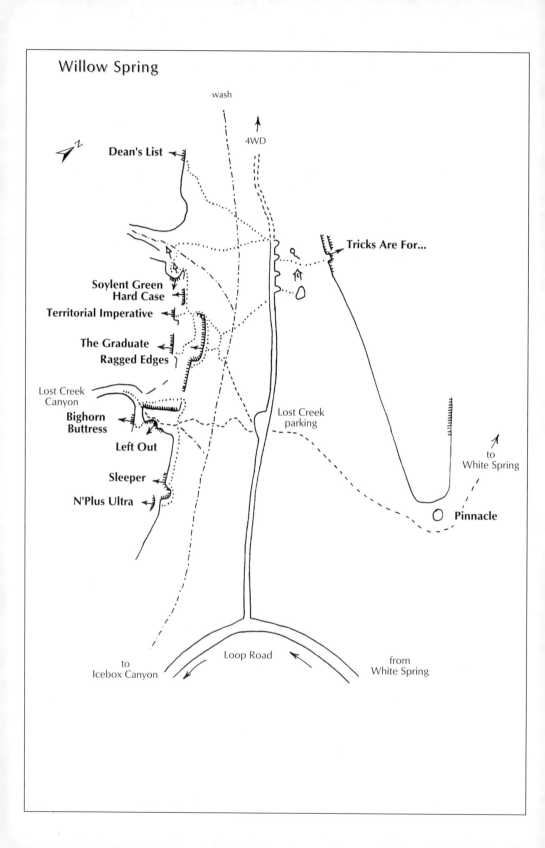

WILLOW SPRING

While not as in vogue as The Gallery or Wall of Confusion, Willow Spring offers many short routes of good quality. The turnoff for Willow Spring is found 7.3 miles down the scenic loop road. This spur road is paved for 0.6 mile – after that it's four-wheel drive territory all the way through toward the town of Pahrump.

Most of the routes described are one pitch long, though at times you may need two ropes to easily get back to your gear. Those longer convenience rappels are noted. The typical rack for Willow Spring includes a set of Friends, TCUs and wired stoppers – it's mostly a traditional area.

At the end of the pavement is a picnic area on the right. There are a few picnic tables under the big cottonwood trees, a natural spring (no potable water, though) and an outhouse. Just to the right (east) of the outhouse building is some excellent bouldering, but stay off the Native American rock art!

Nadia's

Three routes are described just outside the mouth of the Willow Spring canyon. These routes are located roughly halfway between Lost Creek Canyon and Icebox Canyon at the base of the hillside. They are best seen (and approached) from the intersection of the scenic loop road and the Willow Spring road, then walking straight west toward the hillside. All three routes are on a dark, northeast-facing formation. The routes are described from left to right.

1. **Nadia's Nine** 5.9   FA: Joe Herbst, Mark Moore –Spring 1977.
   This route gets rave reviews in the Urioste guide, but I have yet to do it. It climbs a left-facing (toward Icebox Canyon) crack and corner system in two pitches.

The next two routes are to the right of Nadia's Nine on a varnished face.

2. **Dark Star** 5.11+   FA: Paul Van Betten, Bob Conz–September 1988.
   After a hard start, climb a thin flake with bolts (80 feet).

Nadia's Niche
2.   Dark Star   3.   Wheat Thick

3. **Wheat Thick** 5.11b   FA: Paul Van Betten, Sal Mamusia–October 1988.
    This is supposed to be a thick version of Yosemite's **Wheat Thin**. Start to the right of
    Dark Star and climb a flake system and black huecos to webbing anchors. Photo, page
    95.

LOST CREEK CANYON/HIDDEN FALLS

After turning off the scenic loop road into Willow Spring, you'll come to a dirt pullout on your left at 0.2 mile. This is the parking for Lost Creek Canyon and Hidden
Falls. Follow the obvious trail for about 300 yards, passing a spring en route to the
mouth of the canyon. To the left (southeast) are routes **N'Plus Ultra** through
Buffalo Balls. These routes are in the shade all day. To the right of the dry waterfall
are routes **The Threat** through **Hot Climb**. These routes get sun in the morning, then
move into the shade in the afternoon.

4. **N'Plus Ultra** 5.10- ◄   FA: (TR) Joe Herbst–1975. First Lead: Randy Grandstaff–1976.
    This route sits on the second tier of cliff bands, about 300 yards left (southeast) of the
    trail. Turn off the trail at the spring (and a couple of wooden benches), and follow a faint
    path toward the cliff. Approach this route by scrambling up an easy gully with a pine
    tree at the base. The route climbs out a huge roof via a fistcrack. Bring multiple #4
    Friends. Descend by walking off right (northwest) around to the base of the roof, then
    back down the approach gully.

Lost Creek Canyon/Hidden Falls

6.	Pillar Talk	10.	Left Out	25.	Captain Crunch
8.	Sleeper	21.	Grippity Gravity	28.	Heatwave

5. **The Abdominizer** 5.11   FA: Paul Van Betten, Richard Harrison, Shelby Shelton–April 1990.
No spare tires allowed. Climb the roof just left of **N'Plus Ultra** along flakes. Two bolts in the roof provide protection.

6. **Pillar Talk** 5.7 R   FA: Joe Herbst–1970s.
Turn off the trail to Hidden Falls as per **N'Plus Ultra** (in the vicinity of a couple of wooden benches) and follow the faint trail about 200 yards to the base of a pillar with an obvious hand-and fistcrack on its right side.

P1 Climb the crack to a roof (large protection needed; **V1**), then hand traverse left (scary) to the arête. Climb up the easy face and belay in one of many cracks. 100 ft., 5.7 PG.

P2 Continue up the easy face to the top of the pillar. 80 ft., 5.4 R.

V1 Continue up the crack through the roof above, then rejoin the regular route. Large Friends needed. 5.10-.

Descent: walk right (west) and rappel with two ropes from a pine tree atop **Sleeper**.

7. **Big Iron** 5.11c   FA: Paul Van Betten, Bob Conz–Summer 1990.
Climb the steep face just around the corner to the right of **Pillar Talk** past seven bolts. Rappel **Sleeper** with two ropes.

8. **Sleeper** 5.9   FA: Wendell Broussard, Rocky Paravia–1981.
Start 30 feet right of **Pillar Talk**, below an obvious fingercrack leading to a pine tree. Climb flakes to a bulge (about 50 feet up) that is split by a crack. Pull the bulge (crux) and follow the crack to the top. Rappel from the pine tree with two ropes.

The next five routes are on the varnished buttress just left of the trail to Hidden Falls, near some big pine trees at the mouth of the canyon. They are in the shade all day.

9. **Killer Klowns** 5.10+   FA: Paul Van Betten, Sal Mamusia, Richard Harrison, Kevin Biernacki–September 1989.
Climb an easy ramp on the left edge of the steep, varnished wall to an alcove 20 feet up. Struggle up through a bombay slot, then up the face and cracks above to the top. Descend by scrambling over the highest part of the buttress, then down a gully just right (south) of the varnished wall.

10. **Left Out** 5.10+ ✒   FA: (TR) Unknown. First Lead: Joe Herbst–circa 1975.
An excellent route that climbs a thin crack on the left side of the varnished face. Not to be left out! Climb steep huecos just left of the obvious central crack on the formation (**V1**), then up the thin crack to its top. Climb the easier face to the top of the formation. Descend as per **Killer Clowns**.

V1 5.11- R/X FA: Bobby Rotert–1983. Start up **Black Track**, then follow a left-leaning seam into **Left Out** (three bolts lead upward from this seam, but the route is apparently incomplete).

11. **Black Track** 5.9 ✒   FA: Joe Herbst early–1970s.
The obvious line on the wall, and a good follow up climb to **Ragged Edges** (see page 103). Climb the central crack on the wall to a ledge at two-thirds height. Either rappel with one rope from the chain anchor, climb the short offwidth to the top or climb the steep face directly above past two bolts (5.11c).

12. **Bigfoot** 5.10a ✒   FA: Yeti and A. Snowman–1990.
A very good face climb just right of **Black Track**. Climb the steep face past four bolts to the chain anchor.

13. **Buffalo Balls** 5.11c   FA: (TR) Bob Yoho–1989; FA: (lead) Don Burroughs, Alan Busby –May 1992.
Four bolts lead up the steep face just right of **Bigfoot**.

Bighorn Buttress
5.11 PG13

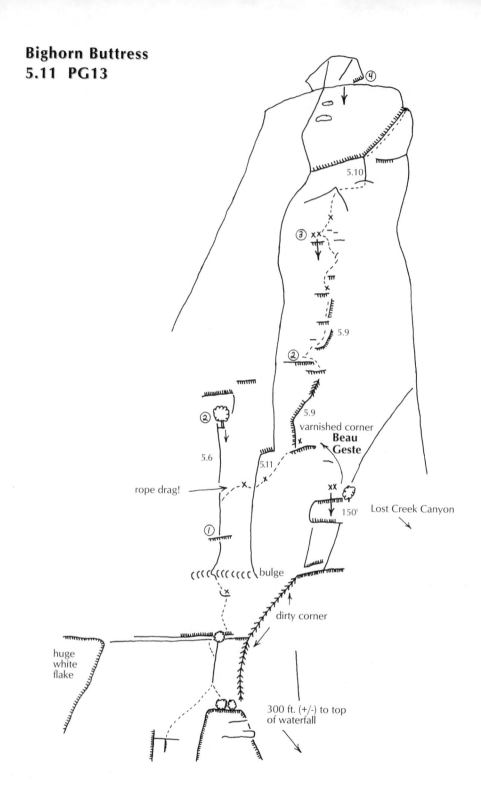

4

5.10

3 XX

5.9

2

5.9

varnished corner

Beau Geste

2

5.6

5.11

rope drag!

XX

150'   Lost Creek Canyon

1

((((((((((bulge

X

dirty corner

huge white flake

300 ft. (+/-) to top of waterfall

Upper Tier

The next two routes are roughly above the **Black Track** buttress. They are located about 200 yards left of **Bighorn Buttress**, at the top of a gully near a large, dead pine tree. Information was sketchy at press time.

14. **Possum Logic** 5.9 R FA: Nick Nordblom, Shelby Shelton–1988.
    Climb the face left of the tree past four bolts.

15. **The Pocket Philosopher** 5.10- FA: Nick Nordblom, Danny Reider–1988.
    This route goes up behind the dead tree and has two bolts.

16. **Bighorn Buttress** 5.11 PG13 ◀ FA: Nick Nordblom, Jenni Stone–Spring 1987.
    This good and scary route is on the left (south) side of the upper Lost Creek Canyon, and starts about 300 feet up and left from the dry waterfall (the top of **The Threat**). The start of the route faces the road, but the majority of the climbing faces right, toward Ragged Edges Cliff. Approach by scrambling up ledges to the right of **Buffalo Balls** or follow the trail up around the top of **Heatwave**. Gear up about 50 feet down and right of a huge, right-facing white flake at a section of chocolate brown rock. Bring equipment up to a #3 Friend and some long slings.

    Start at a short, left-facing corner that is just right of a mossy section of rock and between two opposing corners.

    P1 Climb the short corner then wander up and slightly right on the brown face, aiming for a 20-foot-long vertical crack leading to a prominent bush in a horizontal (**V1**, **V2**). Follow the vertical crack and the face just left to the horizontal, then step right towards the bush. Climb straight up the brown face above to a bolt below a bulge with a thin, vertical seam/crack. Pull the bulge and belay above on a ledge. 140 ft., 5.10- PG13.

    P2 Continue up the crack, exiting right to a bolt. Step around the arête, passing a bolt (crux), then climb a corner to the belay. Watch out for rope drag. 150 ft., 5.11 PG.

    P3 Climb up past a couple of left-facing corners and finish the pitch by face climbing past a bolt to a two-bolt belay. 80 ft., 5.9.

    P4 Go up right past a bolt, turn a small roof into a right-facing corner and go up this to the top. Belay on the summit. 80 ft., 5.10.

    V1 You can also scramble up ledges to the right of the start (below a vegetated corner) and step left to the base of the vertical crack that leads to the bush.

    V2 The original route up this buttress was called **Beau Geste** and climbed up the vegetated corner mentioned in **V1** until one could traverse left into the varnished corners of **P3**. 5.9+.

    Descent: Rappel straight down with two ropes, ending to the right of the route.

The next routes are all located on the other side of Hidden Falls and are described starting at the falls and moving right (north). These routes are in the sun in the morning.

Lower Tier

17. **The Threat** 5.10+ FA: Joe Herbst, Randy Grandstaff –1975.
    Just to the right of the dry falls is an obvious water-polished crack. Move left into the crack (bolt; crux), then up this past another bolt to the top. The easiest descent is to walk left (east) along ledges and scramble down the gully to the right of the **Black Track** buttress. It is also possible to walk off right (north) by **Heatwave**, then circle back around the base of the cliff.

18. **Flight Line** 5.12c FA: Paul Van Betten, Richard Harrison–Summer 1990.
    Climb smooth flakes ten feet right of **The Threat** to a very smooth wave of rock above. Clip the doubled bolts and surmount the wave to gain the top. Don't expect to get this route without a big investment in time – it's technical and tricky.

19. **Mind Bomb** 5.11+ R FA: Paul Van Betten, Richard Harrison–Summer 1990.
A good route – if you can get off the ground! Climb the three-bolt arête 50 feet right of the dry falls and just right of a cave. Bring some natural gear and be prepared to run it out above the top bolt.

20. **Little Big Horn** 5.9+ ◢ FA: Jay Smith, Randy Grandstaff, Doug MacDonald–1981.
A great route – hopefully you won't get massacred by the crux! Walk 100 feet to the right of **Mind Bomb**, past three ugly cracks, until the trail enters the trees. Start in the trees and climb a left-facing corner past an overhang (crux) to the varnished face and the top.

21. **Grippitty Gravity** 5.10 FA: Jon Martinet, Randy Grandstaff–mid 1970s.
A short crux leads to an easy dihedral above. Start atop boulders 100 feet right of **Little...** and below a low roof split by a crack; climb out the roof (crux), then up the low-angled, varnished corner above. Finish up easy cracks and a short face. Photos, below and page 96.

22. **Sportin' A Woody** 5.11+ FA: Paul Van Betten, Sal Mamusia, Bob Conz–February 1990.
About 120 feet to the right of **Little Big Horn** is another good looking, left-facing corner protected by bolts and RPs.

*Roughly 160 feet to the right of **Little Big Horn** is a large, steep face with two bolted routes on it.*

23. **Captain Hook** 5.11+ R FA: Paul Van Betten, Jay Smith–Fall 1988.
This climbs the left side of the face past two bolts to a thin seam/flake. Follow this and clip two more bolts on your way to the top.

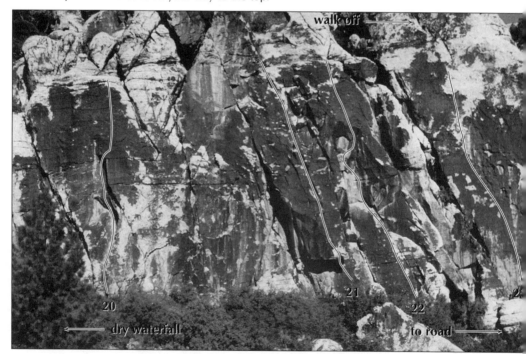

Lost Creek Canyon, Right (west) Side

20. Little Big Horn
21. Grippity Gravity
22. Sportin' A Woody
23. Captain Hook

24. **Captain Curmudgeon** 5.11- R FA: Nick Nordblom, Jenni Stone, Paul Van Betten–Spring 1986.
Climb loose flakes up the center of the steep face just right of **Captain Hook**, passing three bolts en route.

25. **Captain Crunch** 5.10- X FA: Nick Nordblom, Jenni Stone, Paul Van Betten–Fall 1988.
Bring a few small wires (not that you'll get many in!). Climb the right edge of the buttress, ending on the shoulder. Scary and loose. Photo, page 96.

26. **Tuckered Sparfish** 5.10 PG13 FA: Paul Van Betten, Don Burroughs–June 1992.
Rope up 20 feet right of **Captain Crunch** on the next buttress; climb past four bolts to a tree on the top. Bring some wires and TCUs to get you to the first bolt.

27. **Rock Rastler** 5.12+ R FA: Paul Van Betten–Summer 1985.
Climb a hand crack to a roof, then struggle up an offwidth to the top.

28. **Heatwave** 5.10- R FA: Paul & Pauline Van Betten–1988.
At the far right (north) end of the Hidden Canyon, and 200 feet right of **Captain Curmudgeon**, climb the center of a slabby face past three bolts. Photo, page 96.

29. **Hot Climb** 5.10- R/X FA: Nick Nordblom, Wendell Broussard–1989.
This short route climbs a little black varnished wall up and right of **Heatwave**. You'll need some small wires.

NOTE: The hiking trail leading into upper Lost Creek Canyon passes just to the right of this route. This may also be used as the descent.

RAGGED EDGES AREA
Ragged Edges Cliff
This is probably the most obvious cliff in the Willow Spring area. Either park as per Lost Creek Canyon or continue driving down the spur road toward Willow Spring for another 0.3 mile (0.5 mile total from the scenic loop road). On the left side of the road is a large, varnished wall with an obvious vertical crack system in the center. This crack is the classic **Ragged Edges**. After deciding where to park, follow one of the clearly defined trails to the base of the cliff. The following routes are shaded most of the day.

30. **Kemosabe** 5.10- PG FA: Sal Mamusia, Richard Harrison, Paul Van Betten, Wendell Broussard–1983.
An exciting climb. Bring small gear. Begin at the base of an arch 100 feet left of **Ragged Edges**. Climb the face and thin cracks up the arête of the arch to a bolt. Continue up the arête (scary), or weenie out and traverse off left, then up to the top. Walk off to the right (west) as per **Ragged Edges**.

31. **Tonto** 5.5 FA: Joe and Betsy Herbst–1972.
Climb the obvious crack in the slab that is 90 feet left of **Ragged Edges** and just right of the arch mentioned in **Kemosabe**. At the top, move out right onto the face or continue up the crack past a roof (5.7).

32. **Vision Quest** 5.12d FA: Paul Van Betten, Sal Mamusia–October 1988.
Start 75 feet left of **Ragged Edges** and just right of an ugly chimney/corner. Climb up a short crack, then move slightly right to a bolt. Continue up the overhanging wall above, past three more bolts to a chain anchor. The second pitch climbs a left-leaning crack to the top (5.10+). The two ring bolts below were placed by Craig Reason in a failed attempt to do a direct start.

33. **Bodiddly** 5.10 PG FA: Robert Finlay, Richard Harrison–1985.
A very good route, but a tiny bit scary. Start 30 feet left of **Ragged Edges** on the left, front corner of the wall. Climb up the arête and face to a bolt; follow more bolts up left

(V1) past a steep flake. Continue up the easy face above. Walk off right as per **Ragged Edges**.

V1 Bodacious 5.10   FA: Sal Mamusia, Richard Harrison, Wendell Broussard–Spring 1983. From the second bolt, it is possible to traverse straight left, then up past a bolt to rejoin the route. This was how this section of rock was first climbed; **Bodiddly** is the straighter (and perhaps more logical) line.

Ragged Edges Area

30.	Kemosabe	35.	Ragged Edges	**The Graduate Cliff**	
31.	Tonto	36.	Chicken Eruptus	43.	Walk To School
32.	Vision Quest	37.	Gun Boy	44.	The Graduate
33	Bodiddly	38.	Sheep Trail	45.	Acid Jacks
34.	Plan F	42.	Sheep Dip	46.	Circle Jerks

34. **Plan F** 5.11- PG   FA: Sal Mamusia, Richard Harrison, Paul Van Betten, Nick Nordblom–April 1983.
The initial fingercrack is often done by itself, rapping off the bolt in the **Ragged Edges** crack. Begin eight feet left of **Ragged Edges** below an obvious fingercrack. Jam up the crack (5.10-), then angle left up the smooth, slippery face past a few bolts to the top.

35. **Ragged Edges** 5.8   ◄   FA: Joe Herbst–early 1970s.
The classic route in Willow Spring. Bring lots of large gear. Climb the central crack on the varnished wall. The route is a full rope length, so bring an extra long rope to reach the belay tree, or #1.5 and #2 Friends for a belay just below the top. Walk off to the right (west), then back along the base of the crag.

36. **Chicken Eruptus** 5.10 PG   ◄   FA: Richard Harrison, Wendell Broussard, Paul Van Betten, Sal Mamusia–Spring 1983.
Named to commemorate Broussard's meal at Caesar's Palace the previous night! An excellent but sporty route for solid 5.10 leaders. Start five feet right of **Ragged Edges** and climb up a right-leaning ramp for 40 feet to horizontal cracks. Move out right to the nose, then climb straight up the face past a bolt to the summit. Bring #1.5 and #2 Friends for the belay.

37. **Gun Boy** 5.11+ PG   FA: Paul Van Betten, Sal Mamusia, Richard Harrison, Danny Meyers–March 1991.
Start 30 feet right of **Ragged Edges** in a yellow band of rock. Climb past one bolt to a rounded, brown dihedral. Continue straight up the face, keeping just left of a black streak, passing two more bolts to the top. There's a rather scary section that requires some dicey moves off small RPs.

38. **Sheep Trail** 5.10- PG   ◄   FA: John Bachar, Mike Lechlinski, Richard Harrison–Spring 1983.
Wonderful climbing, but make sure you're solid at the grade. This was originally rated 5.8! Begin 40 feet right of **Ragged Edges** at a black streak and a clearing in the vegetation. Weave up past numerous horizontals to a shallow, left-facing corner about 50 feet up. Continue basically straight up the face, exiting the brown rock at a short, vertical crack. Belay on the terrace (small to medium Friends), then walk off right.

39. **Dense Pack** 5.10 PG   FA: Nick Nordblom, Robert Finlay–Spring 1984.
Another excellent but sporty route. Traverse out left on a ledge system 150 feet right of **Ragged Edges** to a right-facing corner. Layback and stem up the corner, then swing out left (V1). Weave up the varnished face above, angling slightly left. Belay on the terrace above, then walk off right.

V1 Twelve Pack 5.10+   FA: Paul Van Betten, Luis Saca–April 1990. From atop the corner, follow an undercling flake out right. Climb up the face past one bolt to the terrace.

40. **Why Left** 5.11b   FA: Sal Mamusia, Paul Van Betten, Luis Saca–August 1992.
Begin about 30 feet to the right of **Dense Pack** below a line of bolts. Climb up and left past four bolts to the terrace.

41. **Why Right** 5.11b   FA: Paul Van Betten, Sal Mamusia, Luis Saca–August 1992.
Clip the first two bolts on **Why Left**, then climb up and right past two more. Walk off right on the terrace.

42. **Sheep Dip** 5.11- R/X   FA: (TR) Randy Marsh–1981; FA: (lead) Richard Harrison, Robert Finlay–1986.
Start as per **Dense Pack** at a black water streak about 150 feet right of **Ragged Edges**. Climb up the black streak on obvious holds (#4 Friend in the horizontal) to gain a white, left-facing corner. Follow this up to the terrace.

NOTE: More topropes have been done to the right, but aren't included here.

The Graduate Cliff

This crag is 100 yards directly above **Ragged Edges** and has huge, bulging roofs on its right side. It's easiest to approach these routes by walking up past the right side of Ragged Edges Cliff, then up a trail to the left of the top of **Ragged Edges**. All three hard routes have rappel anchors and start partway up the cliff atop a varnished, water-streaked slab. The routes are in the shade in the afternoon and are described from left to right. Photos, pages 102 and 105.

43. **Walk To School** 5.7 FA: Jon Martinet, Randy Grandstaff, Scott Gordon–1975.
    Bring medium-sized gear and some long slings. Climb the straight-in crack 40 feet left of **The Graduate** and ten feet right of large white blocks at the mouth of a corridor. At a ledge about 50 feet up, traverse right to the anchor on **The Graduate**. Rappel with one rope.

44. **The Graduate** 5.10 ◂ FA: Randy Grandstaff, Jon Martinet, Scott Gordon–1975.
    Making the **Dean's List** isn't necessary to do this fine route. Bring a good selection of gear including extra #3 Camalots and a few long slings. This climb forms the left margin of the varnished wall and climbs a large, right-facing corner (V1) to the ceiling. There is a natural thread rappel anchor above the ceiling to the left of the top of the corner.

    V1 GED Escape left before the final, steep corner, then up the easy face to the anchor. This makes the climb 5.9.

45. **Acid Jacks** 5.11 FA: Richard Harrison, Kevin Biernacki, Jerry from Colorado–Summer 1989.
    Start 20 feet right of **The Graduate** on the varnished slab below a line of bolts. Bring a #2 Friend, some wires and a long sling to protect the moves above the fourth bolt. Rappel with one rope from a two-bolt belay above the ceiling. This anchor is 15 feet right of **The Graduate**'s anchor.

46. **Circle Jerks** 5.11d FA: Paul Van Betten, Richard Harrison, Kevin Biernacki –Summer 1989.
    Power past six bolts, starting 25 feet right of **Acid Jacks** and just left of some white corners above the varnished slab. There is a two-bolt belay over the roof.

The Case Face

The next routes are 150 yards right and about 50 feet above the top of the Ragged Edges Cliff. They are to the right (northwest) and slightly below the Graduate Cliff. **Hard Case** is easy to spot from the road – it climbs a left-leaning crack on a cliff that has a brown upper and white lower (The Case Face). Approach by walking up the bushy slope just right of Ragged Edges Cliff.

47. **Territorial Imperative** 5.10 R/X FA: Kurt Reider, Randy Grandstaff–1980.
    This scary but excellent route is located in a recess to the left of The Case Face and climbs a black water streak on small edges. Bring small RPs – with a bit of luck (and talent) you can get some in just before the crux, which is between the first and second bolts. Traverse off left.

48. **Just In Case** 5.5 FA: Donette Smith, Todd Swain, George and Catriona Reid (Scots) –October 1994.
    Rope up at the extreme left edge of The Case Face next to a pine tree. Climb up to a bolt, step left (crux), then follow the arête and face up to a short flake/crack. Belay atop the flake, then traverse left across a slab to a corner, which is downclimbed to your pack.

49. **Space Case** 5.7 FRA: Randy Marsh, Pauline Schroeder–1983.
    Originally done without the bolt. Begin ten feet right of **Just In Case** and climb past a bolt into a crack that leads up and slightly left. Traverse left across a slab into a gully/corner, then easily downclimb the gully and low-angled slab.

50. **Head Case** 5.8 FRA (TR) Todd Swain, Donette Smith–March 1994; FA: (lead) Todd Swain, Donette Smith, George and Catriona Reid (Scots)–October 1994.
Start 25 feet right of **Space Case** and 35 feet left of **Hard Case** atop a long, narrow boulder. Climb the white and brown face past four bolts and a few gear placements to a two-cold-shut anchor. Rap with one rope.

51. **Hard Case** 5.9 FA: Joe Herbst, Matt MacMackin–circa 1975.
Bring large gear to protect the wide sections. Start 35 feet right of the last route, below an obvious varnished, left-leaning crack with a ceiling 20 feet up. Follow the crack past an alcove (crux) until it leads to face climbing. Continue up to and around the right side of the summit roof. Walk off right (or traverse left below the roof and rappel from the **Head Case** anchor).

*The next two routes are located down and right from **Hard Case**, and can be approached from that route or from the end of the paved Willow Spring road. To approach from **Hard Case**, traverse 75 feet down and right on a rock rib, then scramble left (west) around some corners. To approach from the end of the pavement, walk 200 yards west into an obvious drainage that has three large pine trees on its left side. Scramble up to the highest pine tree (about 200 feet above the drainage bottom) and rack up.*

52. **Soylent Green Jeans** 5.9+ ◀ FA: Paul and Pauline S. Van Betten–1985.
Bring many TCUs, including at least two of the very smallest. Additionally, bring a good selection of gear up to a #4 Friend and some long slings. Much better than it may first appear. Start at a clean, right-facing corner left of **Sterling Moss** and just above the huge

Ragged Edges Area

42. Sheep Dip

The Graduate Cliff

43. Walk To School
44. The Graduate
45. Acid Jacks
46. Circle Jerks

47. Terratorial Imperative

The Case Face

49. Space Case
51. Hard Case
53. Sterling Moss

pine tree. Climb the cleaved, right-facing corner passing just left of a small pine tree to a yellow, triangular ceiling. Pull the ceiling (intimidating, but not too hard) into a lower-angled dihedral. Stretch the rope to belay at the top of the dihedral off #2 and #3 Friends in a horizontal above a ceiling (180 feet). Scramble down a gully just to the left (north) of the climb.

53. **Sterling Moss** 5.10 R   FA: Richard Harrison, Randy Grandstaff, Wendell Broussard, Nick Nordblom, Sal Mamusia–Spring 1982.
Named for a famous race car driver. Start 40 feet right of the prominent pine tree and climb the face to a bolt (scary). Move a bit right, then up to an obvious left-facing flake (pro here). Step right and climb an easy dihedral to a ceiling. Follow the left-leaning fissure (crux) up into the low-angled dihedral. Stretch the rope to belay at the top of the dihedral off #2 and #3 Friends in a horizontal above a ceiling (180 feet). Scramble down a gully just to the left (north) of the climb. Photo, page 105.

Sumo Greatness Slab
From the end of the pavement on the Willow Spring road, walk 200 yards up the dirt road. About 200 yards to the left (southwest) is a cliff band with a prominent black water streak in its center and a smooth, slabby face at its right end. These climbs are located about 180 feet right of the water streak, on the slabby face, and are in the shade all day. There is Native American rock art about 30 feet right of the water streak, and like all rock art, it should not be climbed on or disturbed in any way. Dozens of routes have been done to the left of the black streak, including the classic corner of **Peaches** (5.5), and the overhanging face just left, **Buckety Goodness** (5.11-).

54. **Sumo Greatness** 5.9+ R   FA: Richard Harrison, Nick Nordblom, Wendell Broussard, Sal Mamusia, Paul Van Betten–Winter 1982.
Start behind a pine tree, at a right-leaning crack/groove with dark varnish on its left side. This is about 150 feet right of the rock art. Climb up the crack/groove for 40 feet, then angle right to a bolt. Climb up past a white splotch to another bolt and the top. Walk off right (west).

55. **Ice Climb** 5.9+ R   FA: John Long, Lynn Hill, Doug Robinson, Randy Grandstaff–1981.
Slippery. Bring some TCUs and wires. Start 20 feet right of **Sumo Greatness** at a short, overhanging wide crack. Climb the face just left of the crack, then follow the thinner, right-leaning crack to a red band. Clip a bolt, then climb up a short seam through a bulge (fixed pin) to an alcove (#3 Friend). Step left and finish up the face above. Walk off right.

56. **Dean's List** 5.11 PG   FA: Paul Van Betten, Richard Harrison, Wendell "the Dean" Broussard, Druce Finlay (8 years old!)–1990.
Can you make the grade? Bring some small wires to protect the moves to the first bolt, and very thin fingers for the pockets past the last bolt. Start 45 feet right of **Sumo Greatness**, atop boulders. Move out left onto a ledge above some low roofs, then angle back right on the slab to a bolt at the right edge of the dark streak. Face climb past two more bolts to the top. Walk off right.

Outhouse Wall

To access this sunny cliff, park at the end of the pavement on the Willow Spring road. On the north (right) side of the road and above the outhouse building is a south-facing cliff. Go directly uphill for 50 yards to an alcove formed by a huge detached boulder. Many other routes have been done here, but only these few are listed. Routes are described from right to left.

57. **Tricks Are For Kids** 5.10- PG13   FA: Paul Van Betten (rope solo)–1982.
Bring your bag of tricks for this one. Start in the alcove above the outhouse building and climb a flake to a ledge at 20 feet. Continue up the left-leaning corner/crack above (cheater stones may be needed to get off the ledge), moving right when the crack doglegs. Walk off right (south).

58. **Spiderline** 5.7 PG   FA: Unknown–circa 1980.
Start in the alcove as per **Tricks Are For Kids** and climb an easy, wide crack on the left to a platform 40 feet up. Climb the left edge of the varnish above, finishing at a notch in a small ceiling. Walk off right (south).

59. **Roasting Affair** 5.10-   FA: Richard Harrison, Wendell Broussard–1983.
The face just left of **Spiderline**, which has some fixed gear on it.

60. **Sin City** 5.11- X   FA: Paul Van Betten, Sal Mamusia–1983.
This route climbs the left edge of the face, about 75 feet left of the **Spiderline** alcove. Start on a ledge and climb over a bulge, protecting in a right-leaning seam. Bring small wires.

61. **Jam Session** 5.11-   FA: Paul Van Betten, Sal Mamusia–1984.
An overhanging crack around the corner and left of **Sin City**.

The Dark Thumb

This sunny formation sits directly across the canyon from the Lost Creek/Hidden Falls parking area. The two climbs listed here are about 175 yards up and left of the Owl (the prominent, squat, free-standing formation at the mouth of the canyon). As you may have guessed, this formation looks like a dark thumb.

62. **Land Of The Free** 5.11c   FA: Greg Mayer–1986.
The left-hand route, which has six bolts and a shared anchor.

63. **Home Of The Brave** 5.11+   FA: Mike Tupper–1986.
The right-hand route, which has at least five bolts and a shared anchor. Bring a small Friend to supplement the bolts.

Icebox Canyon

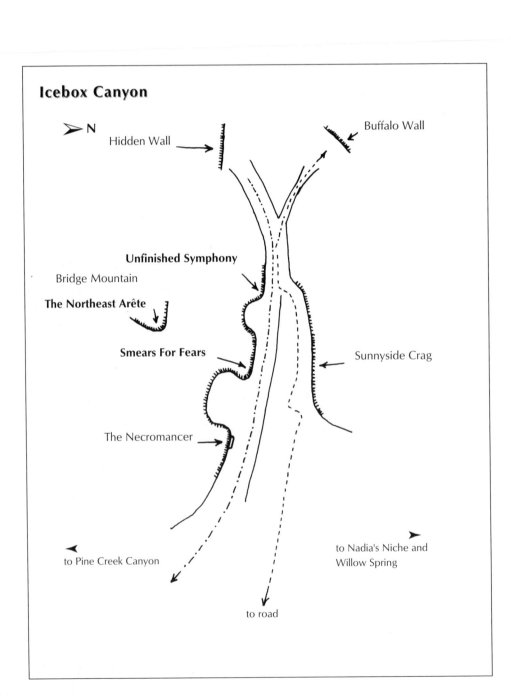

N

Hidden Wall

Buffalo Wall

Unfinished Symphony

Bridge Mountain

The Northeast Arête

Smears For Fears

Sunnyside Crag

The Necromancer

to Pine Creek Canyon

to Nadia's Niche and
Willow Spring

to road

ICEBOX CANYON

The Icebox Canyon routes described here are primarily one-pitch routes, although numerous multi-pitch routes exist. I've also included a few "adventure" climbs for people wishing for true wilderness experiences. Drive 7.8 miles along the scenic loop road until you reach the Icebox Canyon parking area. A well-maintained trail leads from the parking lot into the canyon, with the majority of routes being within 25 minutes of the road. Routes are described from right to left (north to south) throughout the canyon.

Icebox Canyon (view from trailhead)

Bridge Mountain
35. The Northeast Arête
The Necromancer
37. Sensuous Mortician
Smears For Fears Area
34. Lebanese JoJo
33. Smears For Fears

32. Rojo
Refrigerator Wall
28. Amazing Grace
26. Earth Juice
24. Unfinished Symphony
A. Sunnyside Crag

Sunnyside Crag

As you look at the canyon from the parking lot, there are prominent, orange roofs at the bottom of the right (north) wall of the canyon. The climbs described on this crag start about 200 yards to the left, further into the canyon, at a point where the trail comes closest to the cliff. Approach time is about 20 minutes. Routes are described from right to left as you approach on the trail.

1. **Whipper** 5.10   FA: Unknown–circa 1987.
   This routes ascends a prominent roof crack about 100 feet left of a huge boulder with pine trees behind it. Climb the crack out a roof, then up the vertical crack to an anchor. Rappel with one rope.

2. **Backlash** 5.11   FA: Paul Van Betten, Jay Smith–October 1987.
   Begin 45 feet left of **Whipper** at a crack system through a large, bulging roof and just right of a nose. Climb the flake/right-facing corner to a two-bolt anchor.

3. **Whiplash** 5.12- FAP1: Paul Van Betten, Jay Smith–October 1987. FAP2: Paul Crawford, Paul Van Betten–Spring 1988.
   Rope up as per the last route, but trend out left around a corner/nose to a left-leaning crack. Belay above, in an alcove. A second pitch has been done and follows thin cracks on an arête to an anchor under a roof (5.10+). Descend the route in two 75-foot rappels.

Sunnyside Crag

19. Buffalo Wall
17. Tarantula
15. Gotham City

8. Van Allen Belt
5. Cold September Corner
1. Whipper

4. **Meteor** 5.11   FA: Unknown. FFA: Les Hutchinson, Paul Van Betten–1988. FAP2: Jay Smith, Paul Van Betten–1988.

The second pitch was done at a later date and is named **Meteorite**. Start in a cave 40 feet left of **Whiplash**, up on a ledge.

P1 Power out of the cave along an obvious roof crack to a belay stance in a shallow left-facing corner. 60 ft., 5.11.

P2 Climb the vertical seam, then move right into a more pronounced crack/corner system. Climb up toward a roof, then angle about 30 feet up and right to an alcove under the roof. Pull the roof to broken ground and fixed gear (supposedly). 5.10+.

Descent: Rappel with two ropes.

5. **Cold September Corner** 5.8   FA: Joe Herbst, Stephanie Petrilak, Bill Bradley–Fall 1978.

Twenty feet to the left of **Meteor** is an obvious right-facing dihedral. This has been climbed for at least two pitches, but no more is known. If you climb to the top of the crag, it appears you can descend off to the left (as per **Shady Ladies**). Photo, page 110.

6. **Shady Ladies** 5.7   FA: Jineen Griffith, Barbara Euser–May 1978.

Bring long slings and gear up to a #4 Friend. Start 75 feet left of **Cold September Corner** at a varnished dihedral that is just left of a brown face with one bolt on it. Climb the large dihedral for about 90 feet, then traverse straight left along horizontals to the fixed anchor on a ledge (120 feet). Rappel with two ropes. The first ascent party apparently continued upward for three more pitches. If you elect to do this, descend by heading left and rappelling from boulders and trees.

7. **Magellanic Cloud** 5.9+ PG ◀   FA: Unknown–1980s.

Probably the best moderate route on this crag. Carry gear to 4" plus some long slings. Start as per **Shady Ladies** at a varnished dihedral, but after 20 feet of climbing, angle up and left along a crack to the arête. Join **Van Allen Belt** for ten feet, then traverse straight right from a ceiling to a varnished, left-facing corner. Follow this clean corner straight up to the belay ledge. Rappel 120 feet to the ground with two ropes.

8. **Van Allen Belt** 5.7   FA: Unknown–1980s.

I didn't do too good a job guessing the difficulty of this route in the last edition (it was listed as 5.9). Bring up to a #4 Camalot, plus lots of slings. Begin 20 feet left of the last two routes at a smooth, 20-foot-high dihedral. Climb the dihedral and crack to a ceiling 40 feet up. Move left under the ceiling above to the arête, then climb the crack and face up and right to the communal belay ledge (120 feet). Rappel with two ropes.

9. **Unnamed** 5.10   FA: Randy Marsh, Greg Child–1989.

Start 75 feet left of **Van Allen Belt** at a cave with at a very nice-looking varnished nose just to its left. Climb past two bolts and horizontal cracks on the left side of the varnished nose, then up left to a chain anchor.

10. **Tie Me Tightly** 5.10   FA: Nick Nordblom, Jenni Stone–1988.

Start 20 feet left on varnished rock with numerous pockets and huecos. Climb 15 feet up, then move right to a right-facing flake. Climb the flake, then move right and up to the chain anchor on the previous route. Either rap from there or continue up a crack and the face to a two-bolt belay anchor.

11. **Mercedes** 5.11-   FA: Jay Smith–circa 1988.

Begin as per the last route, but climb straight up the steep face past four bolts to a ceiling. Either move right to the chain anchor or continue up to the anchor above.

12. **Water Dog** 5.11+   FA: Paul Van Betten, Jay Smith, Paul Crawford–October 1987.

Rope up ten feet left of **Mercedes** at a thin, slightly left-leaning crack that is ten feet right of a corner. Follow the crack up to a thread at the roof (V1,V2), then up and left through more ceilings to an obvious fixed anchor.

V1 Pit Bull 5.10   Climb the crack just left, joining the regular route at the thread.

V2 Hot Dog 5.10   A toprope up the thin arête/flake just left of **Pit Bull**.

13. **Water Logged** 5.9?   FA: Unknown–circa 1987.
    The obvious dihedral four feet left of **Hot Dog**. Rap from the **Water Dog** anchor with one rope.

14. **Mister Masters** 5.9+ FA: Paul Van Betten, Danny Meyers–1987.
    This route may be used to set up a top-rope for the next three routes. Start just left of the obvious dihedral and climb a varnished face up and left to the arête. Traverse left to a fixed anchor in the horizontal crack.

*The next three routes climb the front of an appealing, varnished buttress that is just left (west) of **Water Logged**. They appear to be the best routes on the crag. Photo, page 110.*

15. **Gotham City** 5.12- PG13 ◄   FA: Paul Van Betten, Robert Finlay–October 1987.
    This route climbs the right side of the face, using a thin seam for protection, to the communal anchor in the horizontal crack. Photo, page 110.

16. **Spring Break** 5.11+ ◄   FA: Paul Van Betten, Sal Mamusia–Spring 1986.
    Ascend the center of the buttress along a thin, vertical seam, then up the face past horizontal cracks, keeping just left of a right-curving fissure.

17. **Tarantula** 5.12- ◄   FA: Paul Van Betten, Sal Mamusia–Spring 1986.
    Get Peter Parker to lead this one! The first ascent party found a tarantula in a horizontal crack about 40 feet up. This route climbs the left arête of the varnished buttress, following very thin seams to the communal belay. Photo, page 110.

*Note: A bolted route has been attempted to the left of **Tarantula**, but as of press time it hadn't been completed. The route has been dubbed **Hideous Taco**, after the talented Japanese climber Hidetaka Suzuki.*

18. **Crossfire** 5.11   FA: Jay Smith, Nick Nordblom–1989.
    Begin at a thin, left-leaning crack that is about 40 feet left of the **Tarantula** arête and 20 feet right of a dirty, broken corner. Follow the left-leaning crack to a ceiling, then up past a bolt to horizontals. Move right into an obvious left-facing corner and follow this to its top. Continue up the short, plated face to the anchor. A two-rope rappel will get you to safety.

Buffalo Wall

This wall is apparently much steeper and more difficult than The Rainbow Wall in Juniper Canyon. Approach by hiking up the canyon beyond the Sunnyside Crags, then take the right (north) fork of the canyon up to the base of the wall. The approach up the north fork will at least require hauling packs up several dry falls. This cliff supposedly looks like a buffalo (hence the name) and is characterized by a huge dark section of rock in its middle.

19. **Buffalo Wall** 5.11 A3   FA: Paul Van Betten, Richard Harrison, Sal Mamusia–April 1991.
    The first ascent party took three days of climbing and used portaledges. The route climbs the center of the wall, finishing on the "hump" of the buffalo. The free-climbing crux was a flaring offwidth arch on pitch three; the aid crux was on pitch six. There are eight pitches total. To descend, hike north to the dirt road running from Willow Spring toward Pahrump. Photo, page 110; topo, page 113.

20. **Tatanka** 5.10 A3   FA: Richard Harrison, Paul Van Betten, Sal Mamusia–April 1993.
    This route took two days and is supposed to be of excellent quality. There are eight pitches, most of which require aid. See topo, page 114.

Buffalo Wall
5.11 A3

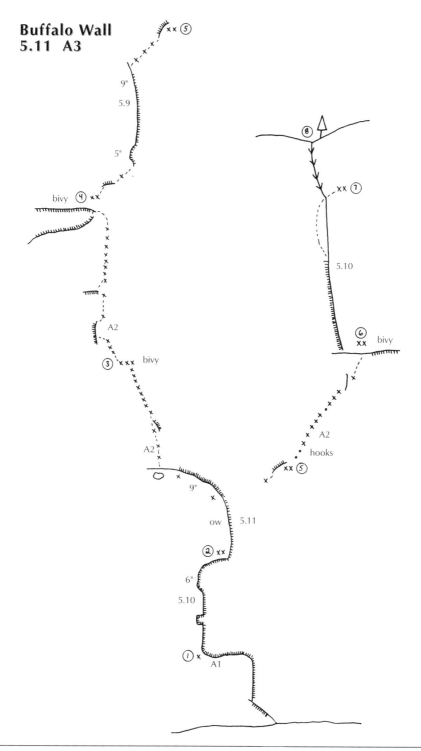

9"

5.9

5"

bivy ④

A2

③ bivy

A2

9"

ow   5.11

② xx

6"

5.10

① x

A1

⑤

⑧

xx ⑦

5.10

⑥ bivy
xx

A2

hooks

xx ⑤

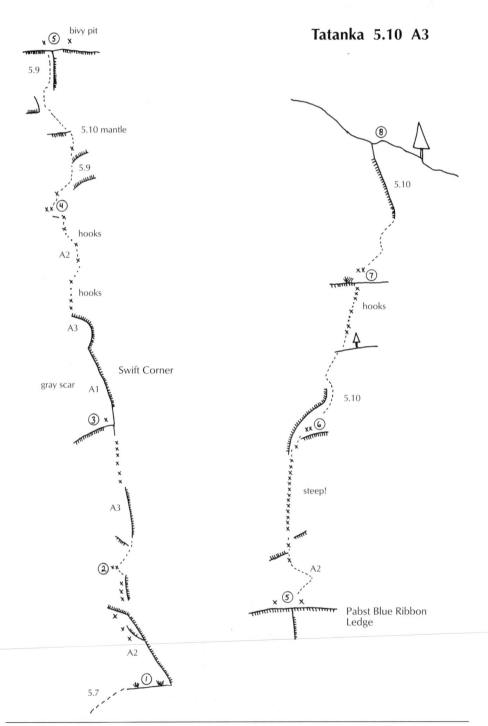

Tatanka 5.10 A3

bivy pit
⑤
5.9

5.10 mantle
5.9
④
hooks
A2
hooks
A3
Swift Corner
gray scar   A1
③
A3
②
A2
①
5.7

⑧
5.10

⑦
hooks

5.10
⑥
steep!
A2
⑤
Pabst Blue Ribbon
Ledge

Hidden Wall

Like Buffalo Wall, this cliff is not easy to approach and may only have been climbed once. Apparently, it sits quite a distance up the south fork of Icebox Canyon, and is only visible from the loop road in the vicinity of White Springs or the Sandstone Quarry.

21. **Blitzkrieg** 5.10+ R   FA: Richard Harrison, Sal Mamusia–1982.
    Follow prominent water streaks up the middle of the wall for seven pitches. There are no bolts on the route. To descend, hike north, then go down all of Icebox Canyon.

Icebox Canyon, South Wall

22. **Weenie Juice** 5.10 ◄   FA: Richard Harrison, Paul Van Betten, Wendell Broussard, Sal Mamusia, Lynn Cronin–1983.
    An excellent one-pitch route. Bring several #4 Camalots (or bigger units if you have them) and two ropes to rappel from the bolt anchor.

    Follow the Icebox Canyon Trail until it enters the wash. Walk up canyon for about 300 yards until below an obvious right-facing arch on the left (south) wall of the canyon. Bushwhack 50 yards up the steep hillside to a platform below the route. Scramble about 50 feet up easy rock to a bushy ledge and belay. Follow the crack/arch/flake to a one-bolt (it's ⅜" at least!) belay. Rappel with two ropes.

Refrigerator Wall

The routes on this cliff are in the shade most of the day (hence the name) and have about a 25-minute approach. To reach this section of the canyon, follow the trail from the parking lot past the Sunnyside Crag. The trail will drop down into the wash, at which point you will cross the wash and head about 100 yards up the bushy hillside on the left (southwest) side of the canyon. The routes are described from right to left, with the first four routes on the right side of a nose, about 100 yards right of three obvious pine trees. The climbs begin roughly across canyon from **Crossfire**. Photo, page 116.

23. **Music To My Fears** 5.10   FA P1, P2: Robert Finlay, Brad Ball–1984.
    Only two pitches of this route are described, although at least five have been done. Nick Nordblom, Paul Van Betten, Jay Smith and Paul Crawford have all turned back on the upper pitches due to loose rock and poor protection.

    Within the highest vegetated area to the right of the obvious pine trees, scramble up to a prominent white block to the right of the obvious drainage/gully (the start of **Unfinished Symphony**).

    P1 From the top of the block, climb a thin crack up to large, loose, white blocks and belay. 80 ft., 5.9.

    P2 Follow the obvious cracks left, then up, then left again, to the top of the crack systems. Belay on a ledge to the left, toward the **Unfinished Symphony** chimney. 150 ft., 5.10.

    Descent: Either traverse left into **Unfinished Symphony** and rappel (two ropes may be needed) or continue up the loose, scary arête directly above the first two pitches (no fixed anchors).

24. **Unfinished Symphony** 5.11   FA: Ross Hardwick, Joe Herbst, Andre Langenbacher–Fall 1978.
    You'll be singing the blues if you don't like wide cracks! Bring lots of large gear and two ropes. Start on the right side of a nose, about 100 yards right of three obvious pine trees, at the highest point of the vegetated hillside. This is directly below a gully leading to a prominent chimney system.

Refrigerator Wall

30. Greased Lightning
30a. Swing Shift
28. Amazing Grace
26. Earth Juice

25. Breakaway
24a. Unnamed crack (5.10 X)
24. Unfinished Symphony
23. Music to My Fears

P1 Climb the drainage/gully past numerous ledges to a belay below the obvious chimney/corner. 150 ft., 5.9.

P2 Move right into the corner, then follow this past a bulge to a large sloping ledge. 5.8

P3 Worm up a chimney to an alcove (5.8), then continue up the nasty offwidth above to a belay stance.

P4 Follow the corner/crack to a belay under a huge roof.

P5 Three bolts lead up the central, overhanging crack. 5.11.

Descent: Rappel the route with two ropes.

NOTE: The prominent crack system just left of **Unfinished Symphony** *has been climbed for six pitches and has red bolt hangers on it. The Uriostes climbed the first five pitches (5.10-); Bob Conz and Nick Nordblom added another pitch (5.10 X) before traversing into* **Unfinished Symphony** *and rappelling.*

25. **Breakaway** 5.10+ PG13 ◀ FA: Danny Meyers, Mike Ward–Summer 1991.
Once you've done the route, you'll know where the name came from! Don't do this route if the rock is at all wet – you may destroy a classic line. This outstanding route climbs the very prominent black water streak to the left of **Unfinished Symphony.** Bring lots of quickdraws and two ropes for the rappel.

Start on the right side of a white pillar at a small, sandy cave about 100 feet down and left of **Unfinished Symphony**.

P1 Climb easy cracks on the right side of the pillar past a few ledges. Follow four bolts up and right on good varnished rock (a bit contrived) to a belay at two vertical cracks at the base of the steep wall with the water streak. Bring medium-sized Friends for the belay, which is about ten feet left of two bolts on the left side of a prominent chimney; crux is by the second bolt. 150 ft., 5.8.

P2 Climb up and left (scary) to the first bolt on the pitch (you can also come in from the left), then face climb up the steep wall past a total of 11 bolts to a three-bolt belay station. 140 ft., 5.10+.

Descent: Rappel the route with two ropes.

The next three routes are on the right side of a small amphitheater and directly behind two prominent pine trees. The routes climb the smooth, varnished wall that is left of a nose and a huge, left-facing flake/corner.

26. **Earth Juice** 5.10+ PG13 FA: Kurt Reider, Chris Robbins, Augie Klein–circa 1979.
A route to get your juices flowing. Start right of the large pine trees below a huge, left-facing corner. Photos, pages 109 and 116.

P1 Scramble up blocks toward the gaping, left-facing flake/chimney, then follow bolts up a varnished face to a crack. Follow the crack to a bolt, then move left to a belay station. 150 ft., 5.10+ PG13.

P2 Go up a steep corner to a bolt, downclimb, then head up and left on a blunt prow to a belay stance below a white ceiling. 140 ft., 5.10+ PG13.

Descent: Rappel with two ropes.

27. **Project** 5.11d FA: (TR) Greg Mayer–October 1994.
The route was attempted long ago and now leads to the second **Earth Juice** belay. Historically, it had a couple of old, bad bolts, but as of press time was being rebolted and finished by Mayer. It climbs the face between **Earth Juice** and **Amazing Grace**.

28. **Amazing Grace** 5.9 PG ◀ FA: Danny Meyers (rope solo)–1985.
Another great pitch that involves sustained climbing. Carry gear to a #3.5 Friend and a few long slings. Begin behind the leftmost pine, 30 feet left of **Earth Juice**. Scramble up to a ledge with a bolt, then climb past two more bad bolts. Move right at the third bolt to the base of the obvious left-facing flake corner. Follow the corner up and left to a three-bolt belay anchor. Rappel with two ropes.Photos, pages 109 and 116.

29. **Grape Nuts** 5.10c PG13   FA: Rick Dennison, Randy Faulk, Alex Malfatto–August 1991.
This route looks scarier than it actually is – although it is runout. Rope up on a ledge 15 feet left of the first bolt on **Amazing Grace**. Follow six bolts to the **Amazing Grace** anchor. Rappel 100 feet to the ground.

30. **Greased Lightning** 5.10 PG13 FA: Nick Nordblom, Randy Marsh–1989.
Across the amphitheater from **Amazing Grace** (toward the road) is a prow with a lightning bolt crack that leads to a ledge. This route is supposedly just left of **Swing Shift**, the prominent crack system leading to clean, light-colored corners near the top of the wall (5.10, 7 pitches). Rappel from a bolted belay anchor on a ledge to the right of the crack with two ropes. Photo, page 116.

SMEARS FOR FEARS AREA

The next three routes are just above wash level and directly across from the right end of Sunnyside Crag. Approach by following the trail in from the parking area for about 15 minutes, then turn left and follow a small drainage down into the main wash. The routes are at the right (west) edge of a large amphitheater that is clearly visible from the road, are all one pitch and are described from right to left. Scramble up through a short, bushy section to reach the ledge on which the routes start.

31. **Romeo Charlie** 5.10+ FA: Sal Mamusia, Robert Finlay–1989.
The furthest right route; it starts on a ledge about 100 feet right of **Rojo** at a right-leaning crack that is just right of a mossy section of cliff. Climb the right-leaning crack, then up the face along a rounded arête that divides brown and black rock. Pull over a bulge and angle slightly up right to a fixed anchor on a mossy slab. Rappel with two ropes.

Icebox Canyon – South Wall

The Necromancer	36. Fold Out	33. Smears For Fears
39. Hop Route	**Smears For Fears Area**	32. Rojo
37. Sensuous Mortician	34. Lebanese JoJo	31. Romeo Charlie

32. **Rojo** 5.11+ PG13   FA: Paul Van Betten, Sal, Mamusia, Mike Ward–1989.
Rope up on a wide, flat ledge below a smooth, varnished face. A prominent, right-facing corner marks the left edge of this face. Climb a right-leaning crack/corner to its top, then face climb to a shallow, right-facing corner. Climb the corner (bolt) and the smooth face above (two bolts) to a bolted anchor. Rap with two cords. Photos, pages 109 and 118.

33. **Smears For Fears** 5.11 PG13 ◄   FA: Sal Mamusia, Mike Ward, Robert Finlay, Paul Van Betten–1989.
A classic one-pitch route, but not for the meek! Start ten feet left of **Rojo** and 15 feet right of a prominent right-facing corner. The left side of the corner forms a jutting prow. Climb a shallow, right-leaning dihedral to a bolt 20 feet up, then go up the face past two more bolts to an overlap. Pull over this and continue past two more bolts to the top (scary!). Rappel from the anchor with dual ropes. Photos, pages 109 and 118.

34. **Lebanese JoJo** 5.9+   FA: Sal Mamusia, Bob Conz, "Frodo" Lybarger, Mike Ward, Paul Van Betten–1990.
Good rock on this one, but the line is rather weird. Start about 75 feet left of **Smears...** at a loose, right-facing corner below the left edge of a roof. Climb up to a pine tree, then traverse out right above the roof to a belay at a thin crack system. Climb the most obvious line up the varnished face above (V1), then rappel with two ropes.

V1 The other three vertical crack systems on the face have been climbed. All are of the same general difficulty.

Bridge Mountain

This is the mountain that separates Icebox and Pine Creek canyons. Numerous routes have been done, but information was available for only one route that should be approached from this canyon. To approach this route, you'll need to somehow climb the Frigidaire Buttress, then wander up through "The Maze" to the base of the arête. Obviously, this is a big undertaking. Photo, page 109.

35. **The Northeast Arête** 5.8   FA: Sal Mamusia, Richard Harrison–1982.
Three pitches up the obvious white arête lead to the top of the mountain. Hike off north to the dirt road leading out from Willow Spring. Photo, page 109.

The Necromancer

This dark, squat formation is on the left (south) side of the canyon and is clearly visible from the parking area. The formation is on the left side of a large amphitheater, with the routes leading to a huge terrace at the top of the formation. From the road, follow the main trail until you are even with the obvious orange roofs to the right (north) of the trail (just before you reach Sunnyside Crag). Turn left (south) and go down a drainage into the main wash. Follow a vague trail about 150 yards up the opposite hillside to the prominent dark brown buttress. Again, this buttress forms the left side of an amphitheater that is clearly visible from the road. Routes are described from right to left, beginning at an obvious crack system near the right margin of the buttress. Photo, page 109.

36. **Fold-Out** 5.8 ◄   FA: Tom Kaufman, Joe Herbst–March 1976.
This climbs the rightmost crack system on the buttress. Excellent rock; good protection will get you to a ledge about 140 feet up. Either traverse left to the **Sensuous Mortician** anchor and rappel with two ropes (you'll need large Friends to set up a belay at the 140 foot high ledge prior to traversing), continue upwards for another pitch or two, or rappel from fixed slings 150 feet up **Fold-Out** on another ledge. If you do go to the top of the buttress, walk off left (toward the road). Photo, page 118.

Breakaway (5.10+): Mike Ward about to place a bolt on the first ascent.

37. **Sensuous Mortician** 5.9 ◀ FA: Nick Nordblom, Jon Martinet–Spring 1979.
One of the best moderate, traditional routes at Red Rocks. Begin 20 feet right of the **Hop Route** handcrack at the next crack line. Climb the obvious crack to its top, then move right to a black streak. Wander up the black face to a ceiling, move left, then climb up to a two-bolt belay. Bring lots of small gear and two ropes for the rappel. Photos, pages 109 and 118.

38. **Black Magic Panties** 5.10- R FA: Nick Nordblom, Jenni Stone, Danny Reider–1988.
Carry gear up to 3" plus a bunch of long slings. Great climbing, but rather scary. This route starts about ten feet right of the handcrack on the **Hop Route**. Wander up the face to a fixed piton about 30 feet up. Continue weaving up the wall, following the obvious weaknesses to a bolt about 100 feet up. Move up and left past another bolt to an obvious crack splitting the roof. Pull this via the crack and belay just above at horizontal cracks (#1.5 to #3 Friends for the anchor). Either traverse down and right to the **Sensuous Mortician** anchor or go left and join the **Hop Route**.

39. **Hop Route** 5.7+ FA: Dave Hop, Joe and Betsy Herbst–March 1975.
The first pitch is very good, the rest a bit less interesting. Photo, page 118.

P1 Climb an obvious handcrack that is 15 feet right of a white, right-facing corner (V1). Follow the crack as it veers left into the corner, then up that past a couple chockstones to a belay ledge on the left. 100 ft., 5.7

P2 and 3 Continue up the easy cracks to the top of the buttress.

V1 You can climb the corner directly – it's a bit harder than the handcrack. 5.7+.

Descent: Walk off left (toward the road).

40. **Crawford's Corner** 5.10 FA: Jay Smith, Paul Crawford–1987.
This three-pitch route climbs a prominent, yellow, left-facing corner system that is located above The Necromancer formation.

*NOTE: At least three other routes are known to have been done to the right of **Crawford's Corner**, but information was lacking at press time.*

Pine Creek Canyon

NOT TO SCALE

➤ N

2. Gemstone
5. Nature Is Fun
19. Terminal Velocity
30. Mushroom People
39. Ripcord
41. Out Of Control
44. Dark Shadows

54. Bloodline
61. Cat In The Hat
64. Crabby Appleton
69. Edge Of The Sun
72. Small Purchase
76. Cartwright Corner
80. Dog Police

South Fork

North Fork

44
61
54
64
69
41
72
39
76
30
19
80
5
2

old
homestead

to road

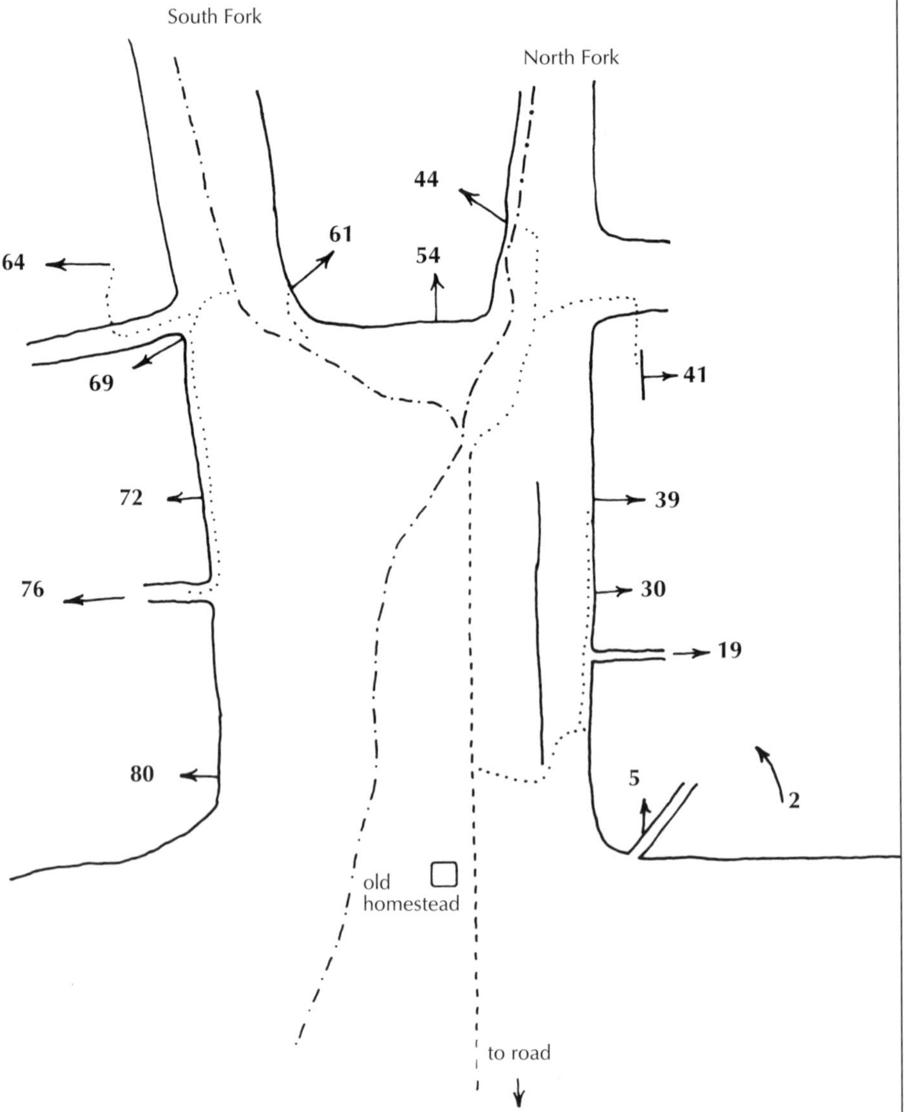

PINE CREEK CANYON

Many fine routes are located in this beautiful canyon. To reach the trailhead, drive 10.3 miles along the scenic loop road. The parking lot is signed and will be just off the road on your right. There are outhouses at the parking lot and the trail is well maintained until the Pine Creek drainage splits.

From the parking lot, follow the obvious trail past the Fire Ecology Trail and an old homestead into the canyon proper (about a 15-minute walk). Ahead, the canyon is split into north and south drainages by a pyramid-shaped formation called The Mescalito. The first routes described in this chapter are on the right (north) side of the canyon well before it is split by The Mescalito. This is actually part of Bridge Mountain, which separates Icebox Canyon from Pine Creek. Routes are then described from right to left, moving across The Mescalito onto the south wall of the canyon.

Bridge Mountain, East Face

Numerous routes have been done on Bridge Mountain, but only handful are described in this edition. I haven't done any of these routes (or even been to the base), so don't blame me if the information isn't correct!

1. **Fear And Loathing** 5.10   FA: Richard Harrison, Nick Nordblom–1982.
    As the story goes, the two prominent corners high up on the east face of Bridge Mountain "had been climbed years ago." One corner was named Fear, the other, Loathing. In 1982, Harrison and Nordblom finally braved the 90-minute approach, only to find that the left corner (which was stuffed full of loose, refrigerator-sized blocks)

Pine Creek Canyon and surrounding areas

Juniper Canyon
5.   Black Dagger (See page 149.)
2.   The Nightcrawler (See page 149.)

Pine Creek Canyon
44.   Dark Shadows
30.   Mushroom People

didn't even reach the ground! They climbed the right-hand, right-facing corner system, which became the original **Fear And Loathing** of Red Rocks.

Bring lots of large Friends for this three-pitch route. There are no fixed anchors or protection on the route.

P1 Climb the face up to the base of the prominent, right-facing corner. 5.10 R.

P2 Climb the corner. 5.9.

P3 Climb the corner and belay atop a block. 75 ft., 5.10-.

Descent: Downclimb somewhere nearby and do one rappel.

*NOTE: Numerous routes have been done on the large cliff to the right of **Fear And Loathing** but no more is known.*

2. **Gemstone** 5.10-   FA: Nick Nordblom, Jenni Stone–1985.
    Down and left of **Fear And Loathing** is another black face with a prominent crack. Bring big Friends for this one.

    P1 Climb the prominent crack, which is wide hands. 5.9.

    P2 Climb the face above. 75 ft., 5.10-.

    Descent: Do two rappels to the right of the route.

*The next four routes are in the gully down and left of **Gemstone**. This gully is easily seen from further south along the ridge, but is not visible from the scenic loop road until you reach Pine Creek. The routes are described going up the gully.*

3. **Stick Right** 5.9   FA: Richard Harrison, Paul Van Betten, Sal Mamusia, Nick Nordblom–1982.
    On the right wall of the gully are two parallel cracks with a roof at their bottom. This 50-foot route climbs the right-hand crack.

4. **Stick Left** 5.10-   FA: Richard Harrison, Paul Van Betten, Sal Mamusia, Nick Nordblom– 1982.
    On the right wall of the gully are two parallel cracks with a roof at their bottom. This 50-foot route climbs the left-hand crack. Apparently, the crux is getting past the roof.

Bridge Mountain, East Face

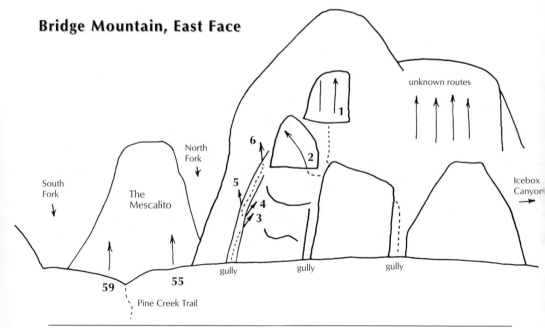

5. **Nature Is Fun** 5.9+   FA: Sal Mamusia, Richard Harrison, Nick Nordblom–1983.
   On the left wall of the gully directly across from the **Stick** routes is a side drainage. This route climbs a long, flared off-width.

6. **The Elephant Penis** 5.10- R   FA: Richard Harrison, Paul Van Betten, Sal Mamusia, Nick Nordblom–1983.
   Further up the gully is a tower attached to the left wall (guess what it looks like). This four-pitch route starts as face climbing and ends on the left side of the tower. There is no pitch easier than 5.8 and you'll have to do multiple rappels to get down.

Straight Shooter Wall

As you enter the Pine Creek drainage, a short, red cliff band will appear on the right. The Beer and Ice Gully is the obvious, huge cleft in the right wall of the canyon and Straight Shooter Wall encompasses the climbs on the right side of this gully. To approach Straight Shooter Wall and Beer and Ice Gully, head off the trail by the homestead, and skirt the right (east) end of the red cliff band. You can also hike directly up to Beer and Ice Gully itself, but this entails a bit of dicey soloing through the center of the red band. A well-beaten path runs along the base of the canyon

Pine Creek Canyon north side (from old homesite)

9. Straight Shooter
11. Forget Me Knot
19. Terminal Velocity
25. Varnishing Point

27. No Laughing Matter
30. Mushroom People
31. Topless Twins

wall in this area, which gets sun all day. The routes are described from right to left. The routes described here are located about 400 feet right of Beer and Ice Gully on a smooth, black face. Allow about 20 minutes for the approach.

7. **The Lazy Fireman** 5.11a FA: Cameron Robbins, Randy Marsh–Spring 1991
   At the right end of a smooth, black face is a boulder/prow that protrudes from the cliff. On the left (west) face is a short, overhanging dihedral with two bolts. Continue up the face above (contrived) past two more bolts to a chain anchor. You may want to bring a #3-Friend-sized piece to place between the second and third bolts.

8. **Sidewinder** 5.11a FA: (TR) Unknown–1980s. FA: (lead) Rick Dennison, Daryl Ellis–April 1991.
   Better than it first appears – it's quite technical. Start 20 feet left of the previous route and just right of a striking fingercrack up the smooth, black wall. Climb the slippery face past six bolts, following small flakes and seams to a shared rappel anchor.

9. **Straight Shooter** 5.9+ ◀ FA: Joe Herbst–circa 1975.
   Climb the perfect, smooth fingercrack splitting the black face to a communal anchor 50 feet up. Bring wires, TCUs and Friends up to #3. Photo, page 125.

10. **Slabba Dabba Do** 5.11b PG13 FA: (TR) Unknown. FA: (lead) Mike Tupper–Winter 1985.
    It's dicey getting to the first bolt; scary and cruxy above the third. Begin about ten feet left of **Straight Shooter** and smear up the glassy face past three bolts with homemade hangers to the ledge 50 feet up. You can set up a directional at the top of the pitch using the ¼" bolt and a #0 TCU.

11. **Forget Me Knot** 5.11 FA: (TR) Unknown. FA: (Lead) Mike Tupper–Winter 1985.
    Shades of Lynn Hill and others who have forgotten to tie in to the climbing rope properly! Start 20 feet left of **Straight Shooter** at a thin, vertical seam. Climb the seam to a bolt, then up a left-facing flake directly above a ⅜" bolt to a ledge (5.10+, possible belay directional here using the ¼" bolt and a #0 TCU). Continue up the right-leaning crack (Bird Crack) on the upper wall to a rap anchor (5.11-). The Bird Crack was first climbed by Paul Van Betten and originally done as a second pitch to **Straight Shooter**. Photo, page 125.

Beer and Ice Gully

Beer and Ice Gully is an obvious, huge cleft in the right wall of the canyon. As you enter the Pine Creek drainage, a short, red cliff band will appear on the right. To approach Beer and Ice Gully, head off the trail by the homestead and skirt the right (east) end of the red cliff band. You can also hike directly up to Beer and Ice Gully itself, but this entails a bit of dicey soloing through the center of the red band. Approach time is about 20 minutes.

12. **Too Pumped To Pose** 5.12 (TR) FA: Paul Van Betten–1987.
    As you enter the Beer and Ice Gully proper, there are a few obvious features on the right wall. This, the rightmost route goes up a line of huecos and is toproped off the **29 Posers** tree.

13. **Posby** 5.12 (TR) FA: Paul Van Betten–1987.
    This toprope route climbs huecos and holes just right of **29 Posers**, and left of the last route.

14. **29 Posers** 5.11+ FA: Paul Van Betten, Bob Yoho–1987.
    This route climbs a flake (Friends) to an overhanging, huecoed face. Power up the face past two bolts and a blind #1.5 Friend placement to a tree. Rappel off the tree back to the ground (or toprope the previous two routes).

15. **Moisture Brau** 5.10+ FA: Paul Van Betten, Bob Conz–1988.
    Start at a left-slanting handcrack. Meet **This Bud's For You**, then go straight up a hand-and fistcrack to its top. Traverse left under roofs and finish up the top corner of **This Bud's For You**.

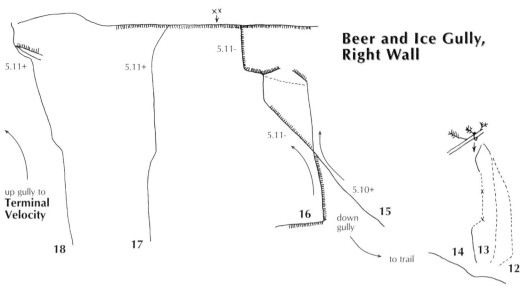

**Beer and Ice Gully,
Right Wall**

16. **This Bud's For You** 5.11- 🦶 FA: Paul Van Betten, Bob Conz–1988.
An excellent route. Start 100 yards uphill from the previous route at a left-facing, left-leaning book with a hand- and fingercrack in its back. Climb the corner to a two-bolt belay station on a ledge (130 feet).

17. **Corona Crack** 5.11+ FA: Paul Van Betten, Sal Mamusia, Bob Conz–Winter 1988.
Begin 50 feet left of **This Bud's For You** at a curving, flaring fingercrack. Bring an assortment of gear for this one. This shares the belay with **This Bud's For You**.

18. **Stout Roof** 5.10+ FA: Mike Ward, Paul Van Betten, Bob Yoho–Winter 1987.
An acquired taste. Climb a crack through an obvious roof to a ledge.

19. **Terminal Velocity** 5.13- 🦶 FA: Mike Tupper, Greg Mayer–March 1989 (after a year of working on it!).
A big undertaking, but a must for the true crack master. Allow about 45 minutes for the approach. Bring gear up to a #3 Friend, including a full set of TCUs and Sliders or Lowe Balls. Scramble up Beer and Ice Gully to its end. Photo, page 125; topo, page 128.

    P1 Scramble up a chimney/gully for 20 feet, then exit onto the left wall. Climb the face and crack above to a one-bolt belay. 160 feet, 5.9.

    P2 Exit right from the belay onto a vertical wall, and crank up the Yosemite **Wheat Thin**-like flake (bolts) to its top. Jog left and climb up a shallow dihedral to a two-bolt belay. 60 ft., 5.11+.

    P3 Traverse 15 feet straight right over the lip of a small roof (exposed). Enter a right-facing dihedral and follow this to another two-bolt belay. 70 ft., 5.11.

    P4 Climb a small dihedral for 30 feet (5.12-), then exit left to the base of a striking, thin fingercrack. Punch up the crack to a two-bolt belay. 60 ft., 5.13-.

    P5 Stem up a slightly overhanging corner past two bolts to a fingercrack in the corner. Continue upward for another 50 feet to the top of the crack. Exit left across a slab to a two-bolt belay. 65 ft., 5.11+.

    Descent: Rappel with two ropes as follows: P5 to P4, P4 to P3, P3 straight down 150 feet to a ledge with bolts, 150 feet to ground.

20. **Chilly Ones** 5.10+ R/X FA: Paul Van Betten, Sal Mamusia–1988.
Start directly across the gully from **This Bud's For You**, on the left wall of the gully. Climb past three bolts to a hand- and fistcrack that leads to a ledge. Rappel with two ropes. Topo, page 128.

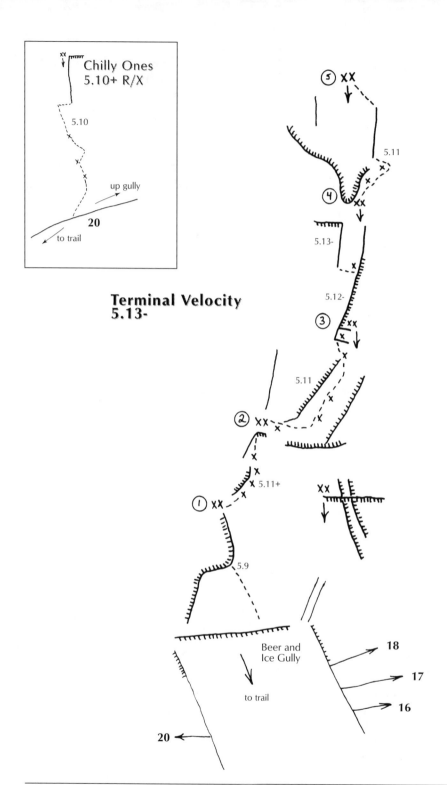

Chilly Ones
5.10+ R/X

5.10

up gully

20

to trail

Terminal Velocity
5.13-

5.11

5.13-

5.12-

5.11

5.11+

5.9

Beer and
Ice Gully

to trail

18

17

16

20

Brass Wall

This is the section of cliff to the left (west) of Beer and Ice Gully, which is the obvious, huge cleft in the right wall of the canyon. As you enter the Pine Creek drainage, a short, red cliff band will appear on the right. To approach Beer and Ice Gully, head off the trail by the homestead, and skirt the right (east) end of the red cliff band. You can also hike directly up to Beer and Ice Gully itself, but this entails a bit of dicey soloing through the center of the red band. Allow about 20 minutes for the approach. Routes are described from right to left.

21. **The Bus Stops Here** 5.8? FA: Unknown–circa 1980.
     This route climbs the right (east) side of a huge, black, pyramidal shaped flake that sits at the left edge of Beer and Ice Gully. Start in the bushy gully and climb the right-facing corner/chimney to a ledge just below the top of the flake. Rappel 140 feet from a natural thread anchor.

22. **Simpatico** 5.10- FA: Jay Smith, Jo Bently, Jenni Stone–circa 1980.
     Begin in the bushy gully ten feet left and around the corner from the last route. Climb up to a ledge that is 15 feet up, then follow a nice, right-facing flake/corner up and right to the arête. Follow the arête and face to a ledge near the top of the huge flake. Rappel with two ropes.

23. **One Stop In Tonopah** 5.10? FA: Paul Crawford–circa 1980.
     Begin 40 feet left at the right edge of bushes and below a 25-foot-high white flake. Climb the right edge of the flake to a bolt. Climb past two ledges then go up and right on dark varnish to finish in a short crack/corner that leads to the arête. Follow the previous routes to the top of the huge flake then rappel with two ropes.

24. **Go Greyhound** 5.11- R/X FA: Paul Crawford–circa 1980.
     Start as per the last route, but climb the left side of the white flake. Step left across a pink scar then climb a thin, right-facing flake to a stance. Climb another, more prominent right-facing flake until it ends. Climb up the face past two bolts. Escape right to the arête by a bush, or persevere straight up to a ledge and the anchor. Rappel with two ropes.

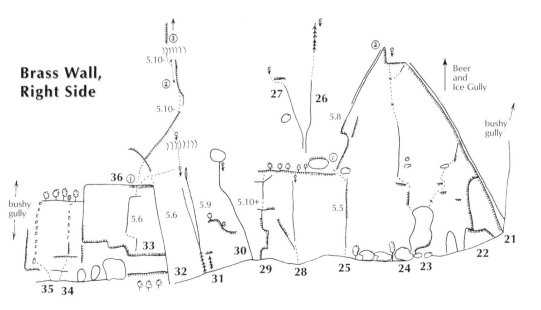

Brass Wall, Right Side

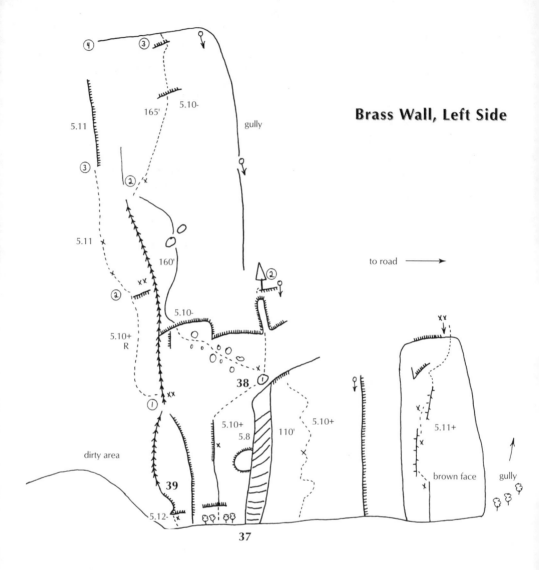

Brass Wall, Left Side

25. **Varnishing Point** 5.8+ ◀ FA: Joe Herbst–circa 1979.
    Start 30 feet left of the last route and ten feet left of an oak tree, below an obvious crack that leads to the right side of a bushy ledge that is 70 feet up. Bring gear to a #4 Camalot and two ropes. Photo, page 125.

    P1 Climb the crack and huecos, stepping left to reach the bushy ledge. Belay in a cave. 70 ft, 5.5.

    P2 Climb the obvious, leftmost, left-facing corner past a ceiling (crux) to the top of the huge varnished flake. 70 ft, 5.8+.

    Descent: Rappel with two ropes.

26. **Serious Business** 5.10+? FA: Unknown–circa 1982.
    Start on the bushy ledge at the top of the first pitch of **Varnishing Point**. Work your way up a thin, vertical seam to reach an obvious dihedral. Follow this up to an anchor.

27. **No Laughing Matter** 5.10-   FA: Greg Child, Randy Grandstaff–1979.
Start 70 feet above the ground on the bushy ledge mentioned in the last route description, and climb the most obvious, slightly left-leaning crack system to a rappel anchor. Photo, page 125.

28. **Fungus Folks** 5.11+   FA: Unknown–circa 1982.
Start 50 feet left of **Varnishing Point** under the center of the bushy ledge that is 70 feet up. Climb the thin, vertical seam up the varnished face to the bushy ledge.

29. **Bush Pilots** 5.8+   FA: Randy Marsh, Paul Van Betten–circa 1984.
Begin 20 feet left of the previous climb at a right-facing corner. Climb the corner to a prominent ceiling, then follow the crack above to the left end of the bushy ledge.

30. **Mushroom People** 5.10+   FA: Dave Diegelman, Randy Grandstaff, Greg Child–1979.
Start about 15 feet left of the last route, directly below the left edge of a bushy ledge about 70 feet up. Climb an obvious, left angling seam up slippery, black rock to a rap anchor just below a huge hueco. Two ropes are needed for the rappel. Photos, pages 123 and 125.

31. **Topless Twins** 5.9 ◀   FA: Randy Grandstaff, Wendell "the Dean" Broussard–1980.
Rope up 50 feet left of **Mushroom People** below a series of short dihedrals leading to thin, parallel, black cracks. Climb a dihedral and the right-hand crack to a rappel station 70 feet up, then zip back to the ground with one rope. You'll need a good selection of wires and TCUs for this route. Photo, page 125.

32. **Heavy Spider Karma** 5.6   FA: Unknown–circa 1980.
Worthwhile. Start ten feet to the left of the last route at the base of a prominent handcrack leading to a ledge. Traverse right from the ledge to the **Topless Twins** anchor or continue up **Raptor**.

33. **Snivler** 5.6 R   FA: Unknown–circa 1980.
A good route. Rope up 20 feet left of **Heavy Spider Karma** at a boulder below a ceiling. Step right off the boulder then go straight up a crack to a ledge. Step left and climb a series of pockets up the varnished face to a ledge. Step right and climb a short face to the big ledge. Traverse right to the **Topless Twins** anchor or continue up **Raptor**.

34. **Zen And The Art Of Web Spinning** 5.4   FA: Unknown–circa 1980.
Start 30 feet left of the last route on the left side of large boulders below a low-angled, "swiss cheese" face and eight feet left of an obvious, left-facing corner. Climb a left-facing corner and "swiss cheese" rock to a tree covered ledge.

35. **Arachnoworld** 5.4   FA: Unknown–circa 1980.
Climb the easy, huecoed face 20 feet left of **Zen...** (and near the arête) to the tree ledge.

36. **Raptor** 5.10- R   FA: Nick Nordblom, Randy Marsh–1990.
This four-pitch route starts atop the block climbed by the last four routes, making it actually a five-pitch route. It is just right of a large gully. Bring a good selection of gear, including two 1" TCUs.

P1 Climb one of the four previous routes to the top of the block. 5.4 or 5.6.

P2 Face climb up to a ramp, which is followed up and right to a left-facing corner. Climb past one bolt to a belay stance. 5.10-.

P3 Climb up past a bolt and a bulge to a belay in a right-facing corner. 5.10-.

P4 Climb the corner, then continue up the face to another right-facing corner and a belay. 5.9 .

P5 Climb the corner above the belay, then go up left past a bolt to the top. 5.10-.

Descent: Go west and descend the gully as per the **Sea Of Holes**, doing three rappels.

NOTE: At least three routes have been done between the gully and **The Black Hole**, but information was lacking at press time.

37. **The Black Hole** 5.8   FA: Jay Smith–1980.
    Start at a chimney a bit to the left of a vegetated gully. Climb up the chimney a bit, then up a shallow corner to a two-bolt rappel anchor. 110 ft. Topo, page 132.

38. **Sea Of Holes** 5.10 R ◄ FA: Nick Nordblom, Jay Smith. P1: 1980. P2 and 3: Fall 1988.
    This route climbs **The Black Hole**, then continues upward for two more pitches. Begin as per **The Black Hole**. Topo, page 132.

    P1 Starting out of a chimney, climb a shallow corner to a two-bolt belay. 110 ft., 5.8.

    P2 Traverse out left using numerous huecos, then up through a roof at a crack on its left side. Friends in huecos for pro. One-bolt belay on arête. 160 ft., 5.10 R.

    P3 Go straight up the black face to a crack in a bulge. Continue up the face to a belay on the shoulder of the buttress. 165 ft., 5.10-.

    Descent: You'll find a rap station in the gully to descend in three rappels.

39. **Ripcord** 5.12- R   FA: Jay Smith, Nick Nordblom–1989.
    This route starts at an arête to the left of **The Black Hole**. Topo, page 132.

    P1 Make desperate moves up the arête past a bolt (crux), then continue up to a bolted belay. 5.12-.

    P2 Move out left and climb up to a bolted belay at a ledge. 5.10+ R.

    P3 Go up past a couple of bolts to a belay at the base of a left-facing corner. 5.11.

    P4 Climb the left-facing corner. 5.11.

    Descent: Rappel down the gully as per **Sea Of Holes** in three rappels.

NOTE: Numerous other routes have been done in the vicinity, but information is sketchy. The topo has some additional information. See page 130.

NORTH FORK OF PINE CREEK CANYON
OUT OF CONTROL AREA

The next few routes are on the right (north) wall of the canyon, but are quite far from the last routes described. From the parking lot, walk up the trail toward the Mescalito, then take the right (north) fork of Pine Creek. The trail becomes faint and braided at this point, but the best route is to head uphill about 100 feet (above The red band of rock), then head left (west), contouring along the hillside on a trail. Roughly 350 yards up this drainage, and past about three huge pine trees, the lowest cliff band on the right is split by a low-angled gully. Head up this gully until you are above the first cliff band, then go right (toward the road) on ledge systems for about 100 yards. You should now be even with the front (east) face of The Mescalito. The following routes are described from left to right, and are in the sun all day. Approach time is about 30 minutes.

40. **American Ninja** 5.10   FA: Paul Van Betten, Robert Finlay–1986.
    Start below a clean, short, dihedral in an alcove that is about 50 feet above the traverse ledge. Climb the corner to rap anchors on the low-angled face above.

41. **Out Of Control** 5.10 ◄ FA: Randy Grandstaff, Dave Anderson–1978.
    Begin about 150 feet up and right of **American...** at the base of a long, straight hand-crack in a smooth, white wall; the crack is about 15 feet left of a huge dihedral. Bring lots of hand-sized gear and two ropes to rappel. Follow the crack past a roof to a rap station.

42. **Remote Control** 5.9? FA: Dave Anderson, Randy Grandstaff–1978.
Rope up 15 feet right of **Out Of Control** at the base of a huge corner. Climb the left-facing dihedral with a smooth, huge, right wall for 165 feet to a rappel anchor.

DARK SHADOWS AREA

The next routes are located on the north face of The Mescalito, the pyramid-shaped formation splitting the canyon into two drainages. The rock is of excellent quality, rivaling the best in Black Velvet Canyon. Bring two ropes to get off all of these shady routes.

From the Pine Creek parking lot, follow the trail into Pine Creek Canyon, going past the Fire Ecology Trail and an old homesite. When the canyon forks, take the right (north) fork. The trail becomes faint and braided at this point. The best route is to head straight uphill on the right (north) side of the canyon for about 100 feet (above the red band of rock), then head left (west), contouring along the hillside on a relatively level trail. Follow one of the many trails heading up canyon for about 600 yards, keeping well above the drainage bottom. Continue up canyon until you are even with the furthest, large pine trees in the drainage. You should now be able to clearly see the varnished, north face of The Mescalito. Pine Creek runs along the base of the wall here and the surrounding vegetation is surprisingly lush and varied.

The climbs described next are all located on this varnished section of cliff and are described from right to left (downcanyon). Depending which trail you chose, you may need to head down (south) to the drainage bottom to see the pools noted in the route descriptions. Total approach time is about 30 minutes.

43. **Slot Machine** 5.10 PG FA: Bob Conz, Sal Mamusia–July 1990.
A worthwhile pitch that rewards those with small fingers. Start as per **Dark Shadows**, atop a flat boulder at the right edge of the pool at the base of the cliff. Bring small RPs and gear up to a #3 Friend. Climb easily past two bolts to the base of a left-leaning ramp (as per **Dark Shadows**). Continue straight up a thin seam in a steep, varnished wall, passing one bolt to the two-bolt anchor. Rappel with two ropes. 150 ft., 5.10. Topo, page 134.

44. **Dark Shadows** 5.8- ◀ FA: Lots of different folks–1973.
One of the best 5.8 routes at Red Rocks, and a popular soap opera in its time. The climb goes to the top of The Mescalito, but only the first four pitches are described here. Bring a variety of gear and be prepared to have fun. Start on a flat boulder atop a small waterfall at the right edge of a pool, and below a huge, black dihedral system capped by a giant roof. Good belay ledges on each pitch. Photo, page 123; topo page 134.

P1 Face climb up and right past two bolts to a left-leaning ramp that leads to the base of a varnished corner. Two-bolt belay anchor. 75 ft., 5.5 PG13.

P2 Climb the clean, varnished, right-facing corner above, moving left to a belay ledge and a bolted belay. (P1 and P2 may be combined.) 75 ft., 5.7-.

P3 Stem up the beautiful dihedral to a ledge with two different bolted belay anchors. 120 ft., 5.7-.

P4 Climb the right-curving crack in the right wall to another two-bolt belay under the giant roof. 75 ft., 5.8-.

Descent: Three rappels, using two ropes, will get you down.

45. **Heart Of Darkness** 5.11 FA: Richard Harrison, John Long, Lynn Hill–Spring 1981.
From the anchor at the top of the last pitch described on **Dark Shadows**, it's possible to climb out left through the giant roof, using an old bolt and manky fixed pegs for pro. The route continues upwards, but the section described is the most worthy of repeating.

Dark Shadows Area

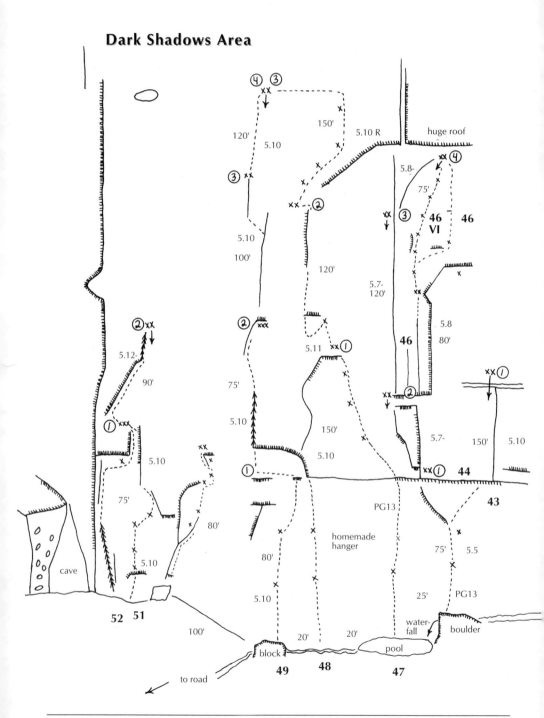

46. **Chasing Shadows** 5.8+ PG13   FA: Randy Marsh, Pier Locatelli–Summer 1990.
This two-pitch route begins at the second belay on **Dark Shadows**. Bring gear to a #4 Camalot for the first pitch of the route. The second pitch was originally done with only the silver bolt!

P1 Climb **Dark Shadows** to the belay at the base of the huge corner (this can be done in one or two pitches). 150 ft., 5.7-.

P2 From the **Dark Shadows** belay, move back right to the right-hand (and widest) of two vertical crack systems. Follow this past a wide section to a two-bolt belay. 80 ft., 5.8+.

P3 Continue straight up the vague arête past a couple of bolts with black hangers, then move out right above a ceiling to a bolt with a silver hanger (V1). Wander up and slightly right along the arête (wires, TCUS, small Friends) to the belay on **Dark Shadows** below huge **Heart of Darkness** roof. 120 ft., 5.8+ PG13.

V1 Edge Dressing 5.10 PG   FA: Randy Marsh, Pier Locatelli, Brett Fishman–November 1993. Move up left to a bolt, then up past six more bolts to the belay on **Dark Shadows** below the right edge of the huge **Heart of Darkness** roof. Bring a #3 Friend to supplement the bolts.

Descent: Do three rappels using two ropes, as per **Dark Shadows**.

47. **Sandstone Sandwich** 5.10c PG13   FA: Bob Conz, George Smith, Jim Lybarger–July 1990.
Don't bite off more than you can chew! A wonderful bolted face climb between the first pitches of **Dark Shadows** and **Excellent Adventure**. Rappel with two ropes from the first belay on **Excellent Adventure**, or continue up that route. Bring #1, #1.5 Friends.

48. **Excellent Adventure** 5.11 R ◀   FA: Mike Tupper, Greg Mayer–Fall 1989.
Perhaps the best route on the wall. Really scary on the last pitch, both for the leader, and follower. Start 20 feet right of **Risky Business** and 25 feet left of **Dark Shadows** at the left edge of the deeper pool at the base of the cliff.

P1 Climb to the right end of the arching ceiling on **Risky Business**, passing two bolts with homemade hangers enroute. Follow the arching ceiling left for 15 feet, then pull the ceiling. Intimidating climbing leads left to a crack system. Follow this up and slightly right past an overhang to a belay stance with bolts. 150 ft., 5.10.

P2 Go up from the belay, then make tricky moves down and left (bolts). Climb up the right side of a vague arête, stepping back out left to a belay anchor. 120 ft., 5.11.

P3 Get ready! Follow bolts up and right along the lip of the giant roof, then straight up (5.10 R). Eventually, you can angle back left to the final rap station on **Risky Business** and rappel the route. Whew!

49. **Risky Business** 5.10+ PG   FA: Mike Tupper, Greg Mayer–Summer 1985
Certainly as good as the movie – maybe better! Begin 20 feet left of the last route and 100 feet right of **Parental Guidance**, where the stream runs along the base of the cliff, and directly in front of some large blocks.

P1 Up a short, left-facing flake, then face climb past two bolts. Move slightly right to a flake (scary), then easily up left (V1) to a belay at the left end of an arching ceiling. 80 ft., 5.10

P2 Follow the shallow dihedral above the left edge of the ceiling, then continue along a seam to a belay station under a small ceiling. 75 ft., 5.10.

P3 Step left and climb up and slightly left, passing numerous bolts to another bolted belay anchor. 100 ft., 5.10.

P4 Continue up the varnished wall above to another rap station. 120 ft., 5.10.

V1 It's possible to undercling the arching ceiling at 5.11+ (but who'd want to?).

Descent: Rappel with two ropes.

50. **Short Circuit** 5.11 PG   FA: Mike Ward, Nick Nordblom–July 1992.
A very sustained and sporty pitch. Unless you have a lot of talent and a cool head, you may short out! Bring a couple tiny TCUs, a large stopper and a couple long slings. Start atop a boulder 20 feet right of **Parental Guidance** and climb a shallow, right-leaning flake/corner past a fixed peg and two bolts to a ledge. Step right, then make very hard moves past another bolt to a short corner and the belay anchor. Rappel with one rope. Topo, page 134.

51. **Parental Guidance** 5.12- PG13   FA: Mike Tupper, Greg Mayer–Winter 1988.
The first pitch is worth doing by itself. Bring numerous small Friends, TCUs and wires for the first pitch. Start about 100 feet left of **Risky Business** and eight feet right of **Lethal Weapon** at a small block leaning against the cliff. Topo, page 134.

P1 Climb the face to an overlap 15 feet up (bolt), then continue past two more bolts to a stance (bolt). Angle up left to an obvious, vertical flake. At the top of the flake, step left to a communal belay. 75 ft., 5.10.

P2 Face climb past bolts to a right-leaning flake/crack, and pull past this into a shallow dihedral. 90 ft., 5.12-.

Descent: Rap the route.

52. **Lethal Weapon** 5.12   FA: Mike Tupper, Greg Mayer–Fall 1989.
The left (east) margin of this wall is defined by a huge, right-facing chimney/corner system, the bottom of which forms a cave (this chimney/corner system is **Negro Blanco**, 5.10+). Start 20 feet right of the cave, in a cleared area that is below several small corners and a huge flake/chimney system. Topo, page 134.

P1 Climb the easy, bigger dihedral to the base of a gaping chimney, then angle right up a corner to a roof. Traverse right under the roof (bolt); follow a flake to a belay station.

53. **Flakes Of Wrath** 5.10+ R/X   FA: Nick Nordblom, Kevin Lowell–1990.
This four pitch route starts to the left of the huge, right-facing chimney/corner system (**Negro Blanco**) that forms the left margin of the varnished wall. Bring two ropes to rappel with. Not much is known about this route, except that it keeps to the right of **Centerfold** (described in the Urioste guide).

P1 Face climb up steep black rock to an anchor consisting of a nut and a piton. 5.8+ R.

P2 Continue up the steep black face to a two-bolt anchor on a ledge. 5.8+ R.

P3 Angle up and left on plates to a white slab. Belay at the base of a left-facing corner at a bolt and peg. 5.10 R.

P4 Go up and left along the crack/corner onto the face (scary) to a bolt and pin belay anchor. 5.10+ R/X.

Descent: Do four rappels with two ropes.

Mescalito, East Face
The next six routes generally face the Pine Creek parking area and are described from right to left (north fork to south fork). Information is vague, as I haven't done any of these climbs.

54. **Bloodline** 5.11- PG   FA: Guys From Colorado–1980s.
Start about 100 feet left of **Negro Blanco** (the giant flake system that forms the left margin of the Dark Shadows Area) on the face left of a deep recess (just left of **Deep Space**, which is described in the Urioste guide). Do an easy pitch up to a ledge, then climb a splitter fingercrack through a bulge to a two bolt belay.

55. **Ride The Tiger** 5.9   FA: Nick Nordblom, Randy Grandstaff–1982.
Start somewhere to the left of the last route at a bushy terrace above the creekbed. Map, page 124.

P1 Climb a broken face through black plates at the base of a big buttress. 5.6.

P2 Continue up the plated face, which gets a little steeper. 5.7.

P3 Layback up a Yosemite **Wheat Thin**-type flake. Belay on a ramp at the top of the flake. 5.9.

P4 Angle left around the arête onto a face which is climbed to the top of the feature. 5.9 R.

Descent: Downclimb. There are no fixed anchors.

56. **Pauligk Pillar** 5.7+ FA: Mr. and Mrs. Roland Pauligk, Randy Grandstaff–1981.
    Guess what Australian Roland Pauligk invented? Bring a good assortment of gear, including RPs. Start about 150 yards left of **Ride The Tiger**. Two long pitches lead up a right-facing corner past trees to a ledge.

57. **Welcome To Red Rocks** 5.12 FA: Sal Mamusia, Paul Van Betten–1986.
    This route is about 100 feet left of **Pauligk Pillar**. Scramble up the hillside to a bushy ramp at the base of the route. Stem up a right-facing, 50-foot-high pink corner past a couple of bolts.

58. **This Ain't No Disco** 5.9+ FA: Randy Grandstaff, Randy Marsh–1982.
    This one-pitch route climbs the black face somewhere between **Mescalito Regular Route** and **CHNO** (Routes #9 and #12 in the Urioste guide).

59. **Pauline's Pentacle** 5.10- R FA: Randy Grandstaff, Randy Marsh, Pauline Schroeder– 1982.
    The following route description will give you an idea of the kind of first ascent information I'm given. Compare the description of this climb with the description of a route I've actually done, such as **Cat In The Hat**. Start between **Black Widow** and **Cookie Monster** (both are described in the Urioste guide).

    Three pitches of steep, black face climbing, with some loose rock on the first pitch. Map, page 124.

SOUTH FORK OF PINE CREEK CANYON
Mescalito, South Face

61. **Cat In The Hat** 5.6+ ◀ FA: Bruce Eisener, Joanne Urioste–April 1976.
    A wonderful, moderate route that can be done during colder weather. Carry a good selection of gear, including long slings and two ropes for rappelling. Topo, page 138.

    This route is located on the south side of The Mescalito – the pyramid-shaped formation splitting Pine Creek Canyon. From the Pine Creek parking lot, follow the trail into Pine Creek Canyon, going past the Fire Ecology Trail and an old homesite. When the canyon forks, take the left (south) drainage for about 75 yards, then follow a trail on the right (Mescalito) side of the creekbed. Continue on this vague trail around the toe of the south buttress, keeping well above the drainage bottom and passing numerous crack systems. A well-worn trail up a talus slope will bring you to the base of this sunny route. Total approach time is about 30 minutes.

    Start at a crack system that is 75 feet left of a prominent chimney. Directly uphill from the start of the climb is a bushy gully that leads to steep, broken, brown rock.

    P1 Climb an obvious, slightly left-slanting crack past numerous huecos, moving right to a ledge with a small bush and slings around a horn (90 feet). Climb the left-slanting fist crack above to another ledge, then continue up the corner/chimney directly above to belay on a sloping terrace. 150 ft., 5.5.

    P2 From the right center portion of the terrace, climb a steep, black wall to a ledge. Step left and follow a left-facing corner to a ledge with a tree (many rappel slings on the tree). 60 ft., 5.5.

    P3 A great pitch. From the first ledge above the rappel tree, climb the black face just left of a left-facing corner along a thin crack. Move left just below a white ceiling and follow

Cat In The Hat 5.6+

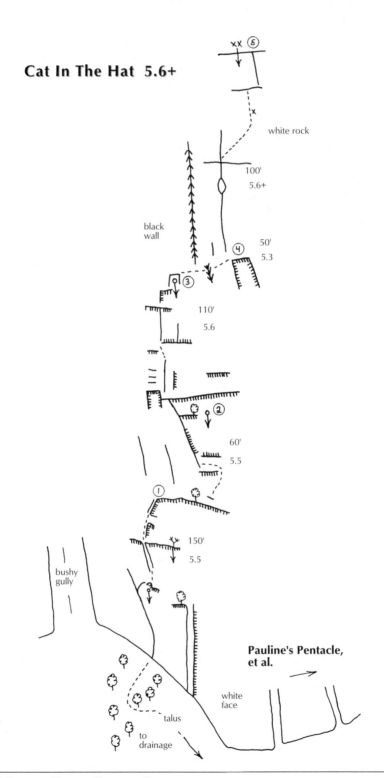

xx ⑤

white rock

100'

5.6+

black
wall

④ 50'

5.3

③

110'

5.6

②

60'

5.5

①

150'

5.5

bushy
gully

Pauline's Pentacle,
et al.

white
face

talus

to
drainage

a fingercrack up the wall to a ledge. Belay on the highest ledge at slings around a block. 110 ft., 5.6.

P4 Step down and traverse around right to a series of blocky ledges with slings. 50 ft., 5.3.

P5 Climb the beautiful crack up the center of the black wall. When it ends in the white rock, angle right around a corner to a bolt, then up the crack above to the top (two-bolt belay). 100 ft., 5.6+.

Descent: Rappel with two ropes as follows:

1) 110-foot rappel to the block atop P3.

2) 110-foot rappel to tree.

3) 60-foot rappel to terrace.

4) Scramble down terrace to bolts on a ledge.

5) 130-foot rappel from bolts to the ground.

*The next two routes are about 150 yards up and left of **Cat In The Hat**.*

62. **OB Button** 5.10-   FA: Paul Obenheim–1982.
    The left-hand of the two routes. Climb a crack through a roof, then continue upward for a total of two pitches. Rappel.

63. **OB Fist** 5.10-   FA: Nick Nordblom, Paul Van Betten–1982.
    Climb the right-hand line – a fist crack through a roof.

CRABBY APPLETON AREA

The next three routes are on a large diamond-shaped face that sits up high on the south side of the canyon. The routes are in the shade most of the day. From the Pine Creek parking lot, follow the trail into Pine Creek Canyon, going past the Fire Ecology Trail and an old homesite. When the canyon forks, take the left (south) drainage for about 400 yards until a prominent gully leading up left is seen on the left (south) wall of the canyon. Scramble up the gully, staying on its right edge, to a small cave. Exit the cave through a hole in its top. Continue up the gully for another 50 feet or so to a big ledge. This approach takes about 90 minutes.

64. **Crabby Appleton** 5.9+ PG ◀   FA: Richard Harrison, Wendell Broussard, Paul Van Betten–1982.
    This is supposed to be an area classic. Topo, page 140.

    P1 Traverse right about 80 feet to the base of an obvious crack system. 80 ft., 5.4.

    P2 Follow the crack, angling right to a big dish with one bolt. 120 ft., 5.7.

    P3 Exit left out of the dish, then follow the crack past an overlap to a ledge with a pin and bolt. 120 ft., 5.8.

    P4 Climb a left-facing arch for 20 feet (V1), step right, then climb a beautiful black face to a huge ledge under a headwall. 100 ft., 5.5.

    P5 Walk right on a ledge for 20 feet (V2). Climb straight up a crack over a bulge (crux). Continue upwards, eventually belaying in a crack. 130 ft., 5.9+.

    V1 Continue up the corner. 5.9.

    V2 Escape left. 5.5.

    Descent: Walk off to the right (west) to the top of an obvious ramp, which is then followed back down toward the road and the base of the route.

65. **Tom Terrific** 5.10- PG   FA: Richard Harrison, Wendell Broussard–1985.
    Don't get whipped into a frenzy. Carry wires, TCUs and Friends up to #4. Start to the right of **Crabby Appleton** on the descent ramp.

64. Crabby Appleton 5.9+ PG
65. Tom Terrific 5.10- PG

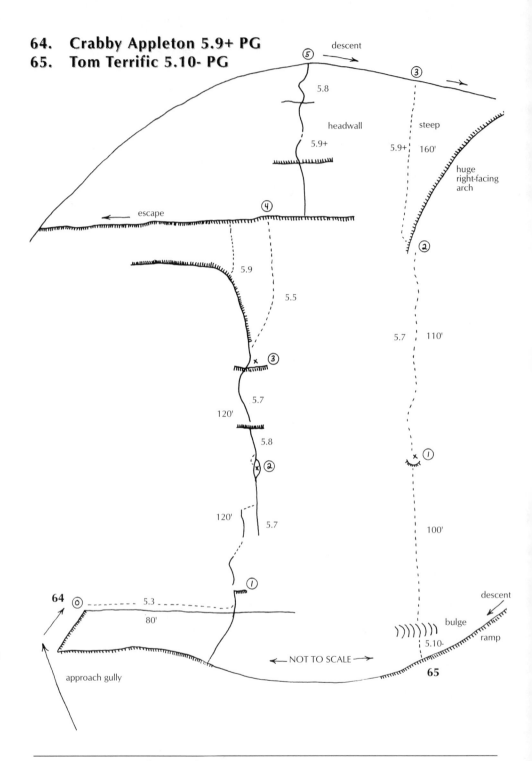

P1 Pull over a bulge (crux), then straight up the face toward the bottom of a right-facing arch. Belay in a dish with one bolt. 100 ft., 5.10-.

P2 Continue straight up the face to the base of the arch (big Friends needed for the anchor). 110 ft., 5.7.

P3 Step left around the arch, then angle left up the face to the top. 160 ft., 5.9+

Descent: Walk off to the right (west) to the top of an obvious ramp, which is then followed back down toward the road and the base of the route.

66. **Creepshow** 5.10 X   FA: Robert Finlay, Richard Harrison–circa 1985.
Climb the face to the right of **Tom Terrific**, along some black water streaks.

67. **The Whitehouse Effect** 5.10+   FA: Dave Wonderly, Warren Egbert–1988.
These guys did a two-pitch route somewhere up here. The crux climbs a real steep bulge with bolts. Good luck! (This route may be the same as **Creepshow**.)

MAGIC TRIANGLE AREA

The next nine routes are located to the left (east) of the **Crabby Appleton** approach gully on the south wall of the canyon. All of the routes are east (toward the road) of the front face on The Mescalito.

From the Pine Creek parking lot, follow the trail into Pine Creek Canyon, going past the Fire Ecology Trail and an old homesite. When the canyon forks, take the left (south) drainage for about 300 yards until you encounter a red slab on your left. A huge boulder with several large pines is about 75 yards upstream. From here, you can see the obvious, left-leaning **Crabby Appleton** gully and other features. Routes are described from right to left, moving toward the mouth of the canyon.

68. **Lunar Escape** 5.11-   FA: Dave Wonderly, Warren Egbert–1988.
Start in the **Crabby Appleton** gully, about 50 feet right of the arête.

P1 Climb a steep, black face to a bolted belay stance. 5.10-.

P2 Traverse right, then wander up the face past about seven bolts to a bolt anchor. 5.10.

P3 Climb up to a steep headwall with bolts, which is climbed to the top of the buttress. 5.11-.

Descent: Rappel the next route with two ropes.

69. **Edge Of The Sun** 5.10+ 🏆   FA: Dave Wonderly, Warren Egbert–1988.
This is supposed to be a very good route. Start at the base of the **Crabby Appleton** gully, just right of the arête. Bring two ropes to rappel with.

P1 Climb the face to a ledge on the prow. 5.10-.

P2 Climb the face on the left of the arête past bolts to a bolted belay below a ceiling. 5.9+.

P3 Go up and left under the ceiling onto a steep white face, then up water streaks (bolts). 5.10+.

Descent: Rappel the route with two ropes.

70. **Clone Babies** 5.10+   FA: Paul Crawford, Richard Harrison–1983.
Start about 75 yards to the left of the **Crabby Appleton** gully. Climb overhanging, twin cracks, then go up and left to the top of a pillar (160 ft). Rappel with two ropes.

71. **Midnight Oil** 5.11-   FA: Richard Harrison, Paul Crawford, Randy Marsh, Nick Nordblom–1983.
Harrison was pictured on the first ascent of this route in the last edition of the guide (page 97). Bring two ropes and a good-sized rack. This climb begins about 150 yards to the left of the **Crabby Appleton** gully below a huge, black triangle of rock (**The Magic**

Triangle, which is described in the Urioste guide). Climb a dihedral with a handcrack, then face climb up along a seam (crux). Mantle a couple of sloping ledges into a corner, which is followed past a bolt to a rappel anchor. 165 ft.

72. **Small Purchase** 5.10 ◀ FA: Joe Herbst–1970s.
An outstanding one-pitch climb on the south wall of the canyon. Bring gear to a #4 Camalot plus extra TCUs in the smaller sizes.

From the red slab described in the approach, you can see this climb – it's a 100-foot-high pillar with a left-leaning dihedral on its right (west) side that sits between two obvious gullies that run up the entire cliff. From the wash, follow any of the numerous social trails about 300 yards up to the base of the climb.

Start at an alcove that is about 40 feet right (west) of a prominent, rectangular block/pinnacle. Climb the classic, right-facing corner to a three-bolt belay atop the pillar. With a 165-foot rope, you can just reach a ledge, then scramble down the initial 20 feet of the climb.

73. **Five And Dime** 5.10+ FA: Unknown–before March 1994.
Climb the knife-edged arête 15 feet left of **Small Purchase** past at least six bolts. Rappel with a 165-foot rope as per **Small Purchase**.

74. **Dukes Of Hazard** 5.9? FA: Randy Grandstaff, Shelby Shelton–circa 1983.
Climb the front of a pillar just right of the **Cartwright Corner/Chocolate Flakes** gully.

*The next two routes climb very obvious, varnished dihedrals that sit midway up the left side of a huge gully. The gully is about 100 feet left of **Small Purchase** and is clearly visible from the approach trail and the old homesite.*

75. **Chocolate Flakes** 5.10+ FA: Robert Finlay, Tom Ebanoff–1985. FFA: Paul Van Betten, Nick Nordblom–1985.
Start at the base of the gully at a nice, flat area surrounded by lush vegetation.

P1 Climb up the dirty chimney system to a big ledge on the left side, below a wide crack in a corner. 130 ft., 5.8.

P2 Climb the crack in the corner to a ledge, then go up another wide crack to a large ledge. 5.9.

P3 Climb the right-hand of two dihedrals to a ledge. 5.10+.

P4 Continue up the corner to its top. 5.10-.

P5 Scramble to the top.

Descent: Go right (up canyon) to the **Crabby Appleton** descent ramp, which is followed back down toward the road.

76. **Cartwright Corner** 5.10 FA: Richard Harrison, Nick Nordblom, Paul Van Betten, Wendell Broussard–1985.
A great route if you can get past the first two pitches. Start as per **Chocolate Flakes** at the base of the gully at a nice, flat area surrounded by lush vegetation.

P1 Climb up the dirty chimney system to a big ledge on the left side, below a wide crack in a corner. 130 ft., 5.8.

P2 Climb the wide crack in the corner to a ledge, then go up another wide crack to a large ledge. 5.9.

P3 Climb the left-hand of two dihedrals to a belay in a pod. 5.10-.

P4 Continue up the corner to a ledge at its top. 5.10.

P5 Scramble to the top.

Descent: Go right (up canyon) to the **Crabby Appleton** descent ramp, which is followed back down toward the road.

75. Chocolate Flakes 5.10+
76. Cartwright Corner 5.10

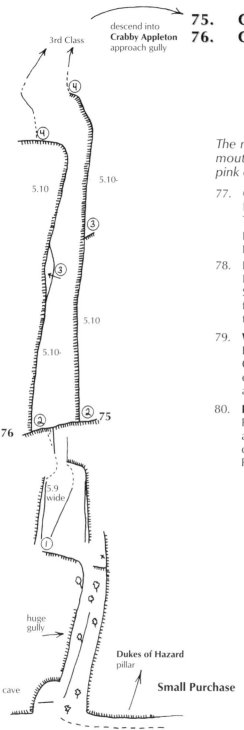

descend into
Crabby Appleton
approach gully

3rd Class

The next three routes are located near the mouth of Pine Creek Canyon at a large, pink corner.

77. **Cold Blue Steel** 5.10
FA: Greg Mayer–1988.
This route climbs the right arête of the pink corner past five bolts and some gear placements to a communal anchor.

78. **Dependent Variable** 5.12
FA: Mike Tupper–1988.
Stem and lieback up the pink corner past four bolts and some gear placements to the communal anchor.

79. **Without A Paddle** 5.11d
FA: Mike Tupper–1988.
Climb the left arête of the corner past eight bolts to the communal belay anchor.

80. **Dog Police** 5.10   FA: Unknown – 1980s.
Rope up to the left of the pink corner at a striking crack system. Climb a superb crack up the center of a white face. Rappel with two ropes.

Juniper Canyon

NOT TO SCALE

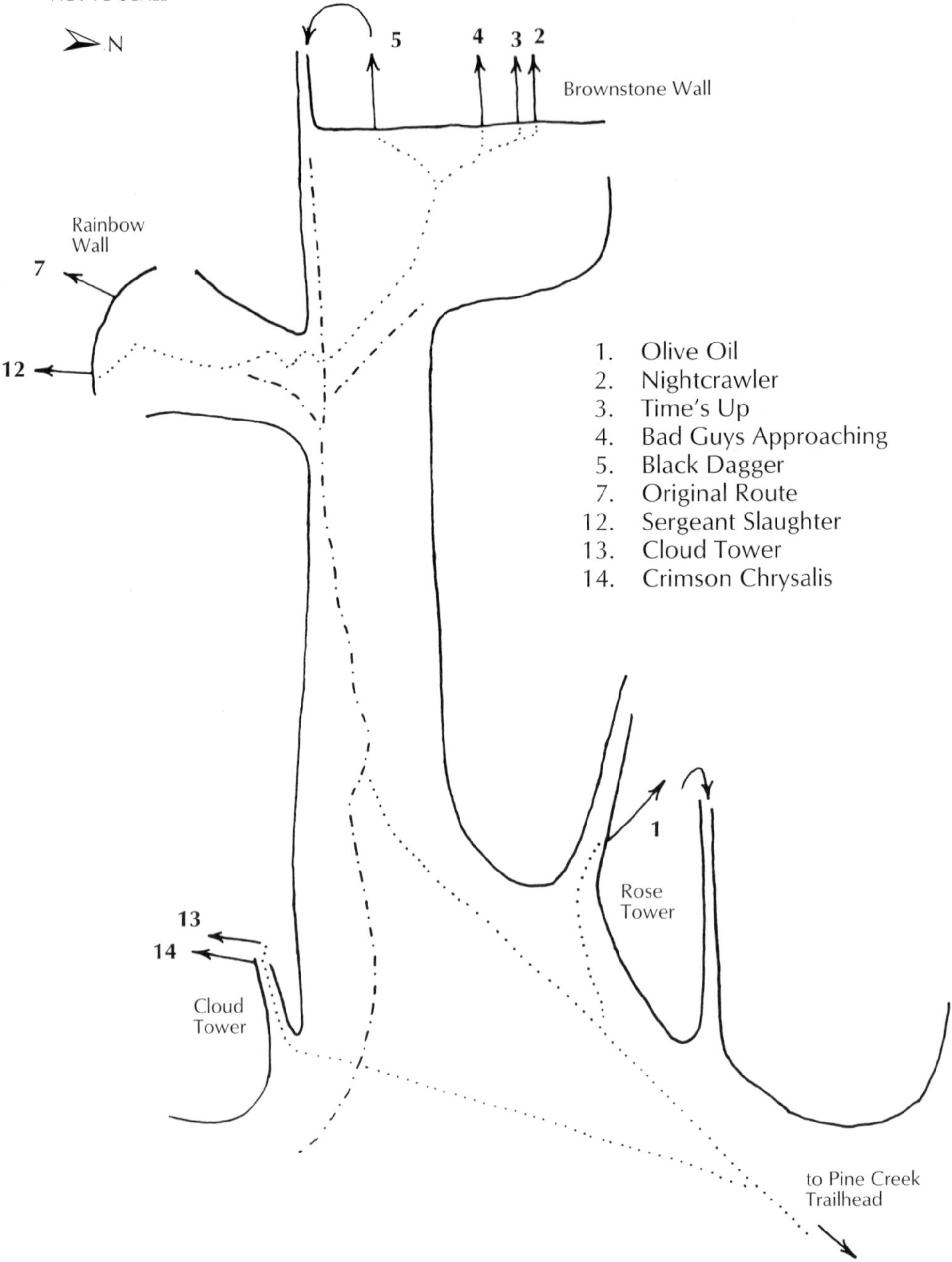

N

Brownstone Wall

5   4 3 2

Rainbow
Wall

7

12

1.   Olive Oil
2.   Nightcrawler
3.   Time's Up
4.   Bad Guys Approaching
5.   Black Dagger
7.   Original Route
12. Sergeant Slaughter
13. Cloud Tower
14. Crimson Chrysalis

1

Rose
Tower

13

14

Cloud
Tower

to Pine Creek
Trailhead

JUNIPER CANYON

It is probably best to approach Juniper Canyon by parking at the Pine Creek Parking Area, located 10.3 miles along the scenic loop road. A new spur road has been built off of the loop road to access Oak Creek Canyon and this may also be used to access Juniper Canyon. From Pine Creek, follow the very well-marked trail down the hill, then angle south across the desert to Juniper Canyon. Once you enter the canyon, follow the main drainage to avoid dense scrub oak. The selected climbs are scattered throughout the canyon – each route has its own detailed description to find its start. Routes are described from right to left (north to south).

Juniper Canyon and surrounding areas

Oak Creek Canyon	Juniper Canyon
A. Solar Slab (see page 167)	5. Black Dagger
	2. The Nightcrawler

Rose Tower

1. **Olive Oil** 5.7 PG FA: Jorge and Joanne Urioste, John Williamson–February 1978.
   A slick route. Bring large gear to protect the last two pitches. Except for the tree atop pitch one, there are no fixed anchors. Topo, page 146; photo, page 147.

   From the Pine Creek parking area, follow the very well-marked trail down the hill, then turn left (south) on the Fire Ecology Trail. Follow this trail until you are closest to the drainage. Cross the drainage, go up a hill on the far side, then angle south across the desert (vague trail) to Juniper Canyon. Just before you reach the mouth of Juniper Canyon, head up right into a tree-filled gully to the left (west) of Rose Tower (a separate formation from the right [north] wall of Juniper Canyon). Scramble about 200 yards up

Olive Oil 5.7

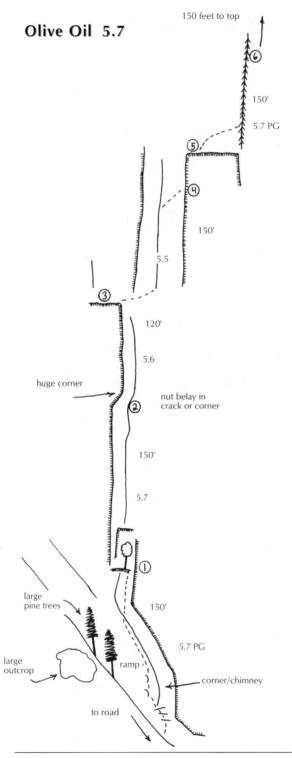

150 feet to top

150'

5.7 PG

150'

5.5

120'

5.6

nut belay in crack or corner

huge corner

150'

5.7

large pine trees

150'

large outcrop

ramp

5.7 PG

corner/chimney

to road

the gully to the base of the route. This approach takes about 45 minutes and the route is in the sun all day.

Start the climb at the base of a left-leaning chimney/corner with an obvious tree about 150 feet up. The base of the chimney/corner forms somewhat of a cave.

P1 Climb up the left-leaning ramp just left of the ugly chimney/corner to a tree and ledge (rap anchors here). 150 ft., 5.7 PG.

P2 Slither up a short chimney, then up the obvious finger-and-hand crack about 15 feet right of a large, right-facing corner. Belay in the crack when you run out of rope. 150 ft., 5.7.

P3 Continue up the crack and face, eventually moving left into the right-facing corner. Belay on a large ledge just left of the corner. 120 ft., 5.6.

P4 Traverse right about 20 feet and follow the central crack upwards. At the end of the pitch, move right into the left-facing corner and belay. 150 ft., 5.5.

P5 Continue up the corner for 30 feet to a huge ledge on the right. Walk right about 25 feet. 55 ft., 5.4.

P6 Angle up right across the face into the huge dihedral above. Continue up this until you've run out of rope. 150 ft., 5.7 PG.

P7 Continue up the corner to the top. 150 ft., 5.6.

Descent: Scramble up slabs about 150 feet, then walk to the top of Rose Tower. Walk left (west) to a notch, then drop down right (north) into the gully. A typically bushy, but easy descent to the valley floor follows.

Olive Oil 5.7

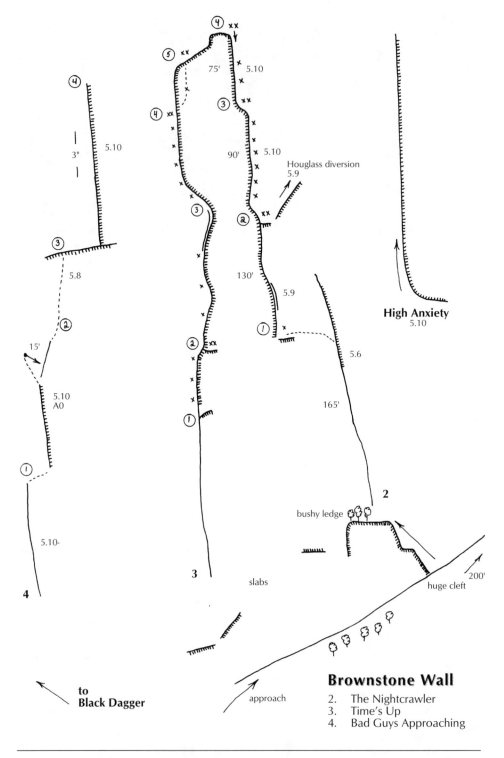

④

3"

5.10

③

5.8

②

15'

5.10
A0

①

5.10-

4

⑤ xx

④ xx

④

③

③

②

①

3

slabs

to
Black Dagger

approach

④ xx

↓

75' 5.10

③ xx

x

90' x 5.10

x

Houglass diversion
5.9

② xx

130'

5.9

① x

5.6

165'

bushy ledge

2

200'

huge cleft

High Anxiety
5.10

Brownstone Wall

2. The Nightcrawler
3. Time's Up
4. Bad Guys Approaching

Brownstone Wall

2. **The Nightcrawler** 5.10 ◥ FA: Jorge and Joanne Urioste–April 1978.

Don't be lured onto this route without a large Friend or two. Like **The Black Dagger**, this route is located on Brownstone Wall – the large, brown wall at the very rear of Juniper Canyon. From the Pine Creek Parking Area, follow the very well-marked trail down the hill, then turn left (south) on the Fire Ecology Trail. Follow this trail until you are closest to the drainage. Cross the drainage, go up a hill on the far side, then angle south across the desert (vague trail) to Juniper Canyon. Hike up the drainage until it is split by a large, white lump of rock with a pine tree on its left side. The Rainbow Wall is up on the left and **The Nightcrawler** is visible about 100 yards right of the white lump; it is just right of a lone pine tree. The route takes the large, right-facing corner system of a huge flake leaning against the wall. Go through bushes below and right of the white lump (cairn), then up an open talus slope. Follow easy slabs up and right to reach the base of the route. The approach takes about 1.5 hours.

Begin on a bushy ledge about forty feet above the ground and 200 feet left of an obvious break in the Brownstone Wall. The route is in the sun most of the day, although the corner pitches will be shaded.

P1 Follow easy cracks up and slightly left for 140 feet, then traverse about ten feet left to a one-bolt belay. 165 ft., 5.6.

P2 Climb the huge, right-facing corner system up to a two-bolt belay stance, worming up a chimney en route. 130 ft., 5.9.

P3 Stem and lieback up the amazing corner, passing six bolts to a two-bolt anchor. 90 ft., 5.10.

P4 Continue up the corner past two bolts and more liebacking to the top of the giant Hourglass flake. Two-bolt belay. 75 ft., 5.10.

Descent: Do four rappels, using two ropes (watch out for stuck ropes in the crack just below the third anchor).

3. **Time's Up** 5.11+ FA: The Uriostes–1985.

This five-pitch route climbs the left side of the huge Hourglass flake leaning against the wall (**Nightcrawler** climbs the right side). Not much is known about the route other than what is shown on the topo on page 148.

4. **Bad Guys Approaching** 5.10+ A0 FA: Paul Van Betten, Robert Finlay, Nick Nordblom–1989.

A four-pitch route that climbs the next major corner system to the left of **Time's Up**. Bring lots of three-inch pieces for the fourth pitch.

P1 Climb a crack system. 5.10-.

P2 Move right, then climb a left-facing corner to its top. Pendulum about 15 feet to the right then climb up to a belay. 5.10 A0.

P3 Climb up to a big ledge. 5.8.

P4 Move right and climb the huge, left-facing corner to its top. 5.10+.

Descent: Rappel?

5. **The Black Dagger** 5.7+ PG ◥ FA: Joe Herbst, Rick Wheeler–1977.

A sharp route. This route is located on Brownstone Wall – the large, brown wall at the very rear of Juniper Canyon. Bring large gear for pitch three.

From the Pine Creek parking area, follow the very well-marked trail down the hill, then turn left (south) on the Fire Ecology Trail. Follow this trail until you are closest to the drainage. Cross the drainage, go up a hill on the far side, then angle south across the desert (vague trail) to Juniper Canyon. Once you enter the canyon, follow the main drainage to avoid dense scrub oak. About halfway up Juniper Canyon, a big, white lump of rock with a pine tree on its left side will divide the drainage in two. The Rainbow Wall is up on the left, and most of **The Black Dagger** is obscured by the white lump. Go

The Black Dagger
5.7+ PG

to
The Gunsight

300' +/-
feet of slabs

⑥

5.6
120'

⑤

5.6
100'

④

tunnel through
4th class

③

5.7+
120'

②

5.7 PG
140'

①

5.4
120'

to
The Nightcrawler

white overhang

slabs

to drainage

approach

through bushes below and right of the white lump (cairn), then up an open talus slope. Follow easy slabs up and left to reach the top of the lump from its right side. Traverse left (south) across more slabs to the obvious right-facing corner system near the left edge of Brownstone Wall. This approach takes about 1.5 hours. The route is in the sun most of the day.

Start just right of a white overhang at an easy-looking crack/dihedral. This is directly below the huge corner mentioned in the approach.

P1 Climb the crack and easy face to a belay atop a block that is just below a prominent white roof. 120 ft., 5.4.

P2 An airy traverse left from the block starts the pitch. Climb up to a crack on the left side of the roof (scary), then traverse back right on varnished plates to the main right-facing corner system. Continue up this to a ledge below the huge, right-facing corner. 140 ft., 5.7 PG.

P3 Layback and stem up the magnificent corner for a full pitch. Belay at the base of a chimney. 120 ft., 5.7+.

P4 Wiggle up the very easy and aesthetic chimney, exiting left through a hole to a huge ledge. 80 ft., 4th class.

P5 From the top of the pillar, climb the plated face to a low-angled, right-facing crack/corner. Belay on the highest ledge, just below a roof. 100 ft., 5.6.

P6 Climb up the face to the roof, then pull over this into the right-facing corner. Follow the corner to a large ledge. 120 ft., 5.6.

Descent: Scramble up about 300 feet of very easy cracks and slabs to the top of Brownstone Wall. Walk left (south) along the top of the formation to the notch (The Gunsight). A very straightforward but bushy descent down the gully will take you back to your pack.

The Rainbow Wall

The Rainbow Wall sits high on the left (south) side of Juniper Canyon and is clearly visible from the Calico Hills and Sandstone Quarry Area. It is characterized by colorful green and black streaks, and huge red arches on the right portion of the cliff. Only one route will be thoroughly described in this guide (the only one I've done), but there are topos included of most of the other recorded routes on the wall. Climbing this formation is not as hideous as it may have been portrayed, although it does require a commitment to hard work. The wall is in the shade most of the day, and depending where you park, takes three to four hours to approach if you're hauling gear. You'll also need to obtain a bivouac permit from the BLM visitor center if you plan to spend the night on the wall. Routes are listed from right to left.

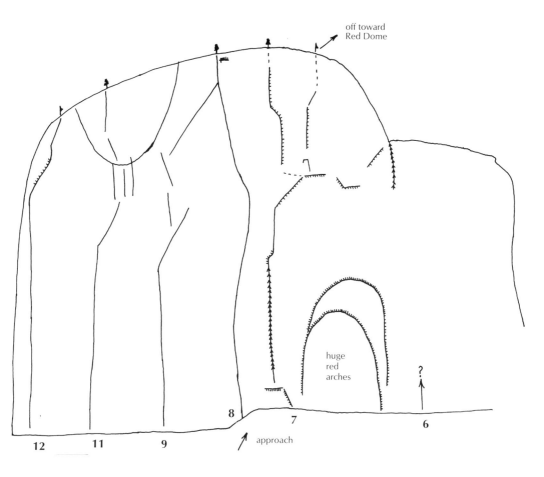

6. **The Kor Route** 5.? A?   FA: Layton Kor, Allison Sheets–1989.
   Supposedly, Kor and Sheets did a route somewhere on the wall to the right of the huge, red arches. The rock appears to be rather dirty and loose in that area.

7. **Original Route**   5.9 A2 or 5.12 ◀   FA: Joe Herbst, Larry Hamilton–April 1973. FFA: Leo Henson–April 1994.

It can be done in a day, but the view of the Las Vegas lights from the bivi ledge can't be beat. In 1993, the route had a number of bolts added to it for free climbing purposes. This has significantly reduced the aid climbing difficulty on most of the pitches. The addition of the bolts has also made it possible to rappel the entire route. See *Onsight Magazine* (issue 2) for an account of the first free ascent. (At press time, all of the new bolts had reportedly been chopped, returning the route to its former aid rating.) Bring a set of Friends, a #4 Camalot, a set of TCUs, one set of wires, a set of RPs, five knifeblades, five Lost Arrows, a couple smallish angles and lots of slings (if you plan on an aid ascent).

Depending on where you park (Pine Creek Trailhead, the Oak Creek spur road or at Oak Creek Campground), you'll need to hike cross country to the mouth of Juniper Canyon. Follow the Juniper Creek drainage upstream for about an hour, to a big, white lump of rock with a pine tree on its left side that divides the drainage in two. The Rainbow Wall is up on the left and Brownstone Wall will be straight ahead (west), at the top of the main canyon. Climb slabs up left (south) for about 600 lung-searing yards to the base of the wall. Photo, page 163.

The route starts roughly 100 feet left of the prominent red arches on the right side of the wall, at an obvious dihedral system.

P1 Start left of a pine tree and wander up the face to a belay ledge with one bolt and a piton. 75 ft., 5.6.

P2 Free climb up, then aid a blank section of the dihedral (bolts). Continue up to a bolted belay anchor. 75 ft., 5.7 A2 or 5.12-.

P3 Lieback a wide crack (5.8); aid up the corner to a sloping ledge. 75 ft., 5.8 A2 or 5.11.

P4 Free and aid up the dihedral past a ledge to a three bolt belay stance above a wide crack. 85 ft., 5.9 A2 or 5.11+.

P5 Free climb up a loose flake, then aid and free up around a ceiling. Belay off bolts in the dihedral above. 110 ft., 5.7 A1 or 5.11-.

P6 Continue up the dihedral past bushes to an easy chimney, and climb this to a ledge with small trees and two bolts. 100 ft., 5.4 A1 or 5.10.

Note: This is the lower left edge of Faith Ledge, a long, multi-stepped ledge that provides an adequate bivouac spot at its upper end (at the mouth of Bat Cave). There is room for two to sit, but if you bring hammocks, better accommodations can be had.

P7 Follow broken ledges up right, then climb a left-facing dihedral to a stance just left of a chimney. Belay from TCUs and Friends. 150 ft., 5.8.

P8 Struggle up the short chimney to a ledge (bolt), then traverse around right and climb an easy but dirty face to a long, flat ledge with a huge pine tree on its right end. Belay from two bolts. 100 ft., 5.7.

Note: This is Over The Rainbow Ledge. It is about 75 feet long, seven feet wide, and can sleep three people comfortably. This is the bivi ledge to shoot for – the view is great!

P9 From the left end of the ledge (V1), traverse left (occasionally with tension) on ledges past a bolt, then face climb up to the base of the red dihedral and a bolt belay. 5.7.

P10 Aid up the huge, left-facing corner, belaying off gear. A2 or 5.12-.

P11 Continue up the arching corner past a couple bolts to a bolted belay. A2 or 5.12.

P12 Negotiate the summit roofs to belay in a cave, or if the rope drag isn't bad, continue up to a tree just below the top of the wall. A2 or 5.12.

P12.5 Scramble to the top. 4th Class.

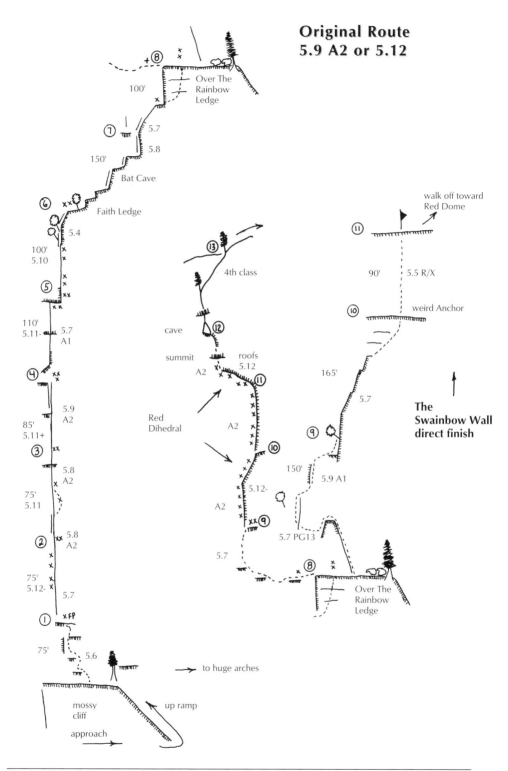

Original Route
5.9 A2 or 5.12

Over The Rainbow Ledge

100'

8

5.7

7

5.8

150'

Bat Cave

6

Faith Ledge

5.4

100'
5.10

5

110'
5.11-

5.7
A1

4

5.9
A2

85'
5.11+

3

5.8
A2

75'
5.11

2

5.8
A2

75'
5.12-

5.7

1 FP

75'

5.6

to huge arches

mossy cliff

up ramp

approach

13

4th class

cave

12

summit

roofs
5.12

A2

11

Red Dihedral

A2

10

5.12-

A2

9

5.7

walk off toward Red Dome

11

90'

5.5 R/X

10

weird Anchor

165'

5.7

9

150'

5.9 A1

5.7 PG13

8

Over The Rainbow Ledge

The Swainbow Wall direct finish

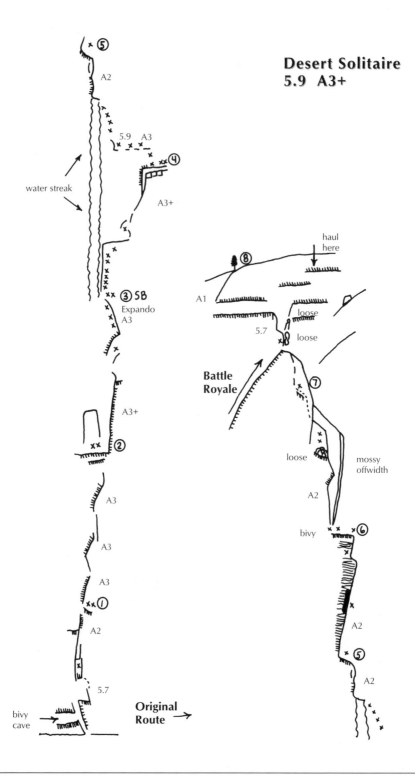

Desert Solitaire
5.9 A3+

⑤

A2

5.9 A3

④

A3+

water streak

haul
here

⑧

A1

loose

③ 5B
Expando
A3

5.7 loose

Battle Royale

⑦

A3+

②

loose mossy offwidth

A2

A3

bivy ⑥

A3

A3 ①

A2 A2

A2

⑤

5.7 A2

bivy
cave **Original Route** →

V1 The Swainbow Wall 5.9 A1 PG13 FRA: Jeff Rickerl, Mark Hoffman, Todd Swain June 1992. A direct (and perhaps more logical) finish to **Original Route**.

P9 From the center of Over the Rainbow Ledge, climb a shallow, left-leaning dihedral to a pedestal. Traverse down and left to the arête (no pro) then up a low-angled face to an obvious, right-facing flake. Climb the flake, angle right into the big, left-facing corner, then up this past a ledge to a hanging belay from a tree (nuts, and Friends). 150 ft., 5.9 A1 PG13.

P10 Follow the corner past numerous ledges, then step around right and angle up right across a face to a belay on a sloping ledge in white, rounded rock. A difficult belay anchor to set up; you'll need lots of TCUs and Friends. 165 ft., 5.7.

P11 Climb the scary vertical face above to the summit. Good training for the Eiger! 90 ft., 5.5 R/X.

Descent: Not as bad as the approach, but it will still take about three hours. Walk south about 300 yards toward the red domes behind The Rainbow Wall, which are at the rim of Oak Creek Canyon. From the top of the red domes, angle slightly southwest down a ridge with rock outcrops. Curve around left (south) onto white rock and follow the ridge and slabs down left to the top of the Oak Creek drainage. It should take about 30-40 minutes from the summit of The Rainbow Wall to the top of Oak Creek Canyon. Follow the drainage down and east (toward the road) past numerous waterholes. You'll eventually exit the drainage on its right (south) bank, and follow a trail and the old road back to your vehicle. If you parked on the spur road, you'll exit left (north) from the drainage, and head towards the road. Not only is this descent quicker than going back down Juniper Canyon, you're much more likely to encounter water in Oak Creek to soak in!

8. **Desert Solitaire** 5.9 A3+ FA: Nick Nordblom (roped solo)–Spring 1989.
    The first major crack system left of the **Original Route**. The gear list and rating suggest that this is the second hardest route on the wall: nine knifeblades; eight Lost Arrows; three small angles; double sets of TCUs, Friends, wires; one set each of RPs and HBs; hooks (including a Bat Hook); one small copperhead; one Crack Tack; one birdbeak; several rivet hangers. There were a total of 40 holes drilled on the route: 14 belay bolts, 18 rivets and eight for pro.

9. **Battle Royale** 5.9 A2 FA: Richard Harrison, Nick Nordblom, Wendell Broussard–Spring 1983.
    Climbs a broken, right-facing corner through the obvious black water streaks. Not recommended.

10. **Crazy World** 5.7 A4 FA: Bart Groendycke, Todd Alston –May 1992.
    The newest and hardest. This climb doesn't go to the top of the cliff and has fixed rappel stations. The route climbs just left of the prominent black water streaks on the wall. The first ascent party recommends fixing three ropes, and sleeping at the base of the route. Gear list: seven short thin knifeblades; 15 RURPs; five Lost Arrows; two hooks, one Fish hook; four ⅜" bolt hangers; 25 #1 copperheads; 30 #2 copperheads; 20 #3 copperheads; 10 #4 copperheads; 25 extra ⅜" copperheads for ladders; three sets of RPs; two sets of Stoppers; three sets of TCUs; two #1 Camalots; one each #2 to #4 Camalots. Topo, page 156.

Holy hideaways: *Bat Cave on Faith Ledge; look for it on the sixth pitch of* **Original Route**, *Rainbow Wall.*

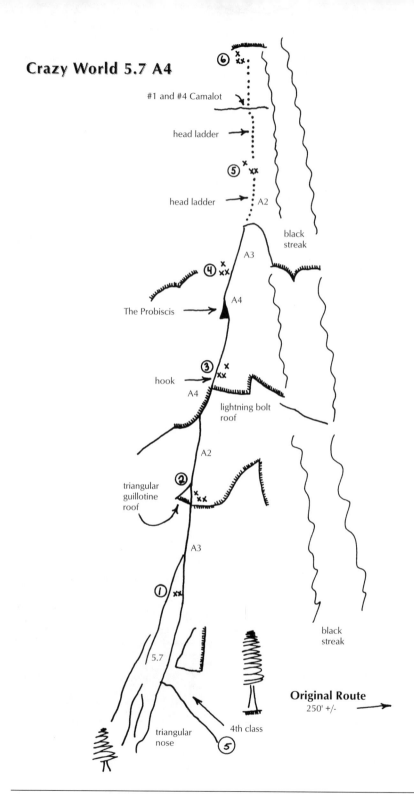

Crazy World 5.7 A4

#1 and #4 Camalot

head ladder

head ladder   A2

black streak

A3

The Probiscis   A4

hook   A4

lightning bolt roof

A2

triangular guillotine roof

A3

5.7

4th class

triangular nose

black streak

Original Route
250' +/-

Emerald City 5.10 A2

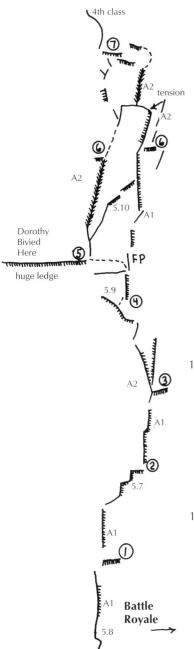
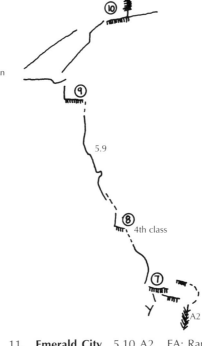

11. **Emerald City** 5.10 A2   FA: Randy Grandstaff, John Thacker–Spring 1983.

The route climbs a series of corners that trend right and lead to the right edge of a large ledge. A big black water streak comes off this ledge. Above, follow either of two corners that start from the right end of the ledge and lead to a shattered recess. Climb through this to the top. Gear needed: four knifeblades; four Lost Arrows; two baby angles; double sets of TCUs and Friends; one set of wires and RPs.

12. **Sergeant Slaughter** 5.10 A3   FA: Richard Harrison, Paul Van Betten–Winter 1984.

This was the first winter ascent of the wall. Follow the corner systems that parallel the left shoulder of the wall for six pitches to a large ledge. Climb behind a large, detached pillar (5.10), gaining the shoulder of the wall. Follow cracks and corners upward, aiming for an obvious right-facing corner capped by a roof. Bring six knifeblades; six Lost Arrows; six angles (up to ¾"); double set of wires; TCUs and Friends (bring a BIG Friend); one set of RPs; and one set of HBs. Topo, page 158.

Sergeant Slaughter 5.10 A3

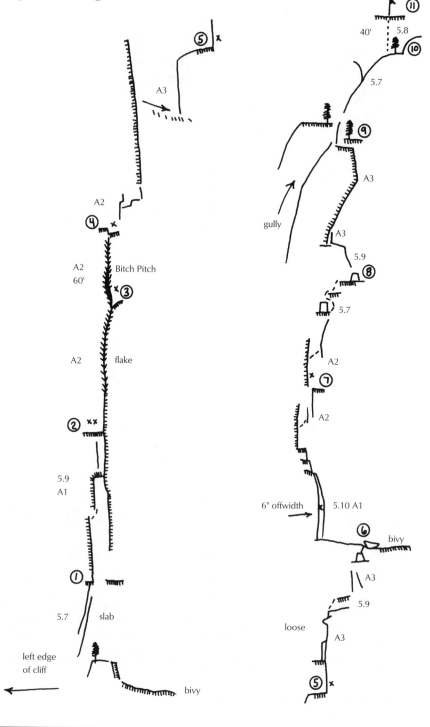

left edge
of cliff

bivy

Sergeant Slaughter 5.10 A3: *Mike Ward and Nick Nordblom on the 11-pitch route (described on page 157). Photo by Kurt Mauer.*

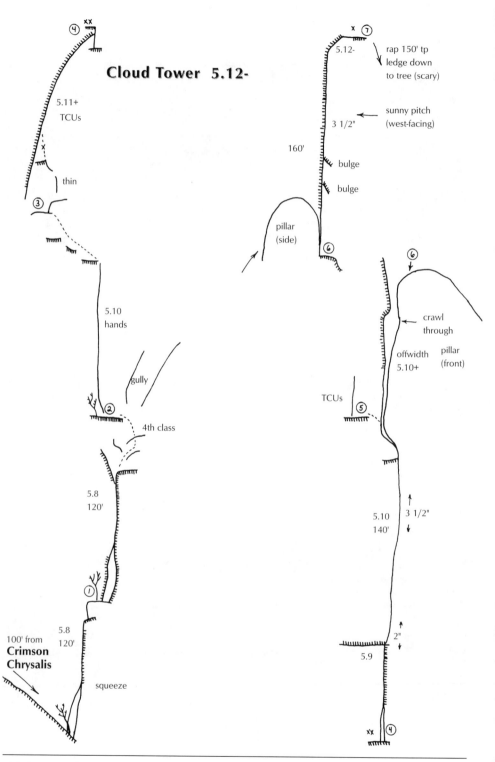

Cloud Tower 5.12-

4 (XX)

5.11+
TCUs

thin

3

5.10
hands

gully

2

4th class

5.8
120'

1

100' from
**Crimson
Chrysalis**

5.8
120'

squeeze

7 (X)

5.12-

rap 150' tp
ledge down
to tree (scary)

3 1/2"

sunny pitch
(west-facing)

160'

bulge

bulge

pillar
(side)

6

6

crawl
through

offwidth
5.10+

pillar
(front)

TCUs

5

5.10
140'

3 1/2"

2"

5.9

XX 4

The Cloud Tower

13. **Cloud Tower**   5.12-   ◄   FA: Paul Van Betten, Richard Harrison, Nick Nordblom–Spring 1983.

Called the **Astroman** of Red Rocks by some; the final pitch is one of the very best in the area.

This climb is located on The Cloud Tower, at the mouth of Juniper Canyon. From the Pine Creek Parking Area, follow the very well-marked trail down the hill, then turn left (south) on the Fire Ecology Trail. Follow this trail until you are closest to the drainage. Cross the drainage, go up a hill on the far side, then angle south across the desert (no trail) to Juniper Canyon. Once you enter the canyon, head up the left (south) slope of the drainage, aiming for a prominent bushy ramp leading up right to the base of a white buttress with a red top (The Cloud Tower). Follow this bushy ramp up right (west) for a couple hundred yards to the top of the ramp, then go down (west) a short way to the base of the route. The approach takes about an hour. Topo, page 160.

Start about 200 feet down from the top of the ramp and 100 feet right of **Crimson Chrysalis**.

P1 Climb a left-facing corner to a belay. 150 ft., 5.8.

P2 Continue up the corner and belay on a bushy ledge. 100 ft., 5.8.

P3 Power up the beautiful straight-in hand crack. 150 ft., 5.10-.

P4 Stem up the right-facing, right-leaning corner with a tips crack in its back to a ledge with two bolts and a loose block. Bring lots of TCUs for this cruxy pitch. 120 ft., 5.11+.

P5 Pull over a roof, then up a hand- and fistcrack in the middle of a face to a belay ledge. 140 ft., 5.10.

P6 Struggle up a scary offwidth to the top of the tower. 60 ft., 5.10+.

P7 Climb the incredible right-facing corner with a hand- and fingercrack in its back. The crux is at the top of the pitch, reaching the bolts. 160 ft., 5.12-.

Descent: Use two ropes to rappel straight down (not down the route), keeping right of the tower. It'll be pretty dicey to reach a couple of the anchors.

14. **Crimson Chrysalis**   5.8+   ◄   FA: Jorge and Joanne Urioste – October 1979.

A superb route that requires crack climbing skills and stamina. Bring two ropes and a good selection of bigger gear. Topo, page 162; photo, page 163.

This long, continuous crack system is located on The Cloud Tower, at the mouth of Juniper Canyon. From the Pine Creek Parking Area, follow the very-well-marked trail down the hill, then turn left (south) on the Fire Ecology Trail. Follow this trail until you are closest to the drainage. Cross the drainage, go up a hill on the far side, then angle south across the desert (no trail) to Juniper Canyon. Once you enter the canyon, head up the left (south) slope of the drainage, aiming for a prominent bushy ramp leading up right to the base of a white buttress with a red top (The Cloud Tower). Follow this bushy ramp up right (west) for a couple hundred yards to the top of the ramp, then go down (west) about 100 feet to the base of the route. This approach takes about an hour.

P1 Climb the obvious crack and right-facing corner to a belay anchor. 125 ft., 5.7.

P2 Continue up the crack/corner past four bolts to another anchor in a recess. 90 ft., 5.8-.

P3 Jam up the same fissure past three bolts and a steep section to a hanging belay from bolts. 60 ft., 5.8+.

P4 Worm up a chimney (bolt), then follow lower-angled thin cracks through two bulges to a belay ledge. 90 ft., 5.8.

P5 Climb a finger- and hand-sized crack past one bolt to a belay station at a small, good ledge. 90 ft., 5.8+.

Crimson Chrysalis 5.8+

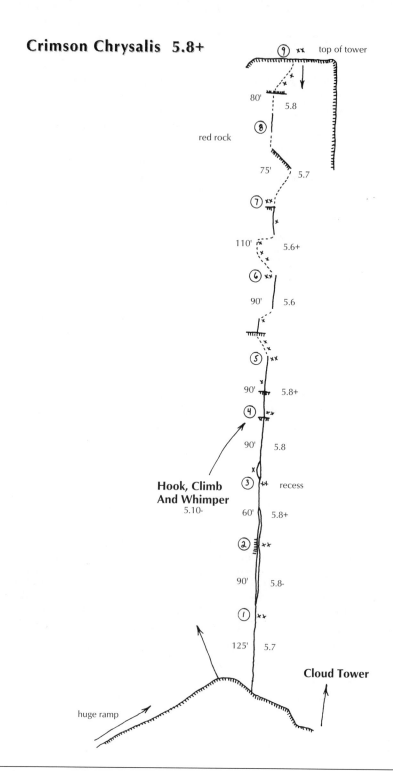

9 xx top of tower

80'

5.8

8

red rock

75' 5.7

7 xx

110' 5.6+

6 xx

90' 5.6

5 xx

90' 5.8+

4

90' 5.8

Hook, Climb
And Whimper
5.10-

3 recess

60' 5.8+

2 xx

90' 5.8-

1 xx

125' 5.7

Cloud Tower

huge ramp

P6 Go up left past two bolts, then up and right past three more bolts to the anchor. 90 ft., 5.6.

P7 Nine bolts will get you to the belay, which is 25 feet into the red rock. 110 ft., 5.6+.

P8 Climb up 25 feet to a ramp (bolt), traverse straight right, then climb up left along a ramp. Climb the chocolate-colored face past three more bolts to the belay. 75 ft., 5.7.

P9 Climb up and right on a plated wall past four bolts and a ceiling to the shoulder of the tower. 80 ft., 5.8.

Descent: Rappel with two ropes, being careful not to get the ropes stuck in the crack.

The Cloud Tower et al.

Cloud Tower
14. Crimson Chrysalis

Rainbow Wall
7.   Original Route

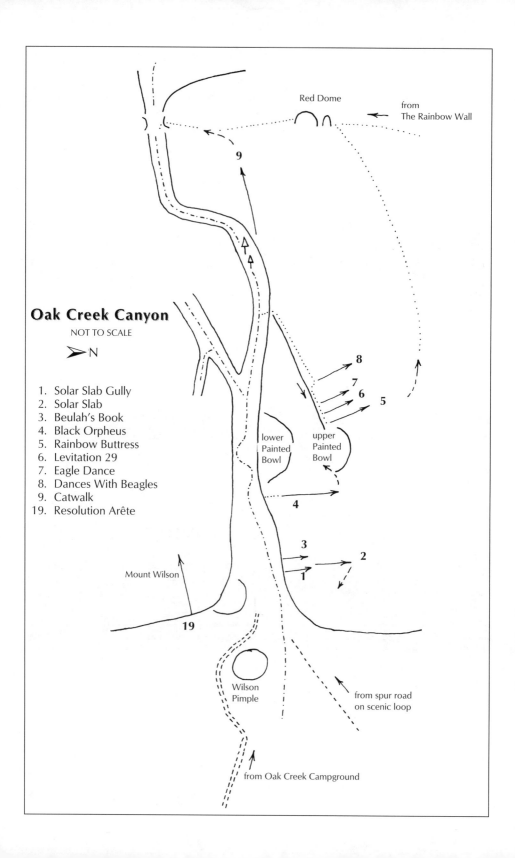

Oak Creek Canyon

NOT TO SCALE

N

1. Solar Slab Gully
2. Solar Slab
3. Beulah's Book
4. Black Orpheus
5. Rainbow Buttress
6. Levitation 29
7. Eagle Dance
8. Dances With Beagles
9. Catwalk
19. Resolution Arête

Red Dome

from
The Rainbow Wall

8
7
6
5

lower
Painted
Bowl

upper
Painted
Bowl

4

3
2
1

Mount Wilson

19

Wilson
Pimple

from spur road
on scenic loop

from Oak Creek Campground

OAK CREEK CANYON

This canyon is on a par with Black Velvet, harboring some of the best routes at Red Rocks; however, the approaches are generally much longer than Black Velvet. Routes are described from right (north) to left (south) starting on **Solar Slab** and ending on Mount Wilson's **Resolution Arête**.

As of press time, there were two ways to approach the climbs in Oak Creek Canyon:

A.) The new spur road leading from near the exit of the scenic loop road toward Oak Creek Canyon has been completed, but can not be accessed before or after normal loop road hours. While this new road and adjoining trail provides a faster approach than via the old Oak Creek Road, the loop road opening and closing times may prove problematic for those attempting the longer routes.

B.) It is also possible to walk the old Oak Creek Road, which begins at the Oak Creek Campground. The campground is located 1.4 miles south (toward Blue Diamond) on Route 159 from the exit of the scenic loop road. From the campground, walk 1.5 miles along the obvious roadbed to the mouth of the canyon.

Both approaches skirt around the huge dirt mound situated at the canyon mouth; the mound is known as the Wilson Pimple. These trails then drop into the main Oak Creek drainage, which is followed some distance up canyon. Each of the following approach descriptions begin at the Wilson Pimple.

Mount Wilson and Oak Creek Canyon

2. Solar Slab
4. Black Orpheus
9. Catwalk

18. Aeolian Wall
19. Resolution Arête

1. Solar Slab Gully 5.3
3. Beulah's Book 5.9-

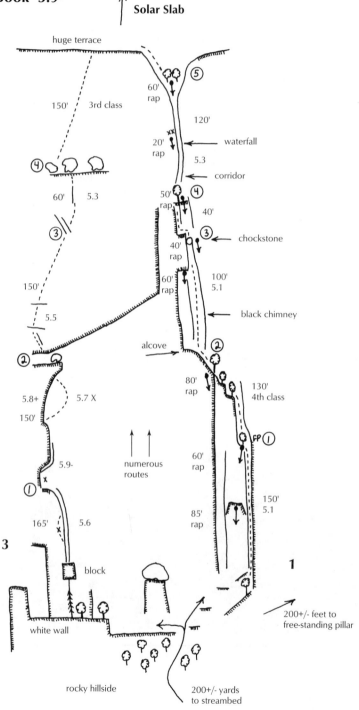

Solar Slab

huge terrace

150'   3rd class

60' rap

⑤

120'

20' rap   ←   waterfall

5.3

←   corridor

④ ○ ○ ○

60' | 5.3

50' rap   ④

③ //   40'

③   ←   chockstone

40' rap

150'

60' rap   100'
5.1

5.5   ←   black chimney

alcove

② ○   ②

5.8+   5.7 X   80' rap   130'
4th class

150'

5.9-   FP ①

① ✕   numerous routes   60' rap

150'
5.1

165'   ✕   5.6   85' rap

3   **1**

block

white wall   200+/- feet to
free-standing pillar

rocky hillside   200+/- yards
to streambed

OAK CREEK CANYON

1. **Solar Slab Gully** 5.3 ◥ FA: Unknown–1970s.

   A great excursion for the novice climber. Most climbers use this as an approach to **Solar Slab** or as a descent from **Beulah's Book**. The route can be rappelled with one rope and all of the anchors are fixed. The crux section is a short waterfall (usually dry) near the top. Photo, page 169; topo, page 166.

   On the far right (north) side of the canyon is a huge, obvious gully running about 500 feet up the cliff to the base of a white face; the gully is the **Solar Slab Gully** and the white face is the **Solar Slab**. From the Wilson Pimple, follow the old roadbed and/or a trail up toward the canyon, until the trail drops into the streambed. Walk up the streambed about 150 yards, then follow a faint trail 200 yards up to the base of the route. The trail ascends the hillside about 75 yards left (west) of the red rock band in the hillside. It takes about an hour to reach the base of the gully from Oak Creek Campground.

   Start at the base of an obvious gully about 100 feet left of a prominent, right-facing corner system (**Beulah's Book**) and 200 feet left of a free-standing pillar (**The Friar**, 5.9).

   P1 Start at the right-hand chimney, near a thin oak tree. Climb straight up a varnished eight-to-twelve-inch wide crack, passing ledges at forty and eighty feet, to yet another ledge with a tree and fixed piton. 150 ft., 5.1.

   P2 From the tree and pin, scramble up the bush-filled gully, then angle up left along ledges past a gnarled oak tree with rappel slings (80 ft). Continue up to a huge alcove at the base of a dark, waterworn chimney. 130 ft., 4th class.

   P3 Climb straight up the black gully/corner and belay on a ledge to the left, just above a chockstone with numerous slings around it. About 60 feet up the pitch, you'll pass a rappel anchor made from a natural thread. 100 ft., 5.1.

   P4 A short and easy chimney leads to a tree in a corridor. 40 ft., 3rd class.

   P5 Walk up the corridor, then ascend a 20-foot waterfall (5.3) to a bolt and piton. Scramble up the gully to the huge terrace. 120 ft., 5.3.

   Descent: Rappel the route or continue up **Solar Slab**.

2. **Solar Slab** 5.6 PG ◥ FA: Joe Herbst, Tom Kaufman, Larry Hamilton–January 1975.

   If you do this one in the summer, it would be best named "Sizzle Slab." A long route, with a long descent. Bring a good assortment of gear, as there are no fixed anchors. Photos, see pages 165 and 169; topo, page 168.

   On the far right (north) side of the canyon there is a huge, obvious gully running about 500 feet up the cliff to the base of a white face. This white face is **Solar Slab** and the obvious right-facing corner system about 100 feet left of the gully is **Beulah's Book**. From the Wilson Pimple, follow the old roadbed and/or a trail up toward the canyon, until the trail drops into the streambed. Walk up the streambed about 150 yards, then follow a faint trail 200 yards up to the base of the routes. The trail ascends the hillside about 75 yards left (west) of the red rock band in the hillside. It takes about an hour to reach the base of the approach gully from Oak Creek Campground.

   The **Solar Slab Gully** approach entails climbing up to about 5.3 in difficulty; it is an enjoyable excursion for the novice climber in itself. The gully is about 500 ft. long, with the most difficult section up near the top. There are fixed anchors up the gully, as it is the descent route for **Beulah's Book**. The gully ends on a large terrace below the white **Solar Slab**.

   P1 Begin on the terrace about 100 feet up and left from the top of the approach gully, below a white slab and an obvious handcrack that doesn't reach the terrace. Climb the slabby face to varnished plates left of the crack. Eventually step right into the crack and follow it to a belay ledge with a prominent bush. 165 ft., 5.5.

P2 Follow the left-leaning ramp/-chimney, passing a ledge about 90 feet up (possible belay here). Continue up the corner above, to belay on a ledge with a dead tree. 165 ft., 5.5.

P3 Traverse right 15 feet, then climb a finger-and-hand crack to a ledge. Traverse right ten feet; follow a small, right-facing corner to a belay stance (#2.5 and #3 Friends; and small wires). 130 ft., 5.6.

P4 Traverse ten feet right and climb a left-facing flake/corner (tricky) to a ceiling. Step down and right to a belay ledge. 150 ft., 5.6.

P5 Climb the obvious hand crack directly above, belaying at a stance in the crack. 150 ft., 5.5.

P6 Continue up the crack, which becomes a right-facing corner. Belay at the pillar's top. 60 ft., 5.4.

P7 Angle right across a white face to an obvious low angled crack. Climb the crack to a ledge, then move right 10 feet and climb a right-facing corner to a huge terrace. 150 ft., 5.3.

P8 Walk and scramble up easy slabs to the base of a varnished, left-leaning dihedral. 150 ft Note: If time is short, you can avoid the final pitch by traversing right around the outside corner, then scrambling to the top.

P9 Climb the corner to the top. 100 ft., 5.5.

Descent: Walk about 800 feet up easy slabs to the bright, red rock. Head right (east) and enter a huge gully system. Two or three rappels may be needed, depending on your downclimbing ability. The descent can be done unroped, if you can down-solo 5.6. In winter months, the gully may contain ice and snow, as it is in the shade all day. The bottom of the descent gully is about 400 feet right (east) of the base of the approach gully.

An alternative descent heads down left (west) at the red rock, and down into the Painted Bowl (as per **The Black Orpheus**).

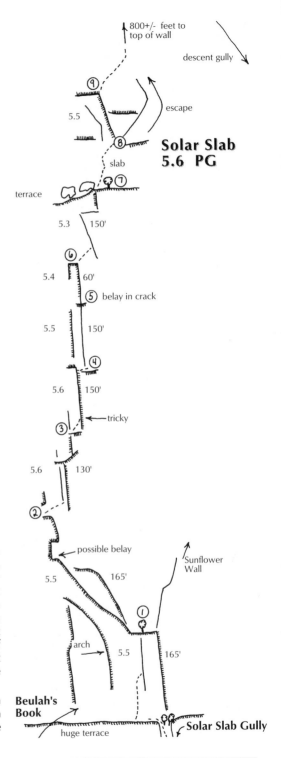

3. **Beulah's Book** 5.9-   FA: Randy Grandstaff, Dave Anderson–1979.
One of the early chapters of this book deals with offwidths. Bring lots of gear, up to a #4 Camalot.

The approach takes about an hour and the climb is in the sun most of the day. For fast parties, it's possible to combine this route with **Solar Slab**, to give nearly 1,500 feet of great climbing. On the far right (north) side of the canyon there is a huge, obvious gully running about 500 feet up the cliff to the base of a white face. This white face is **Solar Slab** and the obvious right-facing corner system about 100 feet left of the gully is **Beulah's Book**.

From the Wilson Pimple, follow the old roadbed and/or a trail up toward the canyon, until the trail drops into the streambed. Walk up the streambed about 150 yards, then follow a faint trail 200 yards up to the base of the routes. The trail ascends the hillside about 75 yards left (west) of the red rock band in the hillside.

Start 100 feet left of **Solar Slab Gully** at a series of dihedrals. This climb begins at the dihedral with a large, jammed block about 20 feet up and an oak tree growing out of the corner's base.

P1 Climb the dihedral past the jammed block (possible belay), then climb the narrow face just left of the chimney past a bolt. Step back right into the chimney, and follow it to a ledge. 165 ft., 5.6.

P2 Continue up the corner/chimney system, passing a flaring bombay section (bolt, #4 Camalot)) to the base of an obvious layback corner. Power up the corner (5.8+, V1) to a ceiling, then step left to a belay ledge in white rock (complicated belay with Friends, TCUs and wires). 150 ft., 5.9-.

P3 Wander up the white face, angling slightly right to eventually belay at some left-leaning cracks. 150 ft., 5.5.

P4 A short, easy pitch leads up to a huge ledge with large boulders on it. 60 ft., 5.3.

P5 Scramble up slabs to the huge terrace that **Solar Slab** starts from. 150 ft., 3rd Class.

V1 It is possible to climb the face to the right of the corner. 5.7 X.

Descent: Either continue up **Solar Slab** or descend the **Solar Slab Gully** by downclimbing and/or rappelling. Only one rope is needed if you decide to rappel the gully rather than downclimb. All the rappel anchors are fixed.

Oak Creek Canyon

1. Solar Slab Gully
2. Solar Slab
3. Beulah's Book

4. **The Black Orpheus** 5.9+ ◄ FA: Joanne and Jorge Urioste– April 1979.

A long route with a short crux. This route is in the sun most of the day, with the approach taking about 1.5 hours. Photo, page 165.

From the Wilson Pimple, follow the old roadbed and/or a trail up toward the canyon, until the trail drops into the streambed. Walk up the streambed as it weaves back and forth across the canyon, then go 200 yards past a buttress that comes down to wash level on the right (north) side of the drainage. A steeper, brown wall is on the left side of the canyon at this point, and it is another 350 yards to the fork in the Oak Creek drainage (if you reach that, you've gone too far). Scramble up brown slabs on the right side of the canyon, aiming for an obvious left-facing corner system with a prominent "V" notch in it. The corner starts about 600 feet above the streambed. The upper part of the approach is over steeper ground, but it's easy.

Start in the first left-facing corner that is right of a large, white, recessed wall at the bottom of a huge, brown buttress. Above, a giant, brown, right-facing corner marks the top of the route. The brown corner is visible from the road, while the rest of the route is hidden until you're in the canyon.

P1 Climb the left-facing corner past two bolts 100 feet up, to a belay in the "V" notch (small Friends for the belay). 165 ft., 5.7.

P2 Continue up the corner (5.8), then climb past two bolts on a ledge to a left-leaning crack. Climb past one more bolt, step right, then up a corner to a large ledge. 165 ft., 5.8.

P3 Diagonal left on a huge ledge for 75 feet, then up vertical and left-leaning cracks to a stance just above varnished rock, on the edge of lower-angled white rock. 165 ft., 5.5.

P4 Scamper up the easy white face to a ledge. 100 ft., 5.0.

P5 Follow a left-leaning crack/ramp to a sloping platform below a steep headwall. 150 ft., 4th class.

P6 Angle left across a smooth, brown slab. Belay at the very left end of the ledges under a small triangular ceiling (Friends for the belay). 200 ft., 4th class.

P7 Make an exposed traverse left for 20 feet to a shallow dihedral (bolt). Climb the dihedral and chimney, then exit right to a belay ledge (nuts and large Friends). 160 ft., 5.9.

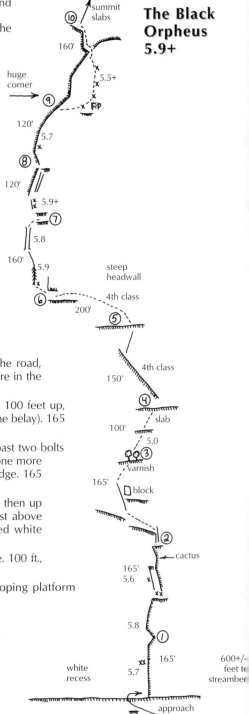

The Black Orpheus 5.9+

summit slabs

⑩

160'

huge corner

120'

⑨

5.5+

RP

5.7

⑧

120'

5.9+

⑦

5.8

160'

5.9

⑥

steep headwall

4th class

200'

⑤

4th class

150'

④

slab

100'

5.0

③

varnish

165'

block

②

cactus

165'
5.6

165'
5.8

①

165'

600+/- feet to streambed

white recess

5.7

approach

P8 Scramble up ledges, then climb a short, steep, thin crack (5.9+, two bolts) to a corner. Jam up beautiful cracks to the second ledge above. 120 ft., 5.9+

P9 Layback up the huge dihedral past one bolt, then traverse right 35 feet to a belay anchor (bolt and drilled piton). 120 ft., 5.7

P10 Climb up the loose pink face past bolts to the dihedral, then exit left out of that into another corner. Follow this to easy summit slabs. 160 ft., 5.5+

Descent: If you have your gear with you, it's probably best to descend down the gully to the right (east) of the buttress, as per **Solar Slab**. This can be done without a rope if you are good at downclimbing; a few rappels can be done if you aren't. In winter months, the gully may contain ice and snow, as it is in the shade all day.

If you left your gear at the streambed below the climb, contour left (west) along ledges in the summit slabs, then go down a ramp. Do an 80-foot rappel (bolt and fixed wire) to a ledge, then walk right (west) 150 feet to the end of the ledge. Another 80-foot rappel (thread and fixed nuts) down a chimney leads to a ledge with lots of vegetation, where yet another 80-foot rappel will put you in the lower section of the Painted Bowl (there are other ways to get here, including a route using two 150-foot rappels directly down from the first anchor).

From the base of the rappels, head down white slabs toward an obvious bench with a large boulder (looks like an IBM Selectric typewriter ball). From the boulder, head right (west) down a low-angled ramp to the streambed. You should now be about 700 yards upstream from your gear and 350 yards above the fork in Oak Creek; head downstream to your packs, and the road.

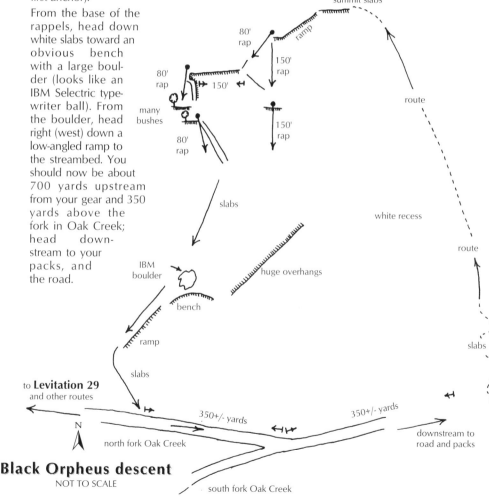

Black Orpheus descent
NOT TO SCALE

5. Rainbow Buttress
6. Levitation 29
7. Eagle Dance
8. Dances With Beagles

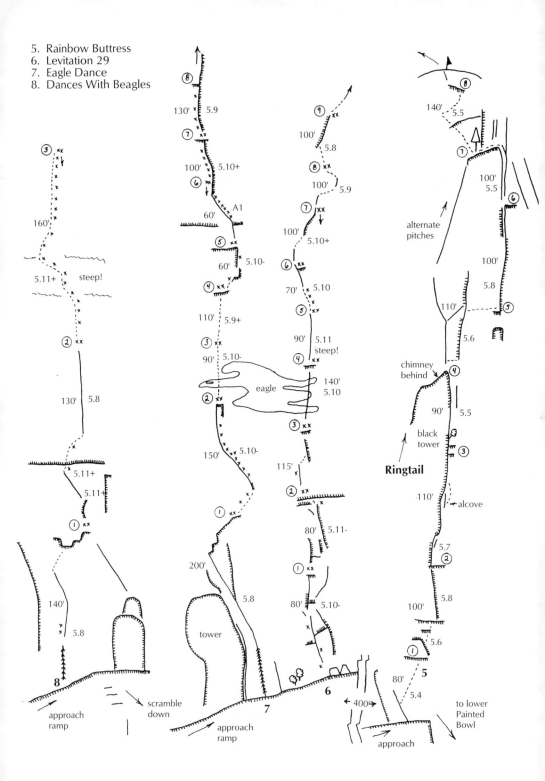

5. **Rainbow Buttress** 5.8 PG ◄ FA: Joe Herbst–1970s.

A great route, but with the long approach and descent you'll need to move fast! Bring a good selection of gear for the belays as well as the climbing (including extra #3.5 and #4 Friends for pitch six).

From the Wilson Pimple, follow the old roadbed and/or a trail up toward the canyon, until the trail drops into the streambed. Hike up Oak Creek Canyon for about an hour, until it splits. Continue up the right (north) fork, until a huge, slabby ramp leads back up right toward the huge cliff band on the right. It is probably best to leave your pack here (see the descent description, page 171). Follow the ramp (some cairns) upward (east) for about 15 minutes to the base of the route. Total approach time is about two hours.

Start at the very top of the huge approach ramp, about 400 feet uphill from **Levitation 29** and left (west) of the upper Painted Bowl. Topo, page 172.

P1 Climb a shallow, varnished, left-facing corner that leads to a wider section of crack. Angle right across the white face to a belay ledge. Friends for the belay. 80 ft., 5.4.

P2 A good pitch. Climb the corner to a huge ledge (5.6) then continue up the left-facing corner to a big ledge with a bush. Nuts and the bush form the belay. 100 ft., 5.8.

P3 Swim up the offwidth above (5.7), then up a corner system to a chimney. Exit right out of an alcove onto the face, then up the main, right-facing corner system to a belay ledge that is 20 feet below a bush. TCUs for the belay. 110 ft., 5.7.

P4 Climb the corner system past a ledge with bushes to a chimney, which leads to the top of The Black Tower. Slings around the summit of the tower and a #3 Friend for the belay. **Ringtail** (5.10) climbs the left side of the tower and terminates at this point. 90 ft., 5.5.

P5 Step across from the top of the tower to a crack, then traverse 15 feet right to a right-facing corner. Climb this for about 40 feet, then traverse 40 right across a slab to the base of an obvious left-facing corner. Belay in the corner (#3.5 and #4 Friends) at a point about 30 feet above a huge pedestal. 110 ft., 5.6.

P6 Climb the obvious left-facing corner past a scary stemming section, a fistcrack and numerous bushes in a chimney. Belay above on a large ledge. 150 ft., 5.8 PG.

P7 Continue up the easy, loose and low-angled crack/chimney system to a huge, sloping ledge with a pine tree. Belay from the tree. 100 ft., 5.5.

P8 Climb the lower-angled face to the left of a left-facing corner, angling up and left to a ledge. Wander back up and right to a belay on a terrace that is 50 feet below the summit. 140 ft., 5.5 X.

Descent: Scramble about 100 yards up toward the canyon rim, then contour left (west). Aim for ramps that lead toward a large, red pinnacle at the right edge of a red blob on the canyon rim. Go around the right (north) side of the pinnacle and blob, then follow a trail down along the canyon rim to the top of the Oak Creek drainage. This should take about 30 minutes. Follow the drainage down and east (toward the road) past numerous waterholes to the base of the approach ramp, a huge pine and your packs. From the top of the route, it should take about an hour to reach your pack at the base of the ramp.

6. **Levitation 29** 5.11 PG ◄ FA: Jorge and Joanne Urioste, Bill Bradley–April 1981. FFA: Lynn Hill, John Long, Joanne Urioste–May 1981.

Considered by many to be the best route at Red Rocks. The climb is on a section of cliff that gets sun all day, and is visible from the road. Bring lots of quickdraws, and the usual assortment of wires, TCUs and Friends up to #3. Photo, page 175; topo, page 172.

From the Wilson Pimple, follow the old roadbed and/or a trail up toward the canyon, until the trail drops into the streambed. Hike up Oak Creek Canyon for about an hour, until it splits. Continue up the right (north) fork, until a huge, slabby ramp leads back up right toward the huge cliff band on the right. Follow the ramp (some cairns) to the base of the route, which is about 400 feet down from the ramp's top. Approach is about two hours.

Start about 200 feet right of a huge, black pillar and 400 feet down from the top of the approach ramp at some varnished cracks leading to a giant roof about 100 feet up.

P1 Climb thin, varnished cracks past four bolts to an anchor. 80 ft., 5.10-

P2 Move right, then go up to the roof. Fire this (bolts) and belay up and left from bolts. 80 ft., 5.11-.

P3 Climb a crack for 75 feet, then angle up right past bolts to a bolted belay at a stance. 115 ft., 5.8.

P4 Follow a crack up the face past seven bolts to an anchor just below a steeper section of the wall. 140 ft., 5.10.

P5 The pumpfest. Follow the obvious crack and 13 bolts to a bolt anchor. 90 ft., 5.11.

P6 Climb seams up left past five bolts to the fixed belay. 70 ft., 5.10.

P7 Pussyfoot up and left along a white, rounded seam to a depression. A bit of "power liebacking" will get you up the right edge of the depression and to the safety of the belay anchors. 100 ft., 5.10+.

P8 Go up and right to a thin crack; when it ends, go left to a belay on a slab. 100 ft., 5.9

P9 Climb up and right along corners and cracks to a right-slanting, right-facing corner. Belay from two bolts, after clipping seven on the pitch. 100 ft., 5.8.

P10 Some 4th class climbing leads to the top of the wall.

Descent: Many people rappel with two ropes after the seventh pitch. If you elect to hike down, walk left (west) along the top of the wall, curving around left (south) onto white rock; follow the ridge and slabs down left to the top of the Oak Creek drainage. It should take about 30 minutes from the summit to the top of Oak Creek Canyon. Follow the drainage down and east (toward the road) past numerous waterholes.

7. **Eagle Dance** 5.10- A1 ◄ FA: Jorge and Joanne Urioste–March 1980.
This route is named for the likeness of a huge eagle (flying west) formed by desert varnish in the center of the wall. This climb goes through the eagle's neck; **Levitation 29** goes through the tail. The climb is on a section of cliff that gets sun all day and is visible from the road. Bring lots of quickdraws, lightweight aiders (or long slings), and the usual assortment of wires, TCUs and Friends up to #2.5.

From the Wilson Pimple, follow the old roadbed and/or a trail up toward the canyon, until the trail drops into the streambed. Hike up Oak Creek Canyon for about an hour, until it splits. Continue up the right (north) fork, until a huge, slabby ramp leads back up right toward the huge cliff band on the right. Follow the ramp (some cairns) to the base of the route. This approach takes about two hours.

Start about 50 feet right of a huge, black pillar that rests against the cliff, at a shallow, varnished dihedral. This is about 450 feet down from the very top of the approach ramp.

P1 Climb the dihedral and crack above to a belay ledge with bolts. This ledge is about 30 feet above the top of the black pillar. 200 ft., 5.8.

P2 Move right and climb past two bolts (use long slings); follow a seam up left past eight more bolts (and a possible belay) to a belay stance atop a block at bolts. 150 ft., 5.10-.

P3 Fly straight up the white face, passing through the eagle's neck and 13 bolts. Belay at a stance with a bolted anchor. 90 ft., 5.10-.

P4 Nine more bolts lead up to a bolt belay on a sloping ledge. 110 ft., 5.9+.

P5 Move up right past one bolt to a ledge at the base of a short, left-facing corner. Climb up loose flakes and a right-facing corner (bolt) to a stance with bolts. 60 ft., 5.10-.

P6 Follow a thin crack up to a bulge, then thrash and dangle out the bulge (8 bolts) to a crack and the belay anchor. 60 ft., 5.8 A1.

P7 Follow the corner/groove and seven bolts to the next anchor (on a ledge). 100 ft., 5.10.

P8 Go up and left in a corner past four bolts to a ledge. 130 ft., 5.9.

P9 Scamper up a corner to the top.

Descent: Either rappel the route from the top of P7 or walk left (west) along the top of the wall, curving around left (south) onto white rock, and follow the ridge and slabs down left to the top of the Oak Creek drainage. It should take about 30 minutes from the summit to the top of Oak Creek Canyon. Follow the drainage down and east (toward the road) past numerous waterholes. You'll eventually exit the drainage on its right (south) bank and follow a trail and the old road back to your vehicle. If you parked on the spur road, you'll exit left (north) out of the drainage to return to your car.

8. **Dances With Beagles** 5.11+ ◀ FA: Jeff Rhoades, Todd Swain–Spring 1993.
Bring gear up to a #1.5 Friend, at least 17 quickdraws(!) and two ropes for the rappel. From the Wilson Pimple, follow the old roadbed and/or a trail up toward the canyon, until the trail drops into the streambed. Hike up Oak Creek Canyon for about an hour, until it splits. Continue up the right (north) fork, until a huge, slabby ramp leads back up right toward the huge cliff band on the right. Follow the ramp (some cairns) to the base of the route. This approach takes about two hours from Oak Creek Campground.

Oak Creek Canyon

Catwalk 5.6+

Start about 300 feet left (west) of **Eagle Dance** at a point 40 feet left of a 50-foot-high pillar and just right of a huge, varnished, left-facing corner.

P1 Climb an easy, varnished dihedral to a steep seam/crack. Follow the seam/crack past two bolts then continue up and slightly left along the fissure to its end. Belay from two bolts on a ledge up and right. 140 ft., 5.8.

P2 Follow a flake above the belay to a thin, left-leaning seam in very smooth rock. Climb the seam and ceiling above (bolt) to an easier face. Move up and right (bolt) to a thin, varnished crack which is followed to a two-bolt belay stance. 130 ft., 5.11+.

P3 Follow 17 bolts up the steep face above, belaying at a two bolt stance. 160 ft., 5.11+.

Descent: Rappel the route with two ropes.

9.   **Catwalk** 5.6+ PG   FA: Margo Young, Joe Frani–February 1975. A good intro to Red Rocks' longer routes. Photos, see pages 165 and 177.

From the Wilson Pimple, follow the old roadbed and/or a trail up toward the canyon, until the trail drops into the streambed. Hike up Oak Creek for about an hour until you reach the point where the canyon splits. Take the right (north) fork, and follow this to the rear of the canyon. The route climbs an obvious left-leaning crack system that passes through two very prominent black water streaks. Total approach time is about two hours. The route is in the sun most of the day.

Start at the base of the water streaks, above several large pine trees in the northern Oak Creek drainage. Scramble up slabs as far as you dare, angling to the right of the rightmost water streak.

P1 Continue up right via roped climbing (if needed) to a belay on a ledge about 400 feet above the pine trees, at the base of the left-leaning crack system. A huge roof is about 80 feet above.

P2 The first of the technical pitches. Follow the left-leaning crack past numerous huecos to a belay ledge just below the roof. 80 ft., 5.4 R.

P3 Continue up the crack past the left side of the roof. Follow the crack to a belay in a pothole, just left of the rightmost black streak. 130 ft., 5.6.

P4 Climb the crack to a right-facing corner with scrub oak. Stretch the rope if you can, to a belay on a spacious ledge (above the bushes) on the left. 165 ft., 5.6.

P5 Continue up the crack into a huge, right-facing corner. Follow this past numerous ledges to a belay below a right-facing chimney/corner on the left. 150 ft., 5.5.

P6 Climb the chimney, exiting left at its top. Belay on the highest of three ledges on the left. 80 ft., 5.6.

P7 The best pitch on the route. Pussyfoot up the steep, black finger-and-hand crack above. As the angle eases, move right to a belay ledge. 150 ft., 5.6+.

P8 Scamper up an easy face to pine trees and the summit. 60 ft., 5.3.

Descent: Head down left (west) into the obvious drainage, and follow the upper part of Oak Creek downstream. The descent is very easy – you'll be back at your pack in less than 15 minutes!

MOUNT WILSON

To the right of the **Resolution Arête** and much closer to the canyon floor is a steep wall with several striking cracks. This 160-foot-high wall is on a satellite peak to the north of Mt. Wilson, west of the Wilson Pimple. The cliff is black on the upper section and lighter-colored near the bottom. It is about 200 yards uphill from the trail leading into Oak Creek Canyon and faces north. Four routes are described, but no more is known about this area since I hadn't been there as of press time.

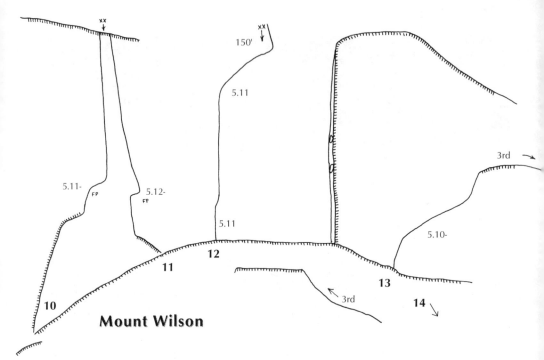

10. **Finger Fandango** 5.11-   FA: Paul Van Betten, Jay Smith, Paul Obenheim–1984.
    Climb a right-facing corner to a fixed peg, then up a fingertip crack. Rappel with two ropes.

11. **Afterburner** 5.12-   FA: Paul Van Betten, Sal Mamusia–1984.
    A thin fingercrack with a fixed pin near the bottom of the crack. It is about 30 feet to the right of the last route.

12. **Eliminator Crack** 5.11+ ◄   FA: Paul Van Betten, Randy Marsh–1984.
    The best pure fingercrack at Red Rocks. Begin 30 feet right of **Afterburner** and climb a straight-in fingercrack. Near the top, angle right for 40 feet to a belay anchor with fixed wires. Rappel with two ropes.

13. **Deguello** 5.10-   FA: Sal Mamusia, Danny Meyers, Paul Van Betten, Brad Stewart–1984.
    Climb the right-slanting handcrack to a ramp. Scramble off to the right.

14. **'34 Ford With Flames** 5.10+   FA: Mike Ward, Bob Yoho–1985.
    Down and right of the last routes is a right-leaning thin crack in perfect white and brown rock. You'll need RPs and small Friends.

Mount Wilson

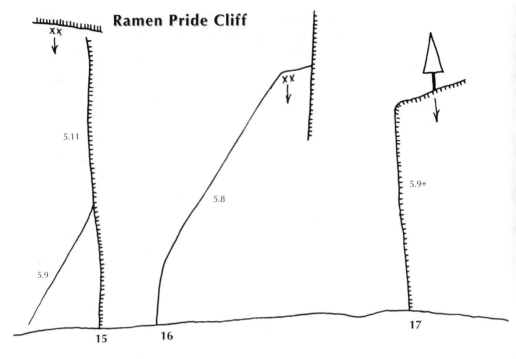

Ramen Pride Cliff

This dark brown cliff is on the very left edge of a gully leading up to the sub-peak of Mount Wilson. This east-facing crag sits very low on the hillside. Routes are described from left to right. As of press time I hadn't been to this crag either.

15. **Ramen Pride** 5.11   FA: Paul Van Betten, Sal Mamusia–1983.
    Climb a right-leaning handcrack (5.9) to a left-facing corner, which is stemmed to the top. Rappel with two ropes.

16. **Zippy** 5.8   FA: Paul Van Betten, Sal Mamusia–1983.
    Start about 20 feet right of the last route. Climb a right-leaning handcrack to an anchor in a left-facing corner. Rappel.

17. **Stemtation** 5.9+   FA: Sal Mamusia, Paul Van Betten–1983.
    Begin about 30 feet right of **Zippy**. Climb the left-facing corner to a pine tree on a ledge.

The east face of Mount Wilson is probably the largest cliff in Red Rocks, although most of it is broken by buttresses and towers. Only two long routes are described on this massive wall, of which I've done neither (yet).

18. **Aeolian Wall** 5.9 A3+   FA: Joe Herbst, Larry Hamilton–March 1975.
    A big route that goes up the center of the face to the right of the **Resolution Arête**. Carry a full rack, including the following pitons: two baby angles, one angle, six Lost Arrows, four knifeblades and two Bugaboos. This route has been done in 11 hours car to car! See the topo on page 180 for what information I could obtain on the route itself.

19. **Resolution Arête** 5.11 or 5.10 A1   FA: Phil Broscovak, Geoffrey Conley–January 1981. FFA: Paul Van Betten, Richard Harrison–1984.
    A big undertaking. Due to the wandering and featured nature of the route, it's nearly impossible to haul gear. Plan to go fast and light, with the second carrying the pack. The

Aeolian Wall 5.9 A3+

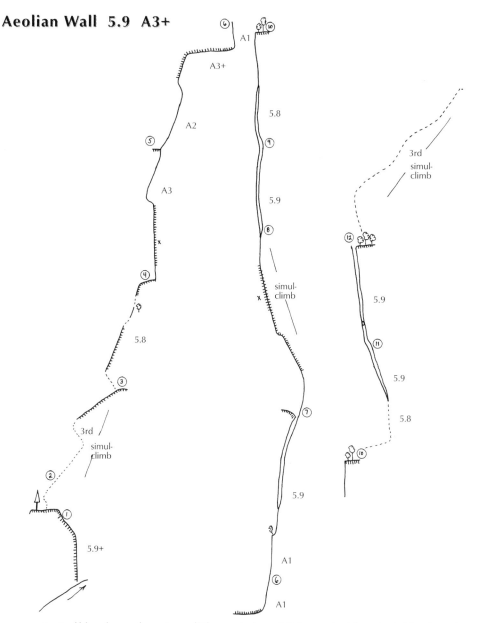

route itself has been done in as little as six hours! Bring a double set of Friends and TCUs, a set of wires and LOTS of slings to cut down on rope drag. There are almost no fixed anchors on the route. Photo, page 165; topo, page 181.

The climb ascends cracks in the right center of a huge, pyramid-shaped buttress, then climbs an obvious pillared buttress that starts just right of a huge, tree-covered ledge (Sherwood Forest).

From Oak Creek Campground, walk along the rough and rocky Oak Creek Road to its end (about 1.5 miles), then follow the old roadbed around the left side of the huge dirt

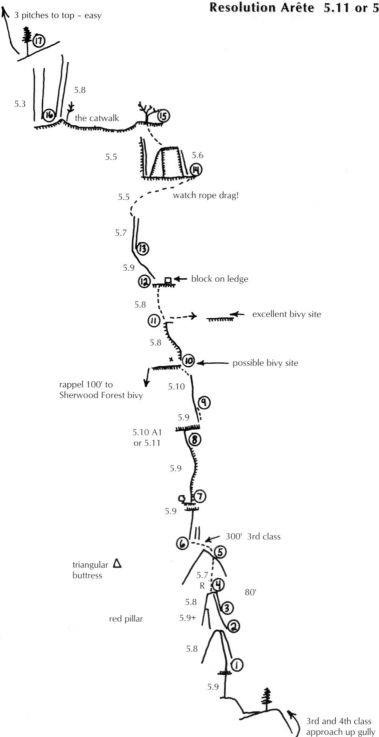

3 pitches to top – easy

⑰

5.8

5.3

⑯ the catwalk ⑮

5.5 5.6

⑭

5.5 watch rope drag!

5.7

⑬

5.9

⑫ ■ ← block on ledge

5.8

⑪ ← → ‒‒‒‒‒‒ ← excellent bivy site

5.8

x ⑩ ← possible bivy site

rappel 100' to 5.10
Sherwood Forest bivy

⑨

5.9

5.10 A1 ⑧
or 5.11

5.9

⑦

5.9

Ⅱ ← 300' 3rd class

⑥ ⑤

triangular Δ
buttress 5.7
R ④
80'
5.8 ③

red pillar 5.9+ ②

5.8

①

5.9

3rd and 4th class
approach up gully

mound blocking the canyon (the hill is called the Wilson Pimple; the large cliff above on the left is Mount Wilson). Angle up left (southwest) toward Mount Wilson, aiming for a gully to the right of a hanging gully/waterfall. Scramble up the gully (4th class) to a ledge with a big tree (possible bivy here). Go left about 50 feet to a chimney that is formed by a huge block and the cliff.

P1 Worm up the chimney, then climb a crack through a ceiling to a dubious bolt. 5.9.

P2 Climb a crack to the top of a red pillar. 5.8.

P3 On the right side of the pillar, climb a very thin corner. Belay in a chimney. 160 ft., 5.9+.

P4 Continue up and left to the top of the next pillar. 80 ft., 5.8.

P5 Climb the white face above, aiming for a point just right of the top of the triangular buttress. 5.7+ R.

P6 Head down and left through a notch behind the buttress, passing a couple of cracks to a steep, loose corner. 300 ft., 3rd Class.

P7 Climb upward, trying to avoid the loose rock in the corner to a ceiling. Pull this and belay in a corner. 5.9.

P8 Climb a right-facing corner to a belay under a large roof. 5.9 PG.

P9 Fire the roof – either free (5.11) or aid – and belay above after some 5.9 face climbing.

P10 Conquer the corner above, then move left to a huge ledge on the left side of a prow. One belay bolt, possible bivy here. 5.10.

Note: Historically, people have rappelled 100 feet down to the Sherwood Forest ledge from here to bivy. Supposedly, there's a shelter there to protect you from the elements.

P11 Head up a left-leaning ramp that leads around a corner, then move up right to a ledge at the base of a steep face. 5.8

Note: If you go right (west) through a notch, there's supposed to be an excellent bivy ledge.

P12 Dance up the steep face and belay on a ledge with a block that's at the base of a left-leaning crack. 5.8.

P13 Hand traverse up the left-leaning crack on friable rock (but good pro) to a belay in a chimney. 5.9.

P14 Slither up the chimney (5.7), then angle up right on a face (5.5) to the right side of a blocky pillar. Belay at the base of the pillar. Watch out for rope drag on this pitch. 5.7.

P15 Climb the chimney (V1), eventually stepping over onto the main wall. Belay up and left on a good ledge with a tree. 5.6.

P16 Shuffle left across a ledge to a chimney on the left (120 ft., 3rd Class, V2). Climb this, then belay at a crack on the left.

P17 Jam up a crack, passing a ceiling to a large, sloping ledge with a big tree. 5.7.

P18-20 Move around left, then climb three easy pitches up to the notch in the summit. 5.2

V1 On the left side of the blocky pillar is an offwidth that leads to the same ledge. 5.8.

V2 The first chimney you encounter (by a dead tree) is 5.8.

Descent: A number of possibilities exist, of which this is one. Walk west to the limestone (about one half mile), then go down a gully to a tree-filled notch (a large, red pillar with a van-shaped block on top marks this particular gully). Descend either gully from here (the right one will require four rappels). Total descent time is about four hours.

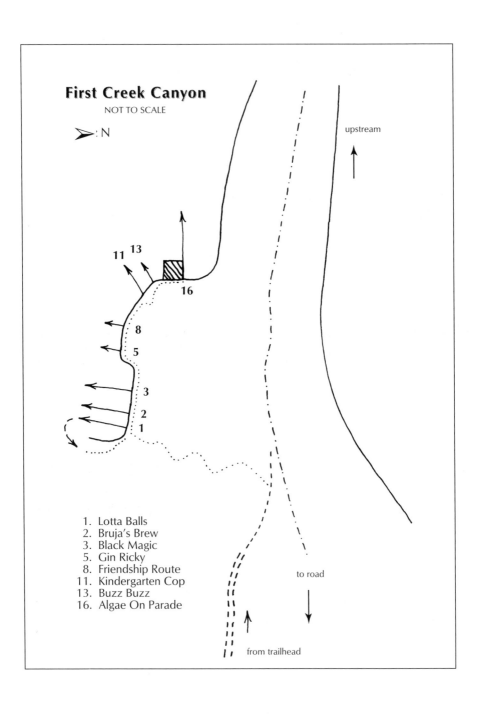

First Creek Canyon

NOT TO SCALE

: N

upstream

11 13

16

8

5

3

2

1

1. Lotta Balls
2. Bruja's Brew
3. Black Magic
5. Gin Ricky
8. Friendship Route
11. Kindergarten Cop
13. Buzz Buzz
16. Algae On Parade

to road

from trailhead

FIRST CREEK CANYON

Lots of rock here, but only a few routes are noteworthy enough to be included in this guide. Park at the First Creek trailhead 0.7 mile south of Oak Creek on Route 159 and follow the old road in toward the canyon (west). When the trail forks, take the Upper Trail (left), then the next left fork when this trail splits again. Stay on the left (south) side of the drainage to the mouth of the canyon. All of the routes included in this book are on the left (south) wall of the canyon as you enter it. Scramble about 150 yards uphill to the base of a varnished buttress with a white top. The approach takes about 45 minutes, and is primarily flat. These routes are in the shade in the afternoon.

Lotta Balls Wall   Romper Room Area

Lotta Balls Wall

1. **Lotta Balls** 5.8 PG ◀ FA: Betsy and Joe Herbst, Randy Grandstaff, Tom Kaufman–March 1977.
   Named for the surrealistic rock formations on the second pitch, not for an inordinate amount of courage needed. Start 50 feet right of a gigantic boulder at the northeast corner of the Lotta Balls Wall and ten feet right of an oak tree growing out of the cliff. Photo, page 186; topo, page 188.

   P1 Climb a series of stacked blocks, then move right to a notch in a ceiling about 20 feet up. Pull through the ceiling into a left-facing corner, then follow a huge white flake up right to a belay stance with two bolts. 100 ft., 5.6.

   P2 Climb the famous marble-studded face above for 40 feet, passing two bolts. Continue up an easy right-facing corner to a spacious ledge. 150 ft., 5.8.

P3 Continue up the easy corner to a roof 75 feet above, then step left and follow an obvious crack. Move left at the end of the pitch to a belay ledge with a tree. 165 ft., 5.5.

P4 Scramble to the top of the buttress. 100 ft.

Descent: Go down a gully to the left (east) of the buttress. Two short rappels and scrambling lead back to the base of the route.

Lotta Balls and Alcohol Walls, Romper Room

Lotta Balls Wall
1. Lotta Balls
2. Bruja's Brew
3. Black Magic

Alcohol Wall
5. Gin Ricky

6. Rob Roy
7. Mai Tai
8. Friendship Route

Romper Room
9. Guise & Gals
10. Girls And Bouys

2. **Bruja's Brew** 5.9 PG   FA: Todd Swain, Debbie Brenchley–December 1991.
    This will cure a powerful thirst! Start eight feet right of **Lotta Balls** below a left-facing corner capped by a roof. Topo, page 188.

    P1 Climb up the corner and crack to the roof, then traverse right to the nose. Continue straight up the face past one bolt, then angle right to a ledge. Go up the obvious crack above for about ten feet, then swing out right on knobs. Climb up a left-facing corner to a belay stance with one bolt and nut placements. 135 ft., 5.9.

    P2 Shoot straight up the varnished face above, to belay about 35 feet below the center of the roof looming above. 150 ft., 5.6.

    P3 Move up to the center of the roof, then angle out left on a ramp system. Belay above in the white rock at a crack. 150 ft., 5.6.

    P4 Continue up the easy white rock to the top of the buttress. 140 ft.

    Descent: Go down a gully to the left (east) of the buttress. Two short rappels and scrambling lead back to the base of the route.

3. **Black Magic** 5.8 PG   FA: Jorge and Joanne Urioste–April 1978.
    Bring your rabbit's foot for the intimidating first pitch. Begin 40 feet right of **Lotta Balls**, atop a boulder and just left of a left-facing corner. Topo, page 188.

    P1 Climb a flake and the varnished face above past two bolts. At the second bolt, traverse right, then up an obvious thin crack. Continue up the crack and varnished face above past one more bolt to a belay stance (natural thread, nuts). 150 ft., 5.8.

    P2 Continue straight up the brown face to a belay in a crack about 35 feet below the right center of the roof. 140 ft., 5.6.

    P3 Climb up to the roof; traverse out right to the nose and a bolt. Move straight up easier white rock to a belay stance in a crack with bushes growing out of it. 140 ft., 5.8.

    P4 Scamper up easy white rock to the top. 140 ft.

    Descent: Go down a gully to the left (east) of the buttress. Two short rappels and scrambling lead back to the base of the route.

Alcohol Wall

This wall plays host to a number of excellent one-pitch routes, all of which are in the shade all day. Bring two 165-foot ropes for the rappel. From the base of **Lotta Balls**, walk right (west) along a ledge system, and go under the boulder that **Black Magic** starts on. Follow the ledge system for 50 feet to the base of a huge right-facing corner. Just right is the start of **Gin Ricky**.

4. **Straight Shot** 5.11+ PG   FA:Paul Van Betten–1983.
    Stem, lieback and power up the short, right-facing corner at the left edge of Alcohol Wall. The top of this corner turns into a big flake.

5. **Gin Ricky** 5.10   FA: Richard Harrison, Paul Crawford, Paul Van Betten, Sal Mamusia, Paul "Obi" Obenheim–1983.
    Bring lots of gear – from wires to a #4 Friend. Begin 55 feet right of **Black Magic**, below a long, right-facing corner. Follow the corner to shaky rappel anchors 180 feet up. Topo, page 188.

6. **Rob Roy** 5.10- PG ◄ 'FA: Richard Harrison, Paul Crawford, Paul Van Betten, Sal Mamusia, Paul Obenheim–1983.
    A bit sporty, but excellent. Bring wires and camming units up to #2.5. Start ten feet right of **Gin Ricky**, below a left-facing corner system. Climb the face past a bolt, then follow the corner past two more bolts to the rappel anchors. 150 ft. Topo, page 188.

7. **Mai Tai** 5.10+ R   FA: Richard Harrison, Paul Van Betten, Paul Obenheim, Sal Mamusia 1983.
    A stiff drink – beware. Begin 12 feet right at a short dihedral capped by a ceiling. Ascend the dihedral to gain the obvious left-facing corner. Follow this past three bolts.

At the third bolt, traverse right past a plethora of knobs to a two-bolt anchor in the large, left-facing corner. 150 ft

8. **Friendship Route** 5.9   FA: Joe Herbst and Friends–Fall 1988.

    Better than it first appears. Bring large gear for the initial wide crack and an attentive belayer for the crux bulge above. Start about 30 feet right of **Mai Tai**, at the right edge of the wall, below an obvious left-leaning corner with a wide crack. Swim up the crack to a ledge (5.8), then climb the steep corner/bulge above past several bolts to a terrace. Belay from a bush and medium-sized Friends. Photo, page 186.

    Descent: Walk up and left on the terrace to the rappel anchor on **Mai Tai** and rappel with two ropes.

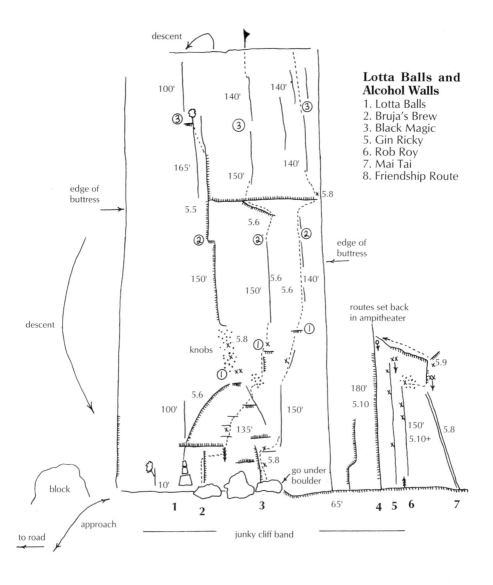

**Lotta Balls and
Alcohol Walls**
1. Lotta Balls
2. Bruja's Brew
3. Black Magic
5. Gin Ricky
6. Rob Roy
7. Mai Tai
8. Friendship Route

ROMPER ROOM AREA

9. **Guise & Gals** 5.4   FA: Jono McKinney, Kimi Harrison, Leslie Appling (NOLS staff)–April 1992.
Sixty feet right of the **Friendship Route** and around an outside corner is a waterpolished dihedral rising from behind a cabin-sized boulder. Climb the dihedral, then move slightly left into a left-facing corner with a bush. Continue up the corner until you can step left to a two-bolt rappel anchor. A 75-foot rappel will get you back to the ground. Photo, page 186.

10. **Girls And Bouys** 5.5 PG   FA: Jono McKinney, Kimi Harrison, Leslie Appling (NOLS staff)–April 1992.
Start 20 feet right of the last route, on the opposite side of the cabin sized boulder at a series of three corners. Climb the leftmost corner for 40 feet to a ledge, then step left and climb the right-hand of two corners (V1) to a two bolt rappel anchor. Carry up to a #3 Friend and rappel with one rope. Photo, page 186.

   V1 Move a bit further left and climb the left-hand dihedral to the anchor (5.4). This can also be reached by starting up the previous route.

11. **Kindergarten Cop** 5.7+ ☙   FA: Donette Smith, Todd Swain–September 1994.
One of the better routes in this area. Bring small Tri-cams, TCUs, Friends to #4 (for placements in pockets) and some long slings. Rope up 30 feet right of **Girls And Buoys**, atop a boulder that sits below a triangular ceiling. Climb through the ceiling at a notch then go up the varnished and white face, past four bolts and gear placements to a communal cold shut anchor. Rappel with two ropes (130 feet).

12. **Magic Mirror** 5.5 FRA Todd Swain, Donette Smith–September 1994.
Carry a good selection of gear for this one. Begin 20 feet right the last route at an obvious left-facing corner that has a varnished right wall. Climb past three ledges, then up the corner to a communal belay consisting of three cold shuts. Rappel with two ropes.

13. **Buzz, Buzz** 5.4   FA: Jono McKinney, Kimi Harrison, Leslie Appling (NOLS staff)–April 1992.
Medium-sized Friends/Camalots needed. Gear up 50 feet right of the last route on the opposite side of a bushy area at a sentry box below a dihedral. This dihedral is 30 feet from a bushy chimney that forms the left margin of an obvious varnished face which is visible from the parking area. Squirm up the sentry box/chimney, then up the dihedral to a two-bolt rappel anchor. Rappel with one rope.

14. **Doobie Dance** 5.6?   FA: Unknown–late 1970s.
Not much is known about this obvious line. Start 40 feet right of the last route at the left side of the obvious varnished face which is visible from the parking area. Climb the crack past a bush to a ledge below a big ceiling. Rappel with one rope.

15. **Romper Room** 5.7+   FA: Unknown–late 1970s.
This one looks harder than it actually is. Bring wires, TCUs and Friends up to #3.5. Watch out for loose flakes in the crack. Climb the crack/flake system in the center of the varnished wall up to a bolt anchor just below a ledge. Rappel with one rope (it just barely reaches).

16. **Algae On Parade** 5.7   FA: Jon Martinet, Jeff Gordon–1978.
Bring a good selection of big gear for this route. Start at the right edge of the obvious varnished wall at a left-facing corner. Climb the corner in three or so pitches to the top of the buttress. Walk off left, going over the top of **Lotta Balls**, then descend as per **Lotta Balls** down a gully (a couple of short rappels are needed).

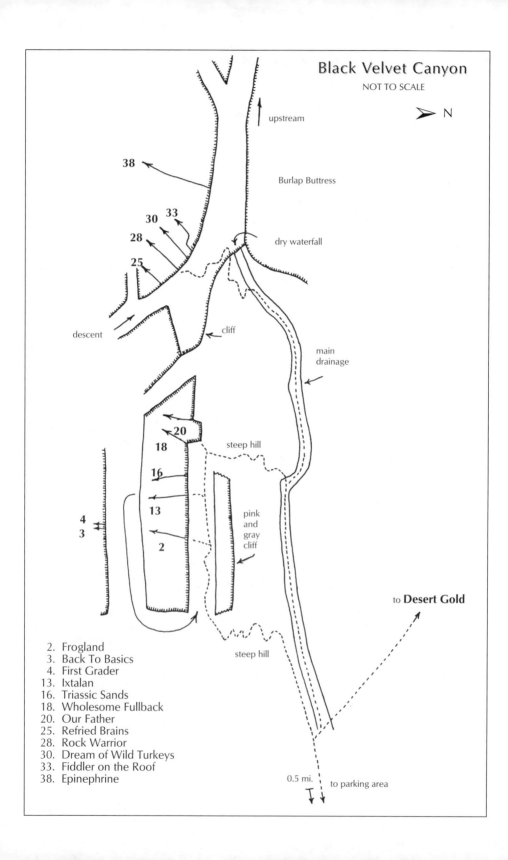

Black Velvet Canyon

NOT TO SCALE

N

upstream

Burlap Buttress

38

30 33

28

25

dry waterfall

descent

cliff

main
drainage

20

18

steep hill

16

13

4
3

2

pink
and
gray
cliff

to **Desert Gold**

steep hill

2. Frogland
3. Back To Basics
4. First Grader
13. Ixtalan
16. Triassic Sands
18. Wholesome Fullback
20. Our Father
25. Refried Brains
28. Rock Warrior
30. Dream of Wild Turkeys
33. Fiddler on the Roof
38. Epinephrine

0.5 mi.

to parking area

BLACK VELVET CANYON

Black Velvet is home to the most famous and classic routes at Red Rocks. The approach hike isn't too long (compared to some of the other canyons) and is actually quite enjoyable. To reach the trailhead, you must drive west on Route 160 for 4.65 miles (from the intersection with Route 159) to a dirt road. If you reach mile marker 16, you have gone too far. The dirt road is not marked by a sign, so keep your eyes open!

Turn right (north) at a cattle guard and follow the dirt road 1.95 miles to the third dirt road on the left. Make this left turn, drive another 0.5 mile to a "T" intersection, then turn right and drive 0.3 mile to the parking areas at the end of the road. To get here, you'll be driving on rough dirt roads, but there is no need for a special type of vehicle. To continue beyond the normal parking areas (to which there is no real benefit) you'll need 4WD.

As of press time, there was one distinct parking area at the end of the passable road and the BLM allowed camping here on a temporary basis. Check with the Visitors Center for the legality of camping at Black Velvet. There is no water, trash pickup or bathrooms, so please do your part to keep this area clean and unpolluted. Again, if we don't police ourselves, there could be major repercussions!

The first routes described will be on the left (south) side of the canyon, on Whiskey Peak. Routes are described from left to right; each has its own approach and descent descriptions.

Black Velvet Canyon

2. Frogland	18. Wholesome...	33. Fiddler...
13. Ixtalan	30. ...Wild Turkeys	38. Epinephrine

1. **Rain Dance** 5.10+ FA: Dave Wonderly, Don Wilson–Spring 1990.

An excellent pitch to round out the day – just watch out for those dark clouds! The route can by toproped after doing the first pitch of **Frogland**. Bring wires, TCUs, and Friends to #2.5. Rope up as per **Frogland** on a ledge above the main terrace. Make sporty face moves up the wall 20 feet left of the **Frogland** corner to a bolt. Continue up thin, right-facing flakes to a ledge. Step left and climb left-facing flakes to a ledge. Rappel from the middle of three bushy ledges with two ropes.

2. **Frogland** 5.8- 🏴
FA: Mike Gilbert, Joanne and Jorge Urioste–May 1978.

The sustained nature of the route may keep you hopping! Bring a good selection of gear, as all of the pitches are long and wander a bit. Photos, pages 191 and 194.

Follow the roadbed about 300 yards from the parking area, then take a trail that branches off right where the road makes a hard left turn. Hike this trail about 0.5 mile, until it forks. Take the left trail (the right fork drops down a hill into the main drainage) for another 200 yards until you are on a red dirt ridge. Follow a faint trail steeply uphill, headed for the left (east) edge of an obvious red and pink rock band below the main canyon wall. Once atop the rock band, contour right (west) about 200 yards to the base of the route. The approach will take about 30 minutes.

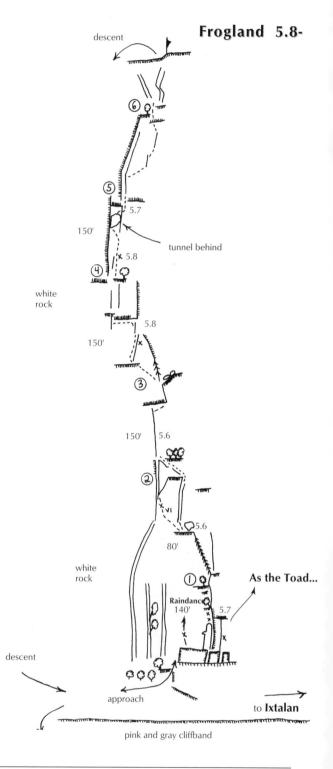

Frogland 5.8-

Start at a clearing on a ledge 100 feet right (west) of a huge, white section of cliff. Between the white section of rock and this route are numerous crack systems filled with bushes and trees. The first pitch of this route ascends a left-facing corner system with a large, white flake at its base.

P1 Scramble atop a block, then climb a left-facing dihedral past three bolts to an obvious sapling. Continue up to the highest ledge with oak bushes on it. 140 ft., 5.7.

P2 Climb a beautiful low angled dihedral above to a ledge (80 ft). Continue straight up the chimney/flake (V1) to another ledge just below a prominent, bushy ledge. 150 ft., 5.6.

P3 Pull a small ceiling, then angle left under the bushy ledge to the main dihedral. Follow this to a bulge, then move right and up to a belay stance in a varnished, left-leaning corner. 150 ft., 5.6.

P4 Angle left across the varnished face to a ledge. Climb the low-angled white dihedral to a bolt, then continue up eight feet to a ceiling. Finger traverse straight left to the arête, then up a thin crack to a stance. Continue up the face and shallow dihedrals above to a stance at a bush. 150 ft., 5.8-.

P5 Face climb up white rock to a bolt, then angle up left into a chimney with a huge chockstone jammed in it. Tunnel easily underneath the chockstone, then step right above it and pull past a white bulge to belay in the easy chimney above. 150 ft., 5.8-.

P6 Scamper up the chimney a bit, then angle right out on the face. Follow thin cracks up to a ceiling and move back left to the corner and a bushy ledge. 120 ft., 5.6 PG.

P7 Scramble up any of the easy routes to the top of the buttress. 100 ft., 4th class.

V1 The original route traversed left to a corner, then went up that to rejoin the line described here.

Descent: From the top of the buttress, head left (east) down a gully toward the road. There are three gullies leading downwards – take the rightmost (southern) one, then contour back around to the base of the route. This is very simple, and surprisingly quick.

There are also two excellent routes on the right wall of the descent gully, about 200 yards from the top of **Frogland***:*

3. **Back To Basics** 5.7   FA: Wendell Broussard, Ed Prochaska–July 1992.
   Start below an obvious, right-facing corner and make difficult moves (using a boulder) into the corner. Rappel with two ropes from a two-bolt anchor.

4. **First Grader** 5.6   FA: Wendell Broussard, Ed Prochaska–July 1992.
   Begin 15 feet right of **Back To Basics**, and climb a beautiful finger crack to face climbing and the bolt anchor.

The following routes are to the right of **Frogland***:*

5. **As The Toad Turns** 5.10+   FA: Nick Nordblom, Jenni Stone, Jay Smith–1989.
   Start as per **Frogland**, on a ledge 100 feet right (west) of a huge, white section of cliff.

   P1 Climb to the top of the initial flake on **Frogland**, then move right into a shallow corner. Go up the corner past a bolt (crux), then right onto the face. Wander up black rock past another bolt to a stance on the arête. 150 ft., 5.10+.

   P2 Go straight up the narrow, black face, eventually moving left into **Frogland**. 90 ft., 5.9.

   Descent: Either finish up **Frogland** or rappel.

6. **Romance Is A Heart Breakin' Affair** 5.10-   FA: Nick Nordblom, Richard Harrison, Brad Ball–circa 1989.
   Begin immediately right of the last route. Climb a crack in the arête that passes through a large hole. Go up and right to ledges (150 ft). Rappel from slings.

7. **Kenny Laguna** 5.10+   FA: Richard Harrison, Paul Crawford, Paul Van Betten, Sal Mamusia–1983.

Begin about 180 feet right of **Frogland**, atop large blocks that are under a huge roof that is about 25 feet above the ground.

P1 Climb a short dihedral under the center of the roof, then follow an obvious break out right through the roof. Climb up to a ledge below a huge dihedral system that starts about 75 feet above the ground. 75 ft., 5.10+.

P2 Follow the obvious corner system upward. 5.10.

Descent: Rappel the route with two ropes.

Frogland et al.

2. Frogland
7. Kenny Laguna
12. Mazatlan
13. Ixtalan
16. Triassic Sands

8. **Perplexity** 5.10+ PG   FA: Todd Swain, Donette Smith–October 1994.
Well worth doing. Sixty feet right of **Kenny Laguna** (and 240 feet right of **Frogland**) at the right edge of a huge roof is a recess with a brown, varnished dihedral 80 feet up. This route climbs the left wall of the recess; **The Misunderstanding** climbs the dihedral. Bring at least doubles of the smaller-sized TCUs, plus wires, Friends to #3 and some long slings.

Scramble up past a couple ledges then step left to a cold shut. Climb past another shut and a right-facing flake to a ledge (bolt). Step left and climb weaknesses to the base of a right-facing corner. Climb the corner and shallow dihedral above past two fixed pegs to a ledge. Move right to the bolted belay atop the second pitch of **The Misunderstanding** (150 feet). Rappel with either one or two ropes.

9. **The Misunderstanding** 5.9   FA: Dave Anderson and partner–Fall 1975.
Two pitches of surprisingly good crack climbing. Begin 60 feet right of **Kenny Laguna** and 60 feet left of the **Mazatlan** corner, at a recess. This recess is at the right edge of a large roof and directly below a brown, varnished dihedral that starts 80 feet up. Bring a full set of Friends, including at least two extra of #3.5, and some long slings.

P1 Scramble up ledges then climb the right-hand crack/corner to a ceiling. Traverse left under the ceiling, then up to a two-bolt belay anchor on a ledge left of the varnished dihedral. 80 ft., 5.9.

P2 Stem, lieback, offwidth and squirm your way up the varnished dihedral to a ledge. Move right around a ceiling then up to a two-bolt belay. 80 ft., 5.9.

Descent: Rappel twice with one rope.

10. **Miss Conception** 5.10   FA Todd Swain, Donette Smith — November, 1994 - June, 1995

Carry a good selection of Friends for the first pitch and lots of quickdraws for the second. Rope up 15 feet right of **The Misunderstanding** below a left-facing corner that leads to a ceiling with white rock on its left side.

P1 Pull past a bulge into the left-facing corner, then up this to a stance below the ceiling. Move up left (bolt) onto a higher, rotten ledge, then go up and right past another bolt to a belay anchor. 75 ft, 5.9.

P2 Climb up along an arête into a right-facing corner, then up the steep face above to a belay anchor. Many bolts to clip and/or hang from. 120 ft, 5.10.

Descent: Rappel with two ropes.

11. **Return To Forever** 5.10+   FA: Richard Harrison, Paul Crawford, Paul Van Betten, Sal Mamusia, Stanley Clarke–1983.

You'll be jazzed after doing this one. Bring two ropes and some BIG gear. Not much is known about this route, as you'll gather once you read the route description. Start about 50 feet right of **The Misunderstanding** and 30 feet left of **Mazatlan** at some huge blocks. Topo, page 195.

P1 Climb the prominent offwidth through the roof and belay above. 5.10+.

P2 Continue upward. 5.10.

P3 Continue upward. 5.8.

Descent: Rappel the route.

12. **Mazatlan** 5.10+ ◀   FA: Dave Anderson, Randy Grandstaff–1978.

A classic pitch to a shaky belay anchor. Bring a good selection of gear, as well as two ropes for the rappel. Photos, pages 194 and 197; topo, page 195.

From the parking area, follow the roadbed toward the canyon for about 300 yards, then take a trail that branches off right when the road makes a hard left turn. Hike this trail about 0.5 mile, until it forks. Take the right fork and drop down into the drainage. Follow the rocky creekbed up for about 300 yards, until you reach a trail leading steeply up left (south). Take this trail upward, skirting the right (west) edge of a pink rockband below the main canyon wall. You should now be roughly below **Wholesome...** and will need to contour left (toward the road; east) about 100 yards to reach the base of this route.

Start 300 feet right of **Frogland** at a clean, varnished dihedral that is six feet left of **Ixtalan** (the obvious offwidth splitting a roof about 100 feet above the ground). Climb the corner/dihedral to a belay station under a ceiling. The crux is right at the start. Two-rope rap.

13. **Ixtalan** 5.11 ◀   FA: Jorge and Joanne Urioste, Dan "Spiderman" Goodwin–June 1981.

Sharpen your off-width skills before trying this one! The bolts next to the offwidth on pitch three were placed on aid, using a giant wooden Friend! Photos, pages 191, 194, 197; topo, page 195.

To approach this route, follow the roadbed for about 300 yards from the parking area, then take a trail that branches off right where the road makes a hard left turn. Hike this trail toward the cliffs for about 0.5 mile, until it forks. Take the right fork and drop down into the drainage. Follow the rocky creekbed upstream for about 300 yards, until you reach a trail leading steeply up left (south). Take this trail upward, skirting the right (west) edge of a pink rock band below the main canyon wall. You should now be roughly below **Wholesome Fullback** and will need to contour left (toward the road; east) about 100 yards to reach the base of this route. Approach time is roughly 30 minutes.

Rope up directly below the obvious offwidth crack splitting a roof about 100 feet above, and six feet right of a beautiful varnished dihedral.

P1 Power up a shallow right-facing corner past four bolts with red hangers, then angle right past three more bolts to a hanging belay at the base of **Ixtalan**'s crack. 70 ft., 5.11c

Mazatlan area

11 Return To Forever
12. Mazatlan
13. Ixtalan
14. Sand Felipe

15 Sandblast
16. Triassic Sands
16 V1. Cole Essence

P2 Layback and jam up the widening crack to another hanging belay. 60 ft., 5.10-.

P3 The longest 60-foot pitch you'll ever do! Struggle up the offwidth, then lieback through the roof to a belay stance with bolts. 60 ft., 5.11-.

Descent: Continue up the easy chimney above (not too interesting) or rappel the route.

*NOTE: There is an old route that climbs the blunt arête between **Ixtalan** and **Sand Felipe**. A belay station is visible about 150 feet up, under a small ceiling. No more is known about the route.*

14. **Sand Felipe** 5.10- PG13 FA: Unknown–Fall 1994.
    Climb the face just left of **Sandblast** past nine bolts to a chain anchor. Take care getting to the second bolt – there's groundfall potential. Rappel with two ropes. Topo, page 195; photo, page 197.

15. **Sandblast** 5.10- R FA: Joe Herbst, Larry Hamilton–May 1972. FFA: Paul Van Betten, Nick Nordblom–Fall 1987.
    The first pitch of this route climbs the original aid line of **Triassic Sands**. It then trends left and continues upward for two pitches of additional climbing. Topo, page 195; photo, page 197.

    Approach this somewhat loose climb by following the roadbed for about 300 yards from the parking area, then take a trail that branches off right where the road makes a hard left turn. Hike this trail toward the canyon about 0.5 mile, until it forks. Take the right fork and drop down into the drainage. Follow the rocky creekbed up for about 300 yards, until you reach a trail leading steeply up left (south). Take this trail upward, skirting the right (west) edge of a pink rock band below the main canyon wall. You should now be roughly below **Wholesome Fullback** and will need to contour left (toward the road; east) about 200 feet until below a striking finger-and-hand crack (**Triassic Sands**).

    Begin at an obvious left-facing flake/corner with a wide crack in its back.

    P1 Climb a left-facing chimney formed by a giant flake (V1) to a ledge. Follow a thin, vertical crack system for about 50 feet to an old bolt. Move right to a wider crack and follow this up to join **Triassic Sands** to a stance with two cold shuts. 150 ft., 5.10-.

    P2 Go left, then climb a thin seam and loose flakes to a belay. 120 ft., 5.9+.

    P3 A short, easy pitch up a wide crack leads to a ledge. 50 ft., 5.7.

    V1 Climb the arête on the right edge of the chimney. 5.9 R.

    Descent: Rappel with two ropes.

16. **Triassic Sands** 5.10 ◀ FA: Joe Herbst, Larry Hamilton–May 1972. FFA: Augie Klien, Tom Kaufman, Randy Grandstaff, Chris Robbins, Joe Herbst–Spring 1979.
    An old route, on even older rock! Bring numerous pieces in the 3" range for the second pitch. Many people rappel with two ropes from the top of the third pitch. If you continue above, there are no fixed anchors. Photos, pages 194 and 197; topo, page 195.

    Approach this route by following the roadbed for about 300 yards from the parking area, then take a trail that branches off right where the road makes a hard left turn. Hike this trail toward the canyon about .5 mile, until it forks. Take the right fork and drop down into the drainage. Follow the rocky creekbed up for about 300 yards, until you reach a trail leading steeply up left (south). Take this trail upward, skirting the right (west) edge of a pink rock band below the main canyon wall. You should now be roughly below **Wholesome Fullback** and will need to contour left (toward the road; east) about 200 feet until below a striking, finger-and-hand crack. You'll be at the base of the climb about 30 minutes after leaving your car.

    Start 100 feet right of the prominent **Ixtalan** crack system and 20 feet right of a left-facing flake/corner; at a left-facing corner with a three-inch crack in it.

P1 Climb the left-facing corner to a ledge at the base of a striped dihedral. 40 ft., 5.7

P2 Step left (V1) and jam the slightly left-leaning fingercrack past a ceiling, then continue up the hand and fist crack to a belay stance with two cold shuts. 100 ft., 5.10.

P3 Continue up the crack past a block, then up one of two cracks to a good ledge with bolts. 160 ft., 5.8.

P4 Climb the right-facing corner to another ledge (no fixed anchors). 160 ft., 5.10-.

P5, P6 Two easy pitches up a series of broken corners lead to the top of the buttress.

V1 Cole Essence 5.11   FA: Charles Cole, Randy Grandstaff–circa 1990. Climb the striped dihedral, exiting right to a belay station on the arête. Either rappel or continue up **Archeopteryx**. Photo, page 197.

Descent: Either rappel from the top of the third pitch (two 150-foot rappels) or from the top of the buttress, head left (east) down a gully toward the road. There are three gullies leading downward – take the rightmost (southern) one, then contour back around to the base of the route. This is very simple and surprisingly quick.

17. **Archeoptryx** 5.11 R   FA: Nick Nordblom, Lynn Robison–Fall 1988.
Named for a fossilized bird-type thing of the Jurassic period (the age of dinosaurs). To approach this route, follow the roadbed for about 300 yards from the parking area, then take a trail that branches off right where the road makes a hard left turn. Hike this trail toward the cliffs for about 0.5 mile, until it forks. Take the right fork and drop down into the drainage. Follow the rocky creekbed upstream for about 300 yards, until you reach a trail leading steeply up left (south). Take this trail upward, skirting the right (west) edge of a pink rock band below the main canyon wall. You should now be roughly below **Wholesome Fullback** and will need to contour left (toward the road; east) to reach the base of this route. This approach should take about 30 minutes.

Start either atop **Cole Essence** (a variation to **Triassic Sands**) or in the gully to the right of the prominent **Triassic Sands** crack. The route basically follows the arête above the **Cole Essence** dihedral for three pitches.

P1 Angle out left from the gully and climb past bolts to a belay. 5.10- R.

P2 Continue up the arête past more bolts to another belay. 5.10-.

P3 Scary and difficult climbing up the arête leads to another belay. 5.11 R.

Descent: Rappel the route with two ropes.

18. **Wholesome Fullback** 5.10-   FA: Cal Folsom, Lars Holbeck–May 1975.
An excellent route that can be done to round out your day. The route name was derived from the first ascent party's last names. Bring gear up to a # 4 Friend, with emphasis on the 1" to 3" sizes. Photos, pages 191 and 200; topo, page 201.

This route can be approached by following the roadbed for about 300 yards from the parking area, then taking a trail that branches off right where the road makes a hard left turn. Hike this trail toward the canyon for about .5 mile, until it forks. Take the right fork and drop down into the drainage. Follow the rocky creekbed upstream for about 300 yards, until you reach a trail leading steeply up left (south). Take this trail upward, skirting the right (west) edge of a pink rock band below the main canyon wall. You should now be roughly below **Wholesome Fullback**, which climbs the left side of a prominent pillar that only goes partway up the cliff. The approach takes roughly half an hour.

Begin 200 feet right of the **Triassic Sands** finger-and-hand crack, and about ten feet right of a right-facing corner, below an obvious fingercrack in a brown, varnished slab.

P1 Climb the slabby face to reach the crack, then follow this past a ledge to an overhang. Jog right, then continue up the crack to a belay at the base of a chimney. 150 ft., 5.10-.

P2 Follow the chimney to the top of the pillar. 100 ft., 5.8.

Descent: Go down **Our Father**, on the right (west) side of the pillar in three short rappels.

Wholesome Fullback Area

18. Wholesome Fullback
19. The Delicate Sound Of Thunder
20. Our Father
21. Tales From The Gripped
25. Refried Brains

NOTE: A route has been done between **Wholesome Fullback** *and* **The Delicate Sound Of Thunder**, *but no more is known.*

19. **The Delicate Sound Of Thunder** 5.11 PG13 ◀ FA: Dave Wonderly, Marge Floyd, Dave Evans–November 1988.

As awesome as it sounds! Not for the faint of heart. Your rack should include a bit of gear up to a #2 Friend.

This route is best approached by following the road from the parking area for about 300 yards, then taking a trail that branches off right where the road makes a hard left turn. Hike this trail toward the canyon for about .5 mile, until it forks. Take the right fork and

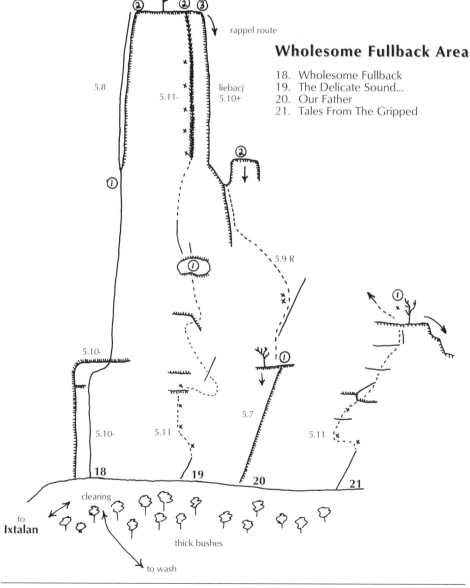

Wholesome Fullback Area

18. Wholesome Fullback
19. The Delicate Sound...
20. Our Father
21. Tales From The Gripped

drop down into the drainage. Follow the rocky creekbed up for about 300 yards, until you reach a trail leading steeply up left (south). Take this trail upward, skirting the right (west) edge of a pink rock band below the main canyon wall. You should now be roughly below **Wholesome Fullback**, which climbs the left side of a prominent pillar that only goes partway up the cliff. This approach should take about 30 minutes.

Start about 50 feet right of **Wholesome Fullback**, at a short, small, right-leaning corner. This left-facing corner is about ten feet left of **Our Father**.

P1 Wander up the face past four bolts, making difficult moves past the second bolt. Traverse right from the fourth bolt, making 5.10 moves way out. Climb up to a ceiling, then swing around right and up the face to an alcove (funky anchors, nothing good fixed). 140 ft., 5.11 PG13.

P2 Climb a short crack above the alcove, then continue up the obvious arête past five bolts to the top of the pillar. Excellent positions! 100 ft., 5.11-.

Descent: Rappel down **Our Father**, on the right (west) side of the pillar in three short rappels (only one rope needed).

20. **Our Father** 5.10+ R   FA: Rick Wheeler, Joe Herbst, Randy Grandstaff, Vern Clevenger (of Tuolumne fame)–Spring 1977.
Say your prayers before leading the second pitch! Bring extra 2" to 3.5" gear. Photo, page 200; topos, pages 201 and 203.

This route is best approached by following the road from the parking area for about 300 yards, then taking a trail that branches off right when the road makes a hard left turn. Hike this trail toward the canyon for about 0.5 mile, until it forks. Take the right fork and drop down into the drainage. Follow the rocky creekbed up for about 300 yards, until you reach a trail leading steeply up left (south). Take this trail upward, skirting the right (west) edge of a pink rock band below the main canyon wall. You should now be roughly below the route, which climbs the right side of a prominent pillar that only goes partway up the canyon wall. This approach will take about 30 minutes.

Begin 60 feet right of **Wholesome Fullback**, at a right-leaning crack/corner and below a prominent, white, right-facing corner marking the right side of a pillar leaning against the main canyon wall.

P1 A fun pitch in itself. Climb the right-leaning crack/corner to a belay ledge with a tree. 60 ft., 5.7.

P2 Climb up the face to doubled bolts, then angle left into the obvious right-facing corner. Belay above, atop a block (fixed anchor). 100 ft., 5.9 R.

P3 Jam and layback up the perfect right-facing corner above. 50 ft., 5.10+.

Descent: Three short rappels (only one rope needed) will get you down.

21. **Tales From The Gripped** 5.11   FA: Todd Swain, Elaine Mathews (of *Vulgarian Digest* fame)–November 1990.
Don't worry, it's not that scary! Bring gear up to a # 2.5 Friend and two ropes to rappel. Photo, page 200; topos, pages 201 and 203.

Approach this route by following the roadbed for about 300 yards from the parking area, then take a trail that branches off right where the road makes a hard left turn. Hike this trail about 0.5 mile, until it forks. Take the right fork and drop down into the drainage. Follow the rocky creekbed upstream for about 300 yards, until you reach a trail leading steeply up left (south). Take this trail upward, skirting the right (west) edge of a pink rock band below the main canyon wall. You should now be roughly below **Our Father**, which climbs the right side of a prominent pillar that only goes partway up the canyon wall. It'll take about 30 minutes to reach the routes in this area. Start 20 feet right of **Our Father** at the next set of parallel, right-slanting cracks.

P1 Climb the crack to its end (bolt), then move straight left to another bolt. Make difficult face moves up to a ceiling, passing a third bolt. Swing right around the ceiling and up to a belay ledge with a bolt and small tree. 60 ft., 5.11.

P2 Go left up a ramp, then climb the arête past two bolts (5.10). Move back right to a flake and a long, right-facing corner. Higher up the corner, follow bolts out right to a hanging belay. 130 ft., 5.10.

P3 Climb past two bolts to an overlap. Pull this (5.10), then angle left to a stance (bolt). Follow two more bolts up left toward a right-facing corner, then angle back right on sloping holds to a vertical seam. Climb up along this to a belay station. 90 ft., 5.11.

Descent: Rappel the two upper pitches with two ropes, then walk off west from the top of the first pitch.

22.. **Only The Good Die Young** 5.11
FA: The Uriostes–1984. This route climbs dihedral systems on the buttress to the right of the **Wholesome Fullback** buttress, and across the gully from **Cutting Edge**. Jay Smith was pictured on the route in an old issue of *Rock & Ice* magazine, but unfortunately, I don't have a lot of info on the route. It has four pitches; they are supposedly rated 5.10+, 5.10, 5.11 and 5.7+. Apparently, the descent is down the gully to the right, between Whiskey Peak and Black Velvet Wall.

20. Our Father
21. Tales From The Gripped

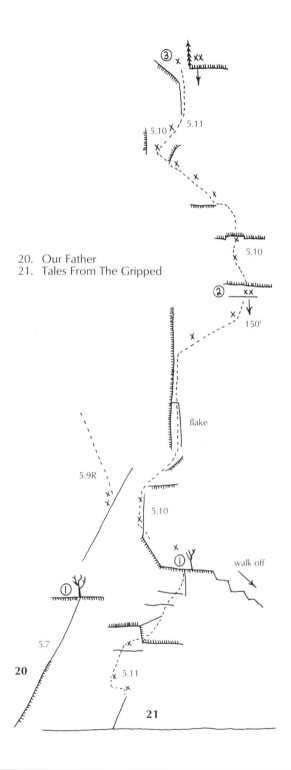

BLACK VELVET CANYON • 203

Black Velvet Wall

25. Refried Brains
27. Sandstone Samurai
28. Rock Warrior
29. The Prince of Darkness
30. Dream Of Wild Turkeys
31. Yellow Brick Road

32. The Gobbler
33. Fiddler On The Roof
35. My Little Pony
36. Velveeta
38. Epinephrine

The next routes are on Black Velvet Wall itself. This wall is separated from Whiskey Peak by a series of large gullies. These 16 routes are described from left to right and are in the shade most of the day (all day in the winter).

23. **Cutting Edge** 5.11   FA: Danny Meyers–1987.
An excellent one-pitch route. The initial 5.10 corner can be climbed up to some fixed nuts to round out a day. Start about 100 yards left of **Refried Brains** and 100 feet uphill from **Smooth As Silk**. Climb a very thin crack up a shallow corner (5.10, V1), step right and do a hand traverse up and right past bolts to a bolted belay (120 ft). Rap off.

   V1 Spark Plug 5.10   FA: Paul Van Betten, Sal Mamusia–1983. Continue straight up the corner to belay slings (150 ft). This was actually done before **Cutting Edge**; and the crux of the route is the initial corner.

24. **Smooth As Silk** 5.10+ PG13   FA: Jay Smith, Paul Crawford, Randy Grandstaff, Dave Diegleman–1981.
Bring small TCUs and wires. Approach this route by following the roadbed for about 300 yards from the parking area, then take a trail that branches off right where the road makes a hard left turn. Hike this trail toward the canyon for about 0.5 mile, until it forks. Take the right fork and drop down into the drainage. Follow the rocky creekbed upstream for about 600 yards until the drainage is blocked by a cliff. Go left (southeast) into the bushes on a path, then scramble up the cliff on big ledges. Follow the trail up left about 100 yards to the base of the large, smooth wall. Continue up along the base of the wall for about another 200 yards, the last of which will be in a large gully.

   Start just right of an obelisk leaning against the wall, at a pair of right-leaning cracks.

   P1 Climb a corner/crack that goes right, then up leaning cracks on a smooth face to a belay anchor in an alcove. 140 ft., 5.10.

   P2 Go up an obvious, big, flaring corner to anchors. 150 ft., 5.10.

   Descent: Rappel with two ropes.

25. **Refried Brains** 5.9   FA: Joanne and Jorge Urioste, Stephanie Petrilak–November 1979.
A good pun – the route is OK, too. Bring two ropes to rappel the route and large gear for the wide cracks. Photo, page 200; topo, page 206.

   Approach this climb by following the road for about 300 yards from the parking area, then take a trail that branches off right where the road makes a hard left turn. Hike this trail toward the canyon for about .5 mile, until it forks. Take the right fork and drop down into the drainage. Follow the rocky creekbed upstream for about 600 yards until the drainage is blocked by a cliff. Go left (southeast) into the bushes on a path, then scramble up the cliff on big ledges. Follow the trails up left about 100 yards to the base of the large, smooth wall. This section of cliff has some of the best routes in all of Red Rocks. **Refried Brains** is at the left margin of this wall and starts near the base of an obvious tree-filled gully leading up left (southeast). Plan on 30 minutes for the approach hike.

   Start about 160 feet right of **Smooth As Silk** and 40 feet left of a huge block leaning against the base of the crag.

   P1 Climb a crack up and right past a bolt to reach an obvious crack. Follow this to a small left-facing corner. At the top of the corner, step left to a belay below a prominent, right-facing corner. 130 ft., 5.8+.

   P2 Step left then climb up via face, crack and a right-facing corner – the last twenty feet of which becomes a chimney/slot. Stretch the rope to belay atop a pillar at the "tree-of-a-thousand-slings." 160 ft., 5.8+.

   P3 Traverse straight right on a shelf for twenty feet to reach a crack. Follow this up past a couple of offwidth sections to a hanging belay in the crack. 145 ft., 5.9.

Refried Brains
5.9

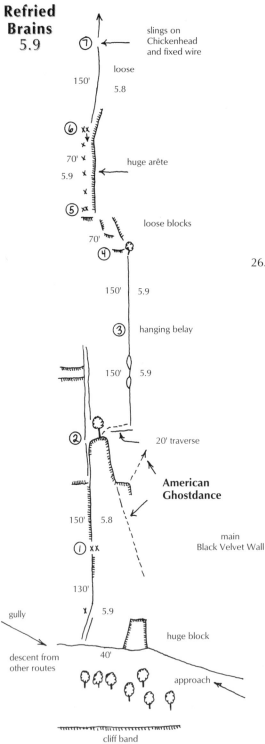

⑦ ← slings on Chickenhead and fixed wire

150' loose

5.8

⑥ xx
70' x
5.9 x huge arête
x
x

⑤ xx
70' loose blocks

④

150' 5.9

③ hanging belay

150' 5.9

② 20' traverse

American Ghostdance

150' 5.8

① xx main Black Velvet Wall

130'

gully

5.9

huge block

descent from other routes

40'

approach

cliff band

P4 Continue up the crack system to a small tree with slings. Wander up and left past blocks to an obvious bolted belay on the arête. 140 ft., 5.9.

P5 Face climb up and left (keeping left of the arête), then straight up past three bolts. Turn a bulge on the left (bolt), then up and right to another bolted belay. 60 ft., 5.8.

P6, P7 These are best avoided, as the rock deteriorates and there are poor fixed anchors atop pitch six. If you want to continue, follow cracks to the top of the pillar. 5.8.

Descent: Rappel the route with two ropes, at times using anchors other than those used for belays on the ascent.

26. **American Ghostdance** 5.12-
FA: Jordy Morgan, Kevin Fosburg–November 1988.
The technical test piece of the wall. Many people rappel after doing the first pitch. If you decide to do the whole route, bring wires, TCUs and Friends up to # 2.5.

Approach this route by following the road for about 300 yards from the parking area, then take a trail that branches off right where the road makes a hard left turn. Hike this trail toward the canyon for about 0.5 mile, until it forks. Take the right fork and drop down into the drainage. Follow the rocky creekbed upstream for about 600 yards until the drainage is blocked by a cliff. Go left (southeast) into the bushes on a path, then scramble up the cliff on big ledges. Follow the trails up left about 100 yards to the base of the large, smooth wall. Approach time is about half an hour.

Begin at a bush just uphill from **Sandstone Samurai** and below a bolt that leads to an obvious rightwards finger traverse below the varnished band.

P1 Climb to a bolt, finger traverse up right, then continue up past four bolts (many difficult moves). Move left (sidepulls) to a bolt, then make more hard moves to escape the varnished band. Continue up past two more bolts (sporty 5.10-) to the anchor. 130 ft., 5.12-.

P2 Climb past four bolts to a belay in a crack. 150 ft., 5.10.

P3 A short pitch up a crack leads to a belay ledge at a right-facing corner. 20 ft., 5.7.

P4 Clip six bolts (moving slightly left after the fifth bolt) to a bolted belay. 150 ft., 5.10.

P5 Three bolts lead to a belay in a crack. 150 ft., 5.9.

P6 Continue up the crack, then move out left and climb past two bolts to a right-facing corner/flake. Belay at a bolt at a corner. 100 ft., 5.9.

P7 Climb up and slightly left past two bolts and a ceiling to a bolted belay on a ledge. 100 ft., 5.10

P8 5th-class climbing and scrambling lead to the top.

Descent: Go left (east; toward the road) until you can walk down to the notch between Whiskey Peak and Black Velvet Wall. Head down the gully between the formations to the base of the climb and your gear.

American Ghostdance 5.12-

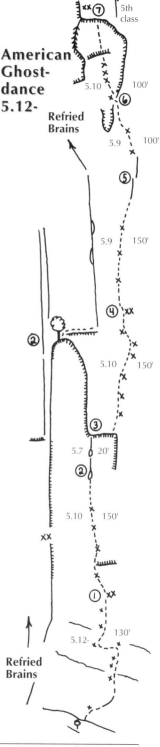

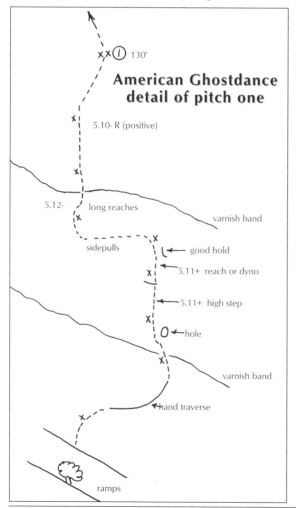

American Ghostdance detail of pitch one

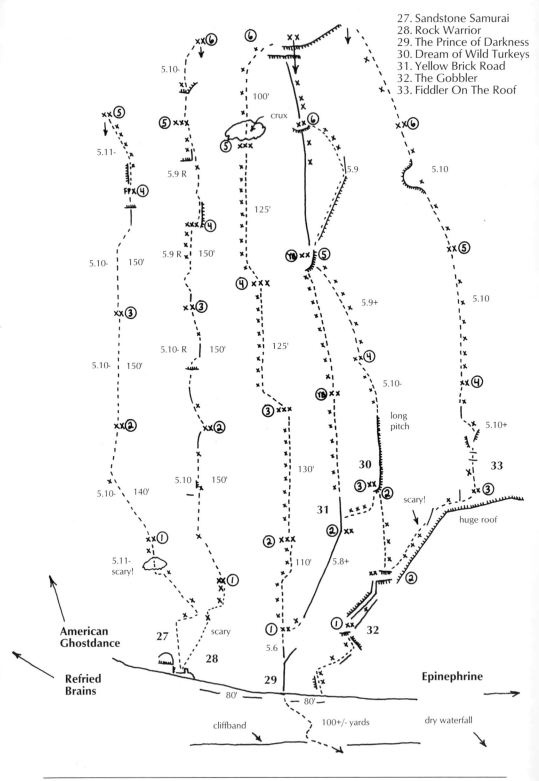

27. Sandstone Samurai
28. Rock Warrior
29. The Prince of Darkness
30. Dream of Wild Turkeys
31. Yellow Brick Road
32. The Gobbler
33. Fiddler On The Roof

5.10-

5.11-

5.9 R

5.10-

100'

crux

5.9

5.10

5.10- 150'

5.9 R 150'

125'

125'

5.9+

5.10

5.10- R 150'

150'

125'

5.10-

long
pitch

5.10+

5.10- 150'

130'

30

33

31

scary!

huge roof

5.11-
scary!

5.10 150'

5.10- 140'

110'

5.8+

American
Ghostdance

27

scary

28

5.6

Refried
Brains

29

32

Epinephrine

80'

80'

cliffband

100+/- yards

dry waterfall

27. **Sandstone Samurai** 5.11- R/X   FA: Paul Van Betten, Nick Nordblom–Spring 1988.
Leading this is akin to hari kari (or so you'll think if you're on the "sharp end"). The route is so runout that a fall long enough to rip out the ¼" bolts is possible. Photo, page 204.

Access this climb by following the roadbed for about 300 yards from the parking area, then take a trail that branches off right where the road makes a hard left turn. Hike this trail toward the canyon for about a half mile, until it forks. Take the right fork, and drop down into the drainage. Follow the rocky creekbed upstream for about 600 yards until the drainage is blocked by a cliff. Go left (southeast) into the bushes on a path, then scramble up the cliff on big ledges. Follow the trail up left about 100 yards to the base of the large, smooth wall. You should be to the base of the route in about 30 minutes.

Rope up at a smooth varnished face to the right of a low ceiling and left of a short pillar forming a left-facing corner. This is the same starting point as **Rock Warrior** and is 30 feet left of **The Prince Of Darkness**.

P1 Climb 40 feet up white rock to a left-leaning white ramp (bolt). Traverse right on the white slab (V1), then diagonal up and left past two bolts to a smooth, varnished section. Make hard and scary moves straight up to another bolt and then the belay (two bolts and wires). 140 ft., 5.11- R/X.

P2 Climb up to a short seam (TCU and wire), then continue up and slightly left (a couple of poor RPs may go in) to a bolt 50 feet above the belay. Head up and slightly right to the next belay anchor. 140 ft., 5.10- X.

P3 Wander straight up the face to a bolt anchor, placing some RPs for pro along the way. 150 ft., 5.10- R.

P4 Continue straight up, then angle right to a crack over a small roof. No bolts on the pitch, but a bolt and pin at the anchor. 150 ft., 5.10- R.

P5 Climb a small right-facing corner, then traverse up and left to the anchor. Five bolts on the pitch. 150 ft., 5.11- R.

V1 There are some newer bolts just left of this route with SMC hangers. I've been unable to determine if this is a totally separate route, or merely variations.

Descent: Rappel the route.

28. **Rock Warrior** 5.10 R ◀   FA: Richard Harrison, Jay Smith, Nick Nordblom–Fall 1983.
A classic route, but LOTS scarier than **The Prince Of Darkness**. Bring a selection of smaller sized gear, two ropes and a cool head. Photo, page 204.

Approach this route by following the roadbed for about 300 yards from the parking area, then take a trail that branches off right where the road makes a hard left turn. Hike this trail toward the canyon for about 0.5 mile, until it forks. Take the right fork and drop down into the drainage. Follow the rocky creekbed upstream for about 600 yards until the drainage is blocked by a cliff. Go left (southeast) into the bushes on a path, then scramble up the cliff on big ledges. Follow the trails up left about 100 yards to the base of the large, smooth wall. This section of cliff has probably the best long routes in all of Red Rocks, including this one. It takes roughly 30 minutes to reach the route from your car.

Rope up at a smooth, varnished face to the right of a low ceiling and left of a short pillar forming a left-facing corner. This is the same start as **Sandstone Samurai** and is 30 feet left of **Dream of Wild Turkeys** and **The Prince Of Darkness**.

P1 Climb 40 feet up and right on white rock (easy, but dangerous) to a slab. Clip a bolt, climb up, then traverse right until beneath the anchor. Climb up past one more bolt and make sporty moves to reach the belay. 150 ft., 5.10- R.

P2 Angle slightly left from the belay to a bolt, then wander straight up to another bolt by a shallow, left-facing corner. Make difficult moves up the arête of the corner to a seam, which is followed up and slightly right past a bit more fixed gear to the anchor. 150 ft., 5.10.

P3 Go slightly left from the belay, then up the face past a little bit of fixed gear to a ceiling. Pull this, and move up to a belay station. 150 ft., 5.10- R.

P4 Wander up the face to a three-bolt belay at a corner (the first ascent party bivied here in hammocks). 150 ft., 5.9 R.

P5 Climb the corner, then up the face past a few bolts to another station. 150 ft., 5.9 R.

P6 Climb over a ceiling, then up along cracks and seams to a belay. 150 ft., 5.10- R.

Descent: Either continue upward (5.8/5.9, then 3rd class) or rappel with two ropes.

29. **The Prince Of Darkness** 5.10 ◀ FA: The Uriostes, Bill Bradley, Mike Ward–Fall 1984.
    This route is impressive – not only for the positions you'll be in, but for the amount of effort needed to drill all the bolts you'll encounter (some say it's over-bolted). Bring lots of quickdraws, a few medium-sized stoppers, butt bag (all the belays are hanging belays) and two ropes for the descent. The bolt hangers are painted black, as the route name might imply (ominous, eh?). Photo, page 204; topo, page 208.

    Approach this route by following the roadbed for about 300 yards from the parking area, then take a trail that branches off right where the road makes a hard left turn. Hike this trail toward the canyon for about 0.5 mile, until it forks. Take the right fork and drop down into the drainage. Follow the rocky creekbed upstream for about 600 yards until the drainage is blocked by a cliff. Go left (southeast) into the bushes on a path, then scramble up the cliff on big ledges. Follow the trails up left about 100 yards to the base of the large, smooth wall. This section of cliff has some of the best routes in all of Red Rocks. **The Prince Of Darkness** follows the left edge of a prominent, black water streak in the center of the smooth wall. Approach time is about thirty minutes.

    Begin as per **Dream Of Wild Turkeys**, below the left end of an obvious, right-leaning crack 100 feet up, and directly below a right-facing crack/corner about 40 feet up.

    P1 Scamper up easy rock to the base of a short, right-leaning crack/corner with a vertical crack leading straight up. Follow either feature up to a slab and a belay station with three bolts. 75 ft., 5.6.

    P2 Follow a crack/seam system up, then slightly right, passing 14 bolts to a three-bolt belay station. 110 ft., 5.10b.

    P3 Continue straight up the seam past 15 bolts to a three-bolt belay. 130 ft., 5.10a.

    P4 Zip up along the crack past 13 bolts (at least two are missing hangers) to a three-bolt belay. 125 ft., 5.9.

    P5 Step left, then follow a crack past eight bolts to a three-bolt belay. 125 ft., 5.9.

    P6 Power up the smooth, varnished slab (crux) past 13 bolts to a large ledge and a two-bolt belay (same belay as **Dream Of Wild Turkeys**). 100 ft., 5.10c.

    Descent: Rappel this route, **Yellow Brick Road** or **Dream of Wild...** with two ropes.

30. **Dream Of Wild Turkeys** 5.10- ◀ FA: The Uriostes–early 1980s.
    One of the earliest routes up this section of cliff. The name is a goof on a famous climb located on a sea cliff in Wales. Bring an assortment of gear up to a #3 Friend and two ropes to rap the route. Photos, pages 191 and 204; topo, page 208.

    Approach this climb by following the roadbed from the parking area for about 300 yards, then taking a trail that branches off to the right when the road makes a hard left turn. Hike this trail toward the canyon for about 0.5 mile, until it forks. Take the right fork and drop down into the drainage. Follow the rocky creekbed upstream for about 600 yards until the drainage is blocked by a cliff. Go left (southeast) into the bushes on a path, then scramble up the cliff on big ledges. Follow the trails up left about 100 yards to the base of the large, smooth wall. This section of cliff has some of the best routes in all of Red Rocks. Give yourself about 30 minutes to reach the base of the wall.

Begin the climb as per **The Prince Of Darkness**, below the left end of an obvious right-leaning crack 100 feet up and directly below a right-facing crack/corner about 40 feet up.

P1 Scamper up easy rock to the base of a short, right-leaning crack/corner with a vertical crack leading straight up. Follow either feature up to a slab and a belay station with three bolts. 75 ft., 5.6.

P2 Angle right past a bolt into the prominent right-leaning crack and follow this to a belay anchor. 110 ft., 5.8+.

P3 Go up the crack a bit, then traverse right past six bolts to the base of a prominent, white flake/corner system and the belay anchors. 80 ft., 5.9.

P4 Climb the flake/corner system to its end (5.8), then face climb left past bolts to a bolt anchor. 165 ft., 5.10-.

P5 Angle up left across a slabby face (six bolts) to a ledge at the base of a left-facing corner. 50 ft., 5.9+.

P6 Follow the left-facing corner/ramp up right to a crack. Go up the crack and face above (bolts), then traverse back left (more bolts) to a vertical crack in a water streak. Belay from two bolts on a scooped ledge. 140 ft., 5.9.

P7 Climb the left-slanting crack/seam past five bolts to a spacious ledge with two bolts. 75 ft., 5.9.

P8 to P12 It's possible to continue up, but most folks rappel from here.

Descent: Rappel with two ropes, using anchors on **Yellow Brick Road** and/or this route.

31. **Yellow Brick Road** 5.10
FA: The Uriostes, Mike Ward, Bill Bradley–Fall 1985.
You don't need to be a wiz to know that the bolt hangers are painted yellow on this one. Really a three-pitch variation to **Dream Of Wild Turkeys**; the climbing is safe and enjoyable. Photo, page 204; topo, page 208.

Approach this climb by following the road from the parking area toward the canyon for about 300 yards, then taking a trail that branches off to the right when the road makes a hard left turn. Hike this trail toward the canyon (west) for about 0.5 mile, until it forks. Take the right fork and

Desert Reality 5.11: *Paul Van Betten and Mike Ward on the 5.11 crack. For route information, see page 219. Photo by Kurt Mauer.*

drop down into the drainage. Follow the rocky creek-bed upstream for about 600 yards until the drainage is blocked by a cliff. Go left (southeast) into the bushes on a path, then scramble up the cliff on big ledges. Follow the trails up left about 100 yards to the base of the large, smooth wall. Allow about 30 minutes for the approach hike.

Start at the base of **Dream Of Wild Turkeys** and **The Prince Of Darkness** below the left end of an obvious, right-leaning crack 100 feet above and directly below a right-facing crack/corner about 40 feet up.

P1 Scamper up easy rock to the base of a short, right-leaning crack/corner with a vertical crack leading straight up. Follow either feature up to a slab and a belay station with three bolts. 75 ft., 5.6.

P2 Angle right past a bolt into the prominent right-leaning crack, and follow this to a belay anchor. 110 ft., 5.8+.

P3 Continue straight up the crack and face above to a hanging belay from bolts. 120 ft., 5.10b/c.

P4 Follow 10 bolts up the face to rejoin **Dream Of Wild Turkeys** at a belay station. 125 ft., 5.10a/b.

P5 Ascend the left-facing flake to a bolt, then move left and up a crack/corner (two more bolts) to a two bolt belay on a scooped ledge.

Descent: Either continue up **Dream Of Wild Turkeys** or rappel the route with two ropes.

32. **The Gobbler** 5.10- FA: The Uriostes, Bill Bradley, Mike Ward–July 1980.
A good way to round out the day or start **Dream Of Wild Turkeys**. Make sure you have some long slings and gear up to 3". Photo, page 204; topo, page 208.

This route is best approached by following the road from the parking area for about 300 yards, then taking a trail that branches off right when the road makes a hard left turn. Hike this trail toward the canyon for about .5 mile, until it forks. Take the right fork and drop down into the drainage. Follow the rocky creekbed upstream for about 600 yards until the drainage is blocked by a cliff. Go left (southeast) into the bushes on a path, then scramble up the cliff on big ledges. Follow the trails up left about 100 yards to the base of the large, smooth wall. It'll take about 30 minutes to reach the base of the route from the parking area.

Start below a right-leaning gash about 60 feet up (rappel anchors are clearly visible) and 40 feet right of **Dream Of Wild Turkeys**. This climb is at the left (east) end of a huge arch/ceiling at the base of Black Velvet Wall.

P1 Climb easy white rock for 30 feet to a bolt in a depression. Go up left ten feet to another bolt then up to a horizontal break. Move up right past two bolts, then finger traverse up right to a left-leaning crack/corner. Follow this past a bolt to a ledge and belay station (watch out for rope drag). 110 ft., 5.9.

P2 Jam up cracks just right of the right-leaning gash/chimney past one bolt to another anchor (5.9, possible belay here). Power up the steep face past more bolts to a belay on **Dream Of Wild Turkeys** at the base of a white, left-facing flake/corner system. 130 ft., 5.10-.

Descent: Either continue up **Dream Of Wild Turkeys** or rap the route. Watch out for stuck ropes in the cracks!

33. **Fiddler On The Roof** 5.10+ PG13 ◀ FA: Dave Wonderly, Warren Egbert, Jenny Rich-ards–November 1990.
Bring your prussiks! This exciting route starts at the second anchor on **The Gobbler** and traverses out right above the lip of the huge arch/ceiling. Mike Ward says it's the best route in the canyon – quite a statement! Photos, pages 191 and 204; topo, page 208.

Start below a right-leaning gash about 60 feet up (rappel anchors are clearly visible) and 40 feet right of **Dream Of Wild Turkeys**. This climb is at the left (east) end of a huge arch/ceiling at the base of the Black Velvet Wall.

P1 Climb easy white rock for 30 feet to a bolt in a depression. Go up left ten feet to another bolt then up to a horizontal break. Move up right past two bolts, then finger traverse up right to a left-leaning crack/corner. Follow this past a bolt to a ledge and belay station (watch out for rope drag). 110 ft., 5.9.

P2 Jam up cracks just right of the right-leaning gash/chimney past one bolt to another belay anchor. 60 ft., 5.9.

P3 Trend out right along the lip of the huge roof (don't fall!), passing two bolts and a few gear placements to a belay station. 165 ft.

P4 Climb pretty much straight up the spectacular face past two bolts to a bolted belay. 150 ft., 5.10+.

P5 Continue up the magnificent varnished face, past six bolts and some traditional gear placements. Fixed anchor. 150 ft., 5.10.

P6 Follow two bolts up the face to ledge (5.10), then continue up past one more bolt to the belay. 150 ft., 5.10.

P7 Two more bolts lead to Turkey Ledge.

Descent: Rappel **Dream Of Wild Turkeys** with two ropes.

*NOTE: Two routes climb the face between **The Gobbler** and **Sour Mash**, but at press time I didn't have complete information on them. The route through the roof is called **Early Times** (5.10-); the bolted face below and right is supposedly 5.10+.*

34. **Sour Mash** 5.10- FA: The Uriostes–July 1980.
A primarily natural line up the wall just right of the huge arch mentioned in **Fiddler...** and **The Gobbler**. Carry a good selection of pro and two ropes. Topo, page 214.

Access this climb by following the roadbed from the parking area for about 300 yards, then taking a trail that branches off to the right when the road makes a hard left turn. Hike this trail toward the canyon for about 0.5 mile, until it forks. Take the right fork and drop down into the drainage. Follow the rocky creekbed upstream for about 600 yards until the drainage is blocked by a cliff. Go left (southeast) into the bushes on a path, scramble up the cliff band as per the other routes, then go up to the base of the wall on one of the trails. Total approach time is about 30 minutes.

Begin below the right end of the huge roof and just left of a large, white, pyramid-shaped buttress. The route ascends the right side of a brown triangle of rock about 60 feet up, then follows crack systems that keep right of the huge roof. Scramble 20 feet up to a ledge with a bush.

P1 Climb up a shallow, right-facing corner, then step right and go up a steeper lieback crack to a ledge with a bush. Climb the left-facing corner/crack above (this is the right side of the brown triangle) past bolts to the top of the triangle. Follow an easier right-leaning crack/corner to a belay stance between two bushes. Large Friends are needed for the belay. 150 ft., 5.10-

P2 Move right from the belay to an arête, then up this past a bolt to the ceiling. Pull the first ceiling to a second bolt, then follow a crack up and right to a belay anchor (possible belay here). Continue up a crack past two bolts. Step left on a ledge to a bolt, then up 20 feet to another ledge with a bolted anchor. 150 ft., 5.8.

P3 Climb the center of three crack systems above to a hanging belay. 50 ft., 5.7.

P4 Follow the crack up and slightly left to a hanging belay. 130 ft., 5.9.

P5 Continue up the obvious, slightly left-leaning seam/crack past bolts to a stance. Lieback a flake up a smooth section past a small ceiling, then angle up and right to a two-bolt belay anchor below another light-colored ceiling. 90 ft., 5.10-.

P6 Step over the ceiling to a bolt. Face climb along a crack past two bolts to a smooth section. Make difficult moves past bolts to a left-facing corner. Step right and up to a

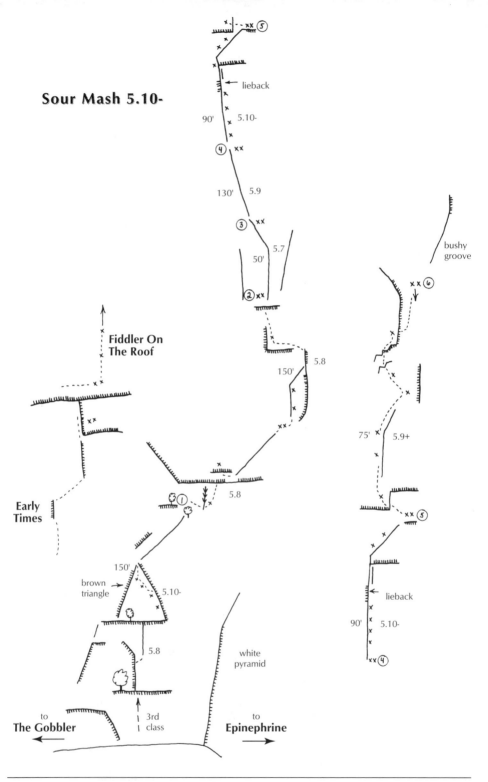

Sour Mash 5.10-

lieback

90'   5.10-

130'   5.9

50'

5.7

bushy groove

Fiddler On The Roof

5.8

150'

75'   5.9+

Early Times

5.8

150'

brown triangle   5.10-

5.8

lieback

90'   5.10-

white pyramid

to The Gobbler

3rd class

to Epinephrine

rappel anchor. 75 ft., 5.9+.

Descent: Rappel with two ropes straight down to **Fiddler on the Roof**'s belay at the lip of the huge roof. Another wild rappel and a bit of downclimbing will return you to your pack at the base of the route.

35. **My Little Pony** 5.11+
FA: Paul Van Betten, Richard Harrison, Shelby Shelton –Summer 1990.
Not much is known about this route. It starts just left of the left side of the **Epinephrine** tower (aka the Black Tower) and goes out the left side of a giant scoop above. The route is seven pitches long and you can rappel with two ropes. See the topo for more details. Photo, page 204.

36. **Velveeta** 5.10+ FA: Richard Harrison, Wendell Broussard –Sum-mer 1990.
This route climbs out the right side of the scoop that is just left of the **Epinephrine** tower (aka the Black Tower). It is six or seven pitches long. Photo, page 204.

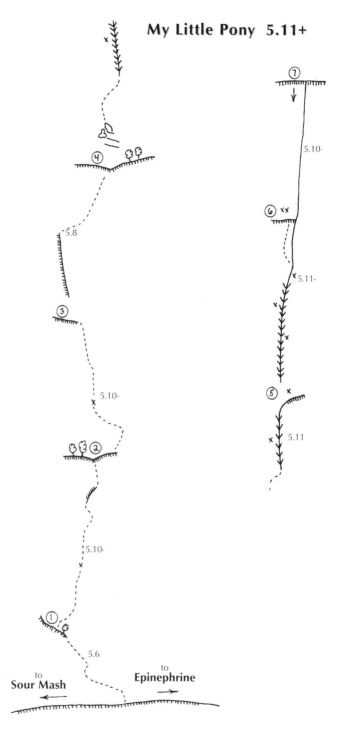

My Little Pony 5.11+

NOTE: The left side of the **Epinephrine** tower (aka the Black Tower) has an off-width route up it called **Malicious Mischief**. It's 5.10 and was first climbed by Joe Herbst, Stephanie Petrilak and Mike Gilbert in May 1978.

37. **Chalk Is Cheap** 5.10+ R: FA Mike Ward, Mike Clifford, Eric Sutton Fall, 1989
Kind of like **The Prince of Darkness**, except the rock is bad and there are no bolts! Bring two ropes and a good selection of gear, as there are no fixed anchors.

Start 50 feet left of **Epinephrine** at a left-slanting ramp on the lowest tier of the cliff. Scramble out left along the ramp then up one of two cracks to the bushy ledge 60 feet up. Start on a small, high ledge beneath a left facing corner that leads to a ceiling.

P1 Climb the left-facing corner to the ceiling, step out right, and climb the scary face to a right-slanting corner that becomes a larger, left-facing corner. Belay amidst blocks below an obvious crack in a dihedral 140 ft, 5.9 R.

P2 Climb the crack in the dihedral, then follow it up the left wall of a broken corner. Just before the crack ends, move around right to a stance below an obvious "V" slot (watch for rope drag). Climb the slot and continue up the easy corner to a belay atop a pillar. 120 ft, 5.8.

P3 Climb the left edge of the steep brown wall (V1), moving out right to a fixed peg. Follow a vertical seam up to the center of a ceiling, and pull through this. Angle slightly left up an easy ramp to a belay at a short, vertical crack. 140 ft, 5.10+ R.

P4 Climb one of the two leftmost cracks up the buttress until you run out of rope. 150 ft, 5.10 R.

P5 An easy pitch leads to the top of the tower. 40 ft, 5.6.

V1 Choss Is Cheaper 5.10- X
FA: Bobby Knight, Todd Swain April, 1995.

P3 From the top of the pillar, go up and left a bit, then go out right on big holds to a vertical seam. Climb the seam to an obvious, right facing flake/corner (this is about ten feet right of the fixed peg). Follow the flake/corner to a good stance then angle up left to reach the vertical seam leading to the ceiling. Follow the regular route over the ceiling and up to the belay. 140 ft, 5.10- X.

P4 Go up and left from the belay, then angle up right to reach the third crack system from the left edge of the tower. Follow this until it ends and belay. 150 ft, 5.10- X.

Descent: Rappel **Epinephrine**. You may need to leave slings and/or some wires to back up the anchors.

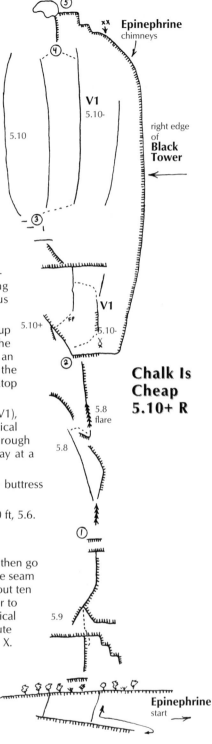

Epinephrine chimneys

V1 5.10-

5.10

right edge of **Black Tower**

5.10+

V1 5.10-

Chalk Is Cheap 5.10+ R

5.8 flare

5.8

5.9

Epinephrine start

38. **Epinephrine** 5.9 ◀ FA: The Uriostes, Joe Herbst–August 1978.
One of the best climbs I've done, but you'd better be solid on 5.9 chimneys! A long route, with sustained climbing and lots of 3rd and 4th class scrambling to get off. As Chouinard says in *Climbing Ice*, published by the Sierra Club, "If you bring bivi gear, you will bivi." (on this route, that may mean twice!) The pitches are described as they were originally done, but it's entirely possible to combine pitches (especially above the top of the tower) to make the climb go faster. Photos, pages 191 and 204.

Approach this fine outing by following the roadbed from the parking area for about 300 yards, then taking a trail that branches off to the right when the road makes a hard left turn. Hike this trail toward the canyon for about 0.5 mile, until it forks. Take the right fork and drop down into the drainage. Follow the rocky creekbed upstream for about 600 yards until the drainage is blocked by a cliff. Go left (southeast) into the bushes on a path, scramble up the cliffband as per the other routes, then go right and down to the pebbly streambed. Approach time is about 40 minutes.

Epinephrine is 60 yards up canyon from the waterfall and starts below a gray face with three bolts (red hangers) that is 15 feet right of a right-slanting crack. If speed is a consideration, you can avoid the first pitch by soloing up easy ledges, starting 50 feet further right (30 feet left of a yellow, left-facing corner).

P1 Climb the gray face past three bolts to a bushy ledge. 60 ft., 5.8.

P2 From the left side of the ledge, follow the obvious features up and slightly left past three bolts to another vegetated ledge. 100 ft., 5.7.

P3 Climb an easy chimney and belay above at one of many trees. 150 ft., 5.6.

P4 Scramble up to the base of the chimneys, which are on the right side of the huge pillar (The Black Tower).

P5 Struggle up the beautiful chimney to a belay station. 150 ft., 5.9.

P6 Continue up the chimney to another anchor (awesome positions). 75 ft., 5.9.

P7 Another pitch of wiggling and thrashing leads to the chimney section's top. 90 ft., 5.9.

P8 Scramble to the top of the tower.

Note: The top of the tower is quite spacious, leans inward and is really the only place to bivi. Many folks climb to here then rappel back down the route.

P9 Face climb past two bolts to a belay. 75 ft., 5.7

P10 Pull a ceiling, then go up to a bushy ledge. 75 ft., 5.7.

P11 Traverse right about 50 feet, then climb up to a belay ledge with one bolt. 75 ft., 5.6.

700'

150'   5.6

90'   5.9

75'   5.7

100'   5.8

75'   5.6

110'   5.9

75'   5.9

75'   5.6

75'   5.7

75'   5.7

Velveeta
5.10+

My Little Pony
5.11+

Malicious Mischief
5.10

90'   5.9

75'   5.9

150'   5.9

Chalk Is Cheap
5.10+

150'   5.6

alternative start

100'   5.7

← downstream

approach

canyon floor

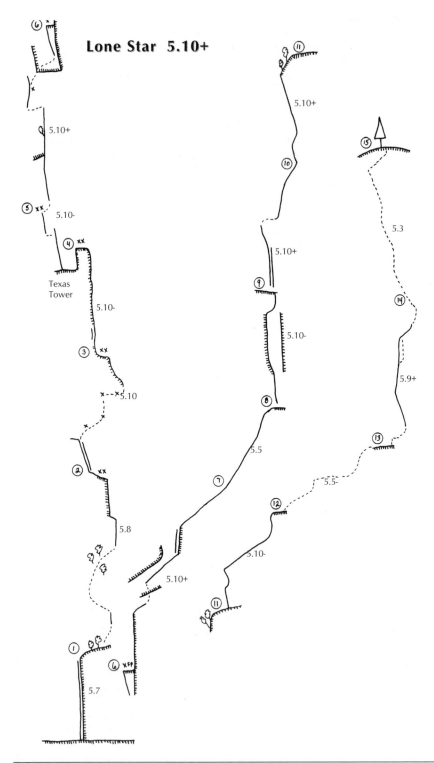

Lone Star 5.10+

P12 A bit of tricky face climbing past two bolts leads to another belay ledge. 75 ft., 5.9.

P13 Climb the prominent dihedral past five bolts to a belay in an alcove. 110 ft., 5.9.

P14 Continue up the dihedral to belay on a ledge. 75 ft., 5.6.

P15 Upward! 100 ft., 5.8.

P16 More of the same. Belay under a roof. 75 ft., 5.7.

P17 Climb the roof on the right (exposed), then up to a belay anchor. 90 ft., 5.9.

P18 Up. Belay on a ledge to the left under a ceiling. Bolt anchor. 150 ft., 5.6.

To the top: Move left from the belay onto a huge, right-leaning ramp (many large ledges to organize on). Follow this ramp up right for about 700 feet, passing numerous places where folks have had to bivi (some for the second time). This involves 4th and easy 5th class climbing, sometimes with big air below. The last bit of the route follows bushy ledges around an amphitheater to the top of the wall.

Descent: Walk up and left (south) to the highest summit (don't be lured down the first gully you come to), then follow the ridge down to the top of Whiskey Peak (you'll be heading down toward the parking area). From the top of Whiskey Peak, drop down into the left (northwest) gully and scramble down past **Refried Brains** and the other routes to your pack. To the right (southeast) is the fastest way to the car – if you have all of your gear with you. The whole descent takes roughly an hour (if you have something other than your tight climbing shoes with you!).

39. **Lone Star** 5.10+ FA: Richard Harrison, Paul Crawford, Paul Van Betten, Paul Obenheim–April 1984.
    This route starts up the **Yellow Rose of Texas** (described in the Urioste guide), then continues up the huge wall to the right. Begin to the right of **Epinephrine** at a left-facing chimney/corner that is about 75 feet left of a pool. Not much is known about this route, other than what is shown on the accompanying topo on page 218.

The next routes are located just outside the mouth of the canyon, to the right (north), on a formation named The Monument.

*As you look at the mountainside, you'll see a large, red band of rock below the brown sandstone. The following routes are above the left (south) end of the widest portion of red rock and climb a thin yellow stripe of rock capped by a roof. The light-colored roof is **Desert Reality** and is visible from the parking area. Many other climbs have been done in the area, but only these ultra-classic routes will be described.*

From the parking area, walk straight across the desert toward a steep drainage that will lead up to the climbs. The approach takes about 45 minutes and the routes are sunny.

40. **Desert Crack** 5.12+ ◀ FA: Paul Van Betten, Sal Mamusia–April 1987.
    The short, but very difficult fingercrack leading up to the huge roof of **Desert Reality**.

41. **Desert Reality** 5.11 ◀ FA: Paul Van Betten, Richard Harrison–February 1984.
    The obvious crack out the huge, light colored roof. This was originally approached from the left via aid (two bolts).

42. **Desert Gold** 5.13- ◀ FA: Stefan Glowacz, Paul Van Betten–May 1987.
    The link-up of the two routes listed above.

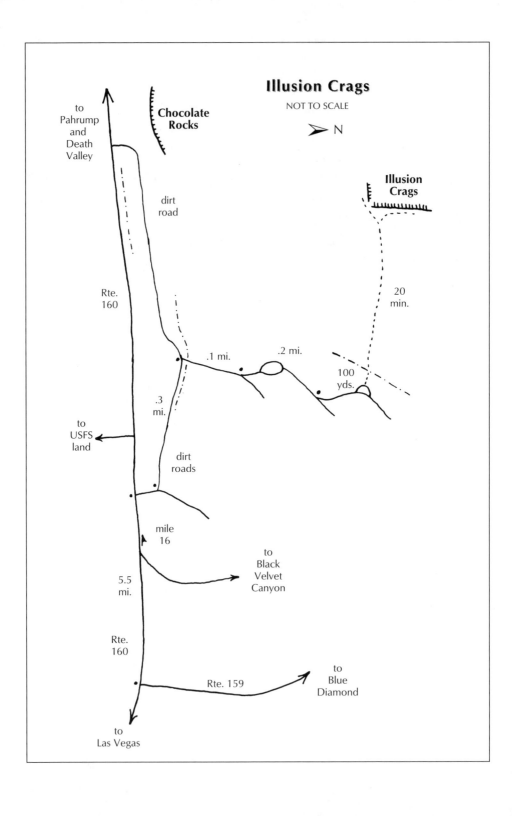

ILLUSION CRAGS

This cliff faces primarily northeast and has some very good varnished rock. Most routes are less than 150 feet high and have established rappel anchors. Despite the good quality rock and advances in bolting technology, it appears that this crag received very little traffic in the 1970s and 1980s. The Urioste guidebook had ten climbs listed here, but I was unable to match the cliff photo and many of the brief descriptions with the features on the crag. The routes listed in this guide are the "best of the bunch" and should provide several days of enjoyable climbing for those that will brave the 20-minute uphill approach.

To reach this cliff, drive west on Route 160 from the intersection with Route 159 for 5.5 miles (passing the turnoff for Black Velvet Canyon). Turn right (north) on a dirt road and parallel the main road for 0.3 mile. Turn right (north) at a wash and go to a fork in the road (0.1 mile). Bear left, pass a large dip, then bear left again (0.2 mile). Continue 100 yards to a parking spot. The cliff is clearly visible across a wash and up the hillside.

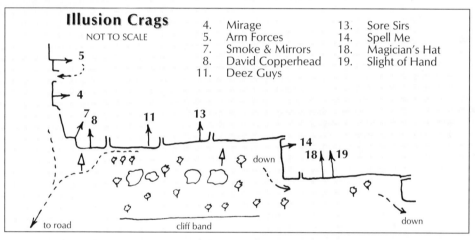

Left Side

The first routes described are on the far left (southwest) side of the formation, overlooking a drainage that is clearly visible on the approach. These routes face southeast and are much more broken than the main wall. These one-pitch climbs are described from right to left (north to south) as you approach up the ridge to the cliff.

1. **Changelings** 5.6 PG   FRA: Donette Smith, Todd Swain–April 1994.
   The first three climbs are on a low-angled, pyramidal formation that has a jutting block several hundred feet above it. Climb the shattered right arête of the low-angled formation, starting 40 feet right of an alcove. Rappel from a natural thread on the ledge 75 feet up.

2. **Chameleon Pinnacle** 5.4   FA: Bill Lowman, Joe and Betsy Herbst, Matt McMackin, Nanouk Borche, Howard Booth–February 1973.
   This route is shown in the Urioste guide as going to the top of the cliff – only the first pitch is described here. Begin 40 feet left of the last route at an alcove with two junky-looking cracks above. Move out right from the alcove onto a low-angled, plated face and climb this to a belay 75 feet up. Rappel from the communal anchor.

3. **Morph Out!** 5.7   FRA: Donette Smith, Todd Swain–April 1994.
For Power Rangers only. Starting in the alcove as per **Chameleon Pinnacle**, swim up the junky looking, left-facing corner/crack to the belay.

4. **Mirage** 5.7   FA: Betsy and Joe Herbst, Joanne Urioste–Fall 1976.
Who would have thought a casino would be named for this climb? Begin 150 feet left of the last two routes on a separate cliff that has cleaner, smoother rock. Climb a crack system that is 15 feet right of the cleanest, most obvious right-facing corner (**Arm Forces**). At the top, go right (east) then descend down the gully separating the two crags.

5. **Arm Forces** 5.9   FA: Joe Herbst, Nanouk Borche–February 1973.
Rope up 15 feet left of **Mirage** and about 165 feet left of **Chameleon Pinnacle**, at an obvious right-facing corner. Climb the clean corner past three ceilings. Walk off right as per the other routes on this formation.

6. **French Bulges** 5.7   FA: Nanouk Borche, Joe Herbst–February 1973.
Begin 20 feet left of the last route at a pine tree. Climb the smaller right-facing corner to a bushy ledge. Walk off right and descend the gully separating the cliffs.

Main Cliff
The next climbs are on the larger, steeper main wall. These climbs face east and are described from left to right (south to north) as you approach the ridge to the crag.

7. **Smoke & Mirrors** 5.9 R FRA: Todd Swain–November 1993.
This route climbs a shallow corner system at the left edge of the main cliff. It is around the left side of an arête and just left of a pine tree. Follow the corner to join **David Copperhead** to the belay ledge. Rappel from fixed anchors with one rope.

8. **David Copperhead** 5.8+ FRA: Todd Swain, Bobby Knight–November 1993.
Start at an obvious wide crack that is just right of a prominent pine tree and just right of the main cliff's left edge. Begin in the wide crack and traverse 15 feet left on a horizontal crack to the obvious arête (V1). Follow the edge past a short vertical crack and a small overhang to the belay ledge. Rappel from anchors with one rope.
V1 Start 15 feet left and climb up the overhanging face to the end of the traverse. 5.10.

9. **Who, Deany?** 5.8   FA: probably Joe Herbst–early 1970s.
Climb the obvious clean, wide crack that is near the left edge of the main cliff and just right of a prominent pine tree. Rappel with one rope from two cold shuts on a ledge.

10. **First Lady Of Magic** 5.9   FA: Todd Swain, Donette Smith–November 1993.
Protection is better than it appears from the ground. Rope up five feet right of the **Who, Deany?** crack at a left-facing corner that curves left to form an arch. Climb the corner for 15 feet, then step right over the arch/corner onto the face. Climb up to a bolt, then up and slightly right to a small ledge. Continue straight up to an obvious crack which is followed to a belay ledge with two cold shuts. Bring gear up to a #2.5 Friend and two ropes for the rappel.

11. **Deez Guys** 5.8+ FRA: Todd Swain, Bobby Knight–November 1993.
Begin 30 feet right of the **Who, Deany?** crack at a small clearing that is just left of an ugly crack system. Wander up the varnished face aiming for a shallow, right-facing flake/corner 40 feet up. Continue up the face along a thin, vertical crack to a belay on a large ledge. Bring a double set of TCUs, extra wires and gear to a #3 Friend. Rappel with two ropes.

12. **Con Jurors** 5.7   FRA: Raleigh Collins, Brandt Allen–October 1994.
Start 90 feet right of the last route and 40 feet left of a pine tree that is just right of an ugly chimney. Scramble 20 feet up to a ledge, then move left to a right-leaning crack that is just right of an ugly chimney. Follow the crack up and right to a shaky belay anchor. Rappel with one rope back to the ledge.

13. **Sore Sirs** 5.8 PG13 FRA: Bobby Knight, Todd Swain–November 1993.
Follow the previous route to a ledge 20 feet up, then climb straight up the varnished face toward a prominent chimney near the top of the cliff. Rappel from a poorly-bolted belay just left of the chimney. One rope will get you down to the ledge that is 20 feet off the ground.

14. **Spell Me** 5.11 ◄ FA: Bobby Knight, Todd Swain–November 1993.
You may want some help leading this excellent route. Bring RPs, TCUs and a #2.5 Friend. Begin at the left edge of a short, south-facing buttress that is 140 feet right of **Sore Sirs**. Climb an easy, left-leaning crack to a small ledge then follow a vertical seam and three bolts to the top. Rappel with one rope from slings around a block.

15. **Illusions Of Grandstaff** 5.11 (TR) FA: Todd Swain, Bobby Knight–November 1993.
Start as per **Spell Me** at a left-leaning crack. Climb the steep face along obvious left-facing flakes. Continue straight up (a bit contrived), keeping left of prominent bushes.

16. **Petit Deceit** 5.8 FRA: Bobby Knight, Todd Swain–November 1993.
Begin as per the last two routes on a bushy ledge below a short, south-facing buttress. Climb the obvious left-facing corner to a stance, then continue up the face, keeping right of two prominent bushes. Continue straight up the final varnished wall above a left-leaning crack to a huge ledge. Rappel with one rope from slings around a block.

17. **Shell Game** 5.9 FA: Todd Swain, Donette Smith, Bobby Knight–April 1994.
Begin 100 feet down and right of the last three routes, at a pine tree that marks the left edge of a varnished wall. Carry gear to 4" and lots of slings to reduce rope drag (and/or use double ropes). Climb up the center of a varnished pillar past horizontals and a vertical seam to a ledge. This pillar forms the left edge of an alcove capped by a ceiling. Move right from the top of the pillar and climb a crack out the roof (as per **Magician's Hat**). Above the roof, move back left toward the arête and follow three bolts up the steep wall to a shallow dihedral. Climb the dihedral to a belay ledge in an alcove. Traverse 20 feet right and rappel from the communal anchor on **False Perception** with two ropes.

18. **Magician's Hat** 5.9 FA: probably Joe Herbst, Bo Hansson–1970s.
Bring lots of large gear and some long slings. Rope up five feet right of a pine tree, at a point below an alcove with two cracks leading through a roof. Climb the left crack past the roof (**Shell Game** joins this route briefly at the roof) to a belay ledge in an alcove 120 feet up. Traverse 20 feet right and rappel from the communal anchor on **False Perception** with two ropes.

19. **Slight Of Hand** 5.9 ◄ FA: probably Joe Herbst–early 1970s.
This classic route may have been listed as **Skinny Mini** or **Sweet Little Whore** in the Urioste guidebook. Climb the obvious crack system 150 feet down and right from **Spell Me**. It starts as a beautiful fingercrack then jogs left and widens. If done in one pitch, you'll need to bring lots of extra gear up to four inches. Rappel with two ropes from cold shuts atop **False Perception**.

20. **False Perception** 5.10+ ◄ FA: Todd Swain, Donette Smith–November 1993.
Perhaps the best route on the crag. Bring TCUs and wires for the upper crack. Begin ten feet right of **Slight of Hand** below a line of bolts. Follow bolts up the chocolate colored varnish, finishing in a spectacular thin crack. Rap from a cold shut anchor with two ropes.

OTHER AREAS

If you tire of Red Rocks, or the weather is uncooperative, there are other climbing areas fairly close to Las Vegas. This section is not meant to be a guide to these areas, but simply to be a source of other climbing options.

CHRISTMAS TREE PASS

This surreal area is located within Lake Mead National Recreation Area, a unit of the National Park Service. The rock is monzogranite (like Joshua Tree), but of a fairly coarse and poor quality. Numerous routes have been done at all grades, with the majority being bolt-protected slabs. The large, domed formations are fairly close to the road and face a variety of directions. See *Summit* magazine (October, 1976) and *Climbing* no. 94.

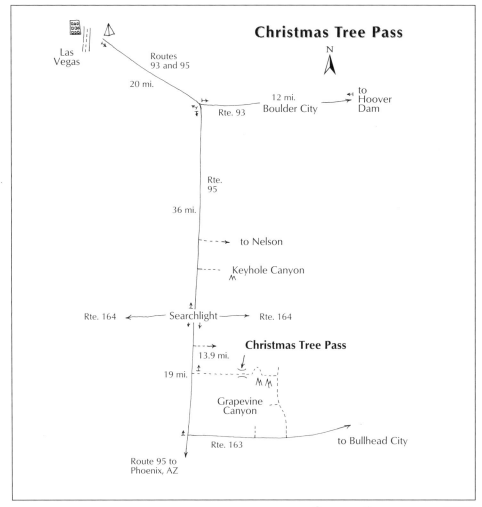

KEYHOLE CANYON

This small area has a wealth of Native American rock art (petroglyphs) and a few good climbs. The rock is a fine-grained monzogranite (like the better rock at Joshua Tree), with the longest route being about half a rope length high. While the climbing is limited, the rock art and canyon make a trip worthwhile.

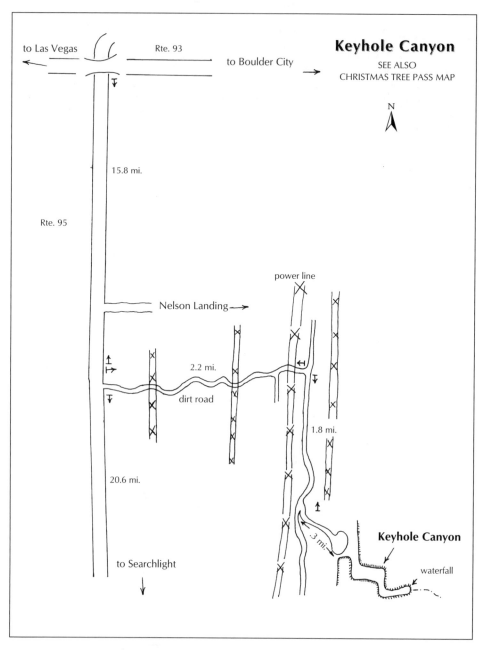

JOSHUA TREE

This renowned area is about a four-hour drive south of Las Vegas. There are more routes in Joshua Tree National Park than in any other climbing area in the country (and perhaps the world). The weather tends to be a little drier than Las Vegas, but the temperatures are about the same.

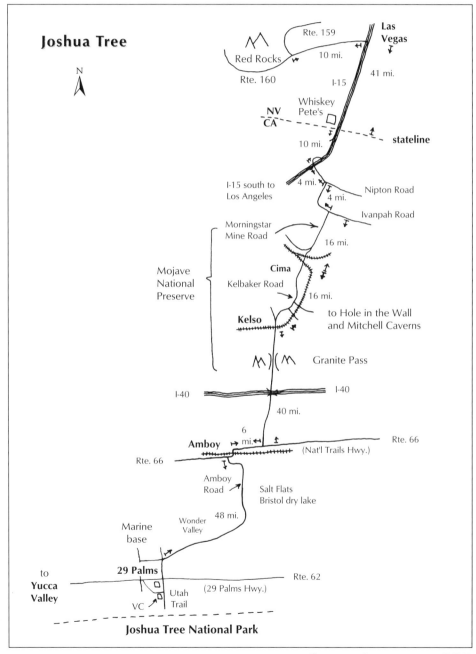

MOUNT CHARLESTON

If overhanging limestone in a mountainous setting appeals to you, this is the place. A relatively new area, it is still being developed. Check out the new guidebook and articles in *Sport Climbing* (vol. 2, no. 4), *Climbing* (no. 142) and *Rock & Ice* (no. 64).

OWENS RIVER GORGE

About a three-hour drive from Las Vegas (via Death Valley National Park), this popular area has its own guidebook, *Owens River Gorge Rock Climbs*, by Marty Lewis.

SNOW CREEK CANYON

This sandstone area is near Saint George, Utah, less than two hours north of Las Vegas. Numerous routes have been done in the area and are described in the new guidebook. Routes are also described in *Climbing* nos. 96 and 102, and *Onsight* magazine no. 2. There are currently two climbing shops in Saint George.

VIRGIN RIVER GORGE

Located just north of Sin City on Interstate 15 in Arizona, this warm, dry limestone area has a bunch of hard routes to dangle on. The only drawback is the proximity to the Interstate. See *Climbing* nos.127 and 148 and *Rock & Ice* no. 44 for details.

ZION

The spectacular sandstone walls of Zion National Park are less than three hours north of Las Vegas. Summer is hot and crowded, but spring and fall are perfect. There are lots of exciting canyoneering trips to do here, as well as big wall free and aid routes. Numerous magazine articles have been written (the most recent being *Onsight* magazine no. 2), plus the park visitor center keeps a notebook with information on the climbs.

RATED ROUTE INDEX

Routes with ratings below 5.7 are not listed. Plus and minus ratings (i.e. 5.10+ or 5.10-) have been grouped with "a" or "d" rated routes, hence a 5.10+ route is listed under 5.10d. Page numbers are in parentheses.

5.7

- ☐ Algae On Parade (189)
- ☐ Back To Basics (193)
- ☐ Bottoms Up (15)
- ☐ Con Jurors (222)
- ☐ Cow Lick Co. Crag (16)
- ☐ Crazy World (155)
- ☐ Ditch Day (44)
- ☐ French Bulges (222)
- ☐ Ghouls Just Wanna Have Fun (15)
- ☐ Group Therapy (91)
- ☐ High Scalin' (83)
- ☐ Hop Route (121)
- ☐ Kindergarten Cop ◄ (189)
- ☐ Ma & Pa In Kettle (10)
- ☐ Mirage (222)
- ☐ Morph Out! (222)
- ☐ Ms. Adventure (87)
- ☐ Nuttin' Could Be Finer (21)
- ☐ Olive Oil (145)
- ☐ Pauligk Pillar (137)
- ☐ Physical Graffiti (12)
- ☐ Pillar Talk (97)
- ☐ Romper Room (189)
- ☐ Shady Ladies (111)
- ☐ Silk Panties (38)
- ☐ Space Case (104)
- ☐ Spiderline (107)
- ☐ Thong (37)
- ☐ Tuna And Chips (37)
- ☐ Tuna Cookies (37)
- ☐ Tunnel Vision ◄ (91)
- ☐ Van Allen Belt (111)
- ☐ Walk To School (104)
- ☐ Wok The Dog (33)

5.8

- ☐ A-Cute Pain (52)
- ☐ The Black Hole (132)
- ☐ Black Magic (187)
- ☐ The Bus Stops Here (129)
- ☐ Bush Pilots (131)
- ☐ Caliban (11)
- ☐ Chasing Shadows (135)
- ☐ Cold September Corner (111)
- ☐ Crimson Chrysalis ◄ (161)
- ☐ Dark Shadows ◄ (133)
- ☐ David Copperhead (222)
- ☐ Deez Guys (222)
- ☐ Ed MacMayonnaise (30)
- ☐ Frictiony Face, Panty Waist ◄ (62)
- ☐ Frogland ◄ (192)
- ☐ Head Case (105)
- ☐ Hip-Hopin' With The Hutterites (73)
- ☐ Human Cannonball (32)
- ☐ Jonny Jamcrack (51)
- ☐ Ken Queasy (46)
- ☐ The Life Chuckle (15)
- ☐ Lotta Ballsp (185)
- ☐ Man In Every Pot, A (10)
- ☐ Mo Hotta, Mo Betta (21)
- ☐ Mojave Green (78)
- ☐ Neon Sunset ◄ (45)
- ☐ The Northeast Arête (119)
- ☐ Old-Out ◄ (119)
- ☐ Parts Is Parts (85)
- ☐ Petit Deceit (223)
- ☐ Ragged Edges ◄ (103)
- ☐ Rainbow Buttress ◄ (173)
- ☐ Sore Sirs (223)
- ☐ Spontaneous Enjoyment (15)
- ☐ The Sport Chimney (24)
- ☐ Sport Climbing Is Neither (56)
- ☐ Technicolor Sunrise (46)
- ☐ Varnishing Point (130)
- ☐ Waterstreak ◄ (37)
- ☐ Who, Deany? (222)
- ☐ Witches' Honor (53)
- ☐ Zipperhead (45)
- ☐ Zippy (180)

5.9

5.10

5.10 cont.

- [ ] Dense Pack (103)
- [ ] Diablo (67)
- [ ] Dime Edging (79)
- [ ] Dog Police (143)
- [ ] Edible Panties (38)
- [ ] Emerald City (157)
- [ ] Fairy Toast (73)
- [ ] Fear And Loathing (123)
- [ ] Friction Addiction (60)
- [ ] Gigantor (14)
- [ ] Gin Ricky (187)
- [ ] The Graduate ◄ (104)
- [ ] Greased Lightning (118)
- [ ] Grippity Gravity (100)
- [ ] Hot Dog (111)
- [ ] Man's Best Friend (33)
- [ ] Miss Conception (196)
- [ ] Music To My Fears (115)
- [ ] The Nightcrawler ◄ (149)
- [ ] One Stop In Tonopah (129)
- [ ] Out Of Control ◄ (132)
- [ ] Panty Raid ◄ (38)
- [ ] Pit Bull (111)
- [ ] Prescription Gription (60)

- [ ] The Prince Of Darkness ◄ (210)
- [ ] RF Gain ◄ (84)
- [ ] Rock Warrior ◄ (209)
- [ ] Sea Of Holes ◄ (132)
- [ ] Sergeant Slaughter (157)
- [ ] Short But Sweet (78)
- [ ] Shut Up And Dance (51)
- [ ] Slot Machine (133)
- [ ] Small Purchase ◄ (142)
- [ ] Spark Plug (205)
- [ ] Sterling Moss (106)
- [ ] Tatanka (112)
- [ ] Territorial Imperative (104)
- [ ] Tie Me Tightly (111)
- [ ] Triassic Sands ◄ (198)
- [ ] Tuckered Sparfish (101)
- [ ] Unknown (68)
- [ ] Unnamed (111)
- [ ] Victoria's Secret (39)
- [ ] Vile Pile (64)
- [ ] Weasel Yeast (18)
- [ ] Weenie Juice ◄ (115)
- [ ] Whipper (110)
- [ ] Yellow Brick Road (211)

5.10a

- [ ] Bigfoot ◄ (97)
- [ ] Black Magic Panties (121)
- [ ] Blonde Dwarf (45)
- [ ] Butt Floss (38)
- [ ] Captain Crunch (101)
- [ ] Cat Walk ◄ (33)
- [ ] Choss Is Cheaper (216)
- [ ] Dancin' With A God ◄ (48)
- [ ] Darkroom, The (70)
- [ ] Deguello (178)
- [ ] Dream Of Wild Turkeys ◄ (210)
- [ ] Eagle Dance ◄ (174)
- [ ] Edward Silverhands (25)
- [ ] Elephant Penis, The (125)
- [ ] Falstaff (65)
- [ ] Gelatin Pooch (56)
- [ ] Gemstone (124)
- [ ] Gobbler, The (212)
- [ ] Heatwave (101)
- [ ] High Class Hoe ◄ (23)
- [ ] High Wire (33)

- [ ] Hot Climb (101)
- [ ] Innocent Bystander (87)
- [ ] Kemosabe (101)
- [ ] Knock The Bottom Out Of It ◄ (15)
- [ ] Mac & Ronnie In Cheese (10)
- [ ] N'Plus Ultra ◄ (96)
- [ ] No Laughing Matter (131)
- [ ] OB Button (139)
- [ ] OB Fist (139)
- [ ] P-Coat Sleeve (15)
- [ ] Pain In The Neck (52)
- [ ] Panty Line (38)
- [ ] Pauline's Pentacle (137)
- [ ] Playing Hooky (44)
- [ ] The Pocket Philosopher (99)
- [ ] Ranger Danger (31)
- [ ] Raptor (131)
- [ ] Red Light ◄ (70)
- [ ] Roasting Affair (107)
- [ ] Rob Roy ◄ (187)
- [ ] Romance Is A Heart Breakin' Affair (193)

5.10a cont.

- [ ] Sand Felipe (198)
- [ ] Sandblast (198)
- [ ] Sheep Trail ☛ (103)
- [ ] Simpatico (129)
- [ ] Sour Mash (213)
- [ ] Spotted Eagle (81)
- [ ] Stick Left (124)
- [ ] Swedish Erotica (66)
- [ ] Texas Tea (48)
- [ ] Tom Terrific (139)
- [ ] Tricks Are For Kids (107)
- [ ] Trigger Happy ☛ (85)
- [ ] Vagabonds (48)
- [ ] Which Hunters? (54)
- [ ] The Whiff (34)
- [ ] Wholesome Fullback (199)

5.10b

- [ ] April Fools (53)
- [ ] Black Gold (48)
- [ ] Doctor's Orders (44)
- [ ] First Born (77)
- [ ] Fool's Gold (48)
- [ ] Hero Worship (87)
- [ ] It's A Bitch ☛ (33)
- [ ] Low Tide (42)
- [ ] Plastic People (64)
- [ ] Pump First, Pay Later (56)
- [ ] The Runaway (57)
- [ ] Tremor (42)

5.10c

- [ ] American Sportsman (57)
- [ ] Crankenstein ☛ (73)
- [ ] Grape Nuts (118)
- [ ] Kokopelli (84)
- [ ] Panty-Mime ☛ (39)
- [ ] Quiet On The Set (30)
- [ ] Roto-Hammer (53)
- [ ] Running Amuck (56)
- [ ] Sandstone Sandwich (135)
- [ ] Some Assembly Required (84)
- [ ] To Bolt Or Toupee (60)

5.10d

- [ ] '34 Ford With Flames (178)
- [ ] Armed And Dangerous (86)
- [ ] Arms Left (17)
- [ ] As The Toad Turns (193)
- [ ] Bad Guys Approaching (149)
- [ ] Baseboy (10)
- [ ] BCR 5L (48)
- [ ] Birthstone (53)
- [ ] Blitzkrieg (115)
- [ ] Brand New Bag (89)
- [ ] Breakaway ☛ (117)
- [ ] Chalk Is Cheap (216)☐
- [ ] Chilly Ones (127)
- [ ] Chocolate Flakes (142)
- [ ] Claim Jumper's Special (25)
- [ ] Clone Babies (141)
- [ ] Crude Boys (47)
- [ ] Earth Juice (117)
- [ ] Edge Of The Sun ☛ (141)
- [ ] False Perception ☛ (223)
- [ ] Fiddler On The Roof ☛ (212)
- [ ] Five And Dime (142)
- [ ] Flake Eyes (78)
- [ ] Flakes Of Wrath (136)
- [ ] The Fox ☛ (14)
- [ ] Goobies For Gumbies ☛ (93)
- [ ] Haunted Hooks (53)
- [ ] Iron Man (44)
- [ ] Kenny Laguna (194)
- [ ] Killer Klowns (97)
- [ ] Left Out ☛ (97)
- [ ] Live Fast, Die Young (48)
- [ ] Lone Star (219)
- [ ] Mai Tai (187)
- [ ] Mazatlan ☛ (196)
- [ ] Moisture Brau (126)
- [ ] Monkey Rhythm (75)
- [ ] Mushroom People (131)

5.10d cont.

5.11

5.11 cont.

5.11a

5.11b

5.11b cont.

- [ ] Prime Ticket (30)
- [ ] Red Storm Rising (88)
- [ ] Sandstone Enema (49)
- [ ] Scorpions (24)
- [ ] Scudder Global (79)
- [ ] Slabba Dabba Do (126)
- [ ] Slave To The Grind (52)
- [ ] Stonehenge (53)

- [ ] Texas Lite Sweet (49)
- [ ] Thunderbird (81)
- [ ] Turtle Wax (24)
- [ ] Wheat Thick (96)
- [ ] When The Cat's Away ◀ (88)
- [ ] Why Left (103)
- [ ] Why Right (103)

5.11c

- [ ] 20th Century Ultra (79)
- [ ] Airlift (45)
- [ ] Big Iron (97)
- [ ] Black Flag (72)
- [ ] Blanc Czech (31)
- [ ] Bone Machine (43)
- [ ] Buffalo Balls (97)
- [ ] C.H.U.D. (74)
- [ ] Cameo Appearance (30)
- [ ] Disposable Blues (89)
- [ ] Everybody's Slave ◀ (73)
- [ ] The Felon (21)
- [ ] Gridlock (56)
- [ ] Guccione (19)
- [ ] Here Kitty, Kitty (33)
- [ ] The Heteroclite (89)
- [ ] Hooligans (72)
- [ ] Hostile Takeover (79)

- [ ] Jimmy Nap (61)
- [ ] Land Of The Free (107)
- [ ] Life Out Of Balance (43)
- [ ] Like Mom Used To Make (78)
- [ ] Livin' On Borrowed Time (49)
- [ ] The Max Flex (32)
- [ ] Native Son (77)
- [ ] Pickled (10)
- [ ] Pinkies For The Dean (79)
- [ ] Poodle Chainsaw Massacre (34)
- [ ] Sand Illusion (87)
- [ ] Sister Of Pain (52)
- [ ] Star Search (30)
- [ ] Sudden Impact (57)
- [ ] Suffering Cats (50)
- [ ] Swilderness Experience (13)
- [ ] Tin Horn Posers (49)
- [ ] Totally Clips (39)

5.11d

- [ ] #1 (74)
- [ ] #2 (74)
- [ ] #3 (74)
- [ ] #6 (74)
- [ ] 29 Posers (126)
- [ ] 911 (45)
- [ ] Arrowhead Arête (19)
- [ ] Autumnal Frost ◀ (21)
- [ ] Black Happy (25)
- [ ] Blackened (24)
- [ ] Cactus Root (31)
- [ ] Captain Hook (100)
- [ ] Circle Jerks (104)
- [ ] Circus Boy (33)
- [ ] Climb Bomb (29)
- [ ] Cold Sweat (16)
- [ ] Corona Crack (127)

- [ ] Cujo (34)
- [ ] Dances With Beagles ◀ (175)
- [ ] Dark Star (95)
- [ ] Disguise The Limit (19)
- [ ] Eliminator Crack ◀ (178)
- [ ] Fear This (10)
- [ ] Fibonacci Wall (65)
- [ ] Fungus Folks (131)
- [ ] GBH (Great Bodily Harm) (72)
- [ ] Golden Nugget (25)
- [ ] Graveyard Waltz ◀ (63)
- [ ] Gun Boy (103)
- [ ] The Healer (77)
- [ ] High Roller (18)
- [ ] Home Of The Brave (107)
- [ ] Mind Bomb (100)
- [ ] My Little Pony (215)

5.11d cont.

- [ ] New Traditionalists (63)
- [ ] Nine Lives (50)
- [ ] Northern Lights (65)
- [ ] Peak Performance (23)
- [ ] Pocket Rocket (43)
- [ ] Rebel Yell (61)
- [ ] Red Skies (35)
- [ ] Resin Rose (56)
- [ ] Rojo (119)
- [ ] Saddam's Mom (88)
- [ ] Second Fiddle To A Dead Man (63)
- [ ] Social Disorder (56)
- [ ] Solar Flare (23)
- [ ] Sonic Youth ◄ (73)
- [ ] Soul Power (89)
- [ ] Sportin' A Woody (100)

- [ ] Spring Break ◄ (112)
- [ ] Straight Shot (187)
- [ ] Stratocaster (69)
- [ ] Synapse Collapse (20)
- [ ] There Goes The Neighborhood (62)
- [ ] Time's Up (149)
- [ ] Tortugas Mutante (83)
- [ ] Water Dog (111)
- [ ] When The Shit Hits The Fan (69)
- [ ] Without A Paddle (143)
- [ ] Yaak Crack ◄ (55)
- [ ] Yucca (50)

5.12

- [ ] Dependent Variable (143)
- [ ] Gay Nazis For Christ (32)
- [ ] Lethal Weapon (136)
- [ ] Midway (33)
- [ ] Original Route ◄ (152)
- [ ] Posby (126)

- [ ] Take The Skinheads Bowling (32)
- [ ] Tier Of The Titans (66)
- [ ] Too Pumped To Pose (126)
- [ ] Toxic Playboy (61)
- [ ] Welcome To Red Rocks (137)

5.12a

- [ ] #4 (74)
- [ ] Abandon Ship ◄ (42)
- [ ] Absolute Zero (89)
- [ ] Afterburner (178)
- [ ] American Ghostdance (206)
- [ ] Americragger (61)
- [ ] Before Its' Time (43)
- [ ] The Bristler (69)
- [ ] Caligula (19)
- [ ] Cannabis (20)
- [ ] Caught In The Crosshairs (82)
- [ ] Chunder Bolt (25)
- [ ] Cloud Tower ◄ (161)
- [ ] Cowboy Cafe (69)
- [ ] Crowd Pleaser (33)
- [ ] Crude Control (48)
- [ ] Dodging A Bullet (82)
- [ ] Fear And Loathing III ◄ (57)
- [ ] Flame Ranger (66)
- [ ] Gimme Back My Bullets ◄ (24)

- [ ] Gotham City ◄ (112)
- [ ] Green Eagle (32)
- [ ] Hodad (31)
- [ ] Integrity Of Desire (70)
- [ ] KGB (20)
- [ ] Loki (72)
- [ ] Man-eater (12)
- [ ] Pain Check (77)
- [ ] Parental Guidance (136)
- [ ] Ripcord (132)
- [ ] Rise & Whine (77)
- [ ] Save The Heart To Eat Later (10)
- [ ] Sound Of Power ◄ (60)
- [ ] Sputnik (80)
- [ ] Standing In The Shadows (43)
- [ ] Steep Thrills (24)
- [ ] Strategic Arms (16)
- [ ] Stukas Over Disneyland (14)
- [ ] Sunny And Steep (24)
- [ ] Sweet Pain ◄ (52)

5.12a cont.

- [ ] Tarantula ◄ (112)
- [ ] They Just Don't Make Outlaws Like They Used To (89)
- [ ] Titan Rocket (66)
- [ ] Tour De Pump (24)
- [ ] Unknown Arête (87)
- [ ] Velvet Elvis (29)
- [ ] Where Egos Dare (77)
- [ ] Whiplash (110)
- [ ] Wizard Of Odds (83)

5.12b

- [ ] #5 (74)
- [ ] Aftershock (42)
- [ ] Agent Orange (73)
- [ ] Big Damage (57)
- [ ] Boschton Marathon (62)
- [ ] Celebrity Roast (30)
- [ ] Churning In The Dirt (60)
- [ ] Commando ◄ (63)
- [ ] Death Before Decaf (88)
- [ ] The Deep West (71)
- [ ] Every Mother's Nightmare ◄ (44)
- [ ] Fear This Sport (11)
- [ ] Fidelity Select (79)
- [ ] K-9 (34)
- [ ] Land Shark (42)
- [ ] Lee Press-On (52)
- [ ] Minstrel In The Gallery (56)
- [ ] Naked And Disfigured (44)
- [ ] Onsight Flight (78)
- [ ] Party Down (68)
- [ ] Pigs In Zen (44)
- [ ] Plastic Pistol (71)
- [ ] Poseidon Adventure (42)
- [ ] Promises In The Dark (57)
- [ ] Sandblaster (50)
- [ ] Smokin' (20)
- [ ] Southern Cross (83)
- [ ] Stand And Deliver (78)
- [ ] Stealin' (44)
- [ ] Stratocaster Direct (69)
- [ ] Turbo Dog (23)

5.12c

- [ ] #.5 (75)
- [ ] Angler (42)
- [ ] Body English (56)
- [ ] Boobytrap (14)
- [ ] Choad Hard (68)
- [ ] The Choad Warrior (69)
- [ ] Computer Virus (87)
- [ ] The Fiend (21)
- [ ] Flight Line (99)
- [ ] Gladiator (45)
- [ ] Glitch (55)
- [ ] The Grinch (87)
- [ ] Indian Giver (81)
- [ ] Jack Officers (14)
- [ ] New Wave Hookers (12)
- [ ] Purple Haze II (69)
- [ ] Ranch Hands (14)
- [ ] Satan In A Can (18)
- [ ] Stargazer (79)
- [ ] Supernova II ◄ (80)
- [ ] Swilderness Permit (13)
- [ ] Threadfin (42)
- [ ] The Trophy (82)
- [ ] Who Made Who (55)

5.12d

- [ ] Cavity Search (21)
- [ ] Cosmos (80)
- [ ] Desert Crack ◄ (219)
- [ ] Flying Cowboys (71)
- [ ] The Gift ◄ (55)
- [ ] Keep Your Powder Dry ◄ (82)
- [ ] Main Attraction (33)
- [ ] Man Overboard! (42)
- [ ] One Man's Kokopelli Is Another Man's [ ]
  - [ ] Side Show Bob (20)
- [ ] Pablo Diablo (67)
- [ ] Pet Shop Boy ◄ (81)
- [ ] Rock Rastler (101)
- [ ] Vision Quest (101)
- [ ] Where The Down Boys Go (55)
- [ ] Wonderstuff (12)

5.13 a/b/c

ROUTES BY NAME INDEX

Bold numbers represent topos or photos.